FISCAL ASPECTS OF
EVOLVING FEDERATIONS

This collection of essays on the economics of fiscal federalism contains original research on a timely topic by leading experts in North America and Europe. Reform of fiscal relations between central and subnational governments is an urgent priority in many countries, because increased economic integration within and among countries means that goods, services, capital, and human resources can flow across political boundaries more easily than before. Theoretical and applied contributions present new conceptual insights, together with discussions of practical policy questions in countries such as Australia, France, South Africa, the United States, the European Union, and transition economies. The structure of intergovernmental transfers and tax competition, as well as the fiscal implications of labor migration, are analyzed for audiences in economics, political science, and public policy. Several of the essays were published in a different form in a recent special issue of *International Tax and Public Finance*.

FISCAL ASPECTS OF
EVOLVING FEDERATIONS

Edited by

DAVID E. WILDASIN
Vanderbilt University

CAMBRIDGE
UNIVERSITY PRESS

CAMBRIDGE UNIVERSITY PRESS
Cambridge, New York, Melbourne, Madrid, Cape Town, Singapore,
São Paulo, Delhi, Dubai, Tokyo, Mexico City

Cambridge University Press
The Edinburgh Building, Cambridge CB2 8RU, UK

Published in the United States of America by Cambridge University Press, New York

www.cambridge.org
Information on this title: www.cambridge.org/9780521148429

First published 1997
First paperback printing 2010

A catalogue record for this publication is available from the British Library

Library of Congress Cataloguing in Publication data
Fiscal aspects of evolving federations / [edited by] David E.
Wildasin

p.   cm.

ISBN 0-521-56382-8 (hb)

1. Intergovernmental fiscal relations. 2. Transfer payments.
3. Revenue sharing. 4. Fiscal policy. 5. Local finance.
I. Wildasin, David E.

HJ197.F568   1997
336 – dc21   97-691
                                      CIP

ISBN 978-0-521-56382-6 Hardback
ISBN 978-0-521-14842-9 Paperback

Contents

PART III   POLICY AND PRACTICE

Preface

This book is based on a conference on "Fiscal Aspects of Evolving Federations" held at Vanderbilt University in August 1994. The conference, which was held under the auspices of the International Seminar on Public Economics (ISPE), provided a forum for the presentation of new research on the principles of fiscal relations, as well as on recent experience and current policy issues relating to fiscal federalism in several countries.

It is a pleasure to acknowledge the contributions of numerous individuals and organizations who provided vital assistance in the planning and administration of the conference and in the publication activities associated with it. The basic idea for a conference first emerged from discussions with Edward M. Gramlich of the University of Michigan. I discussed the idea of the conference with a number of colleagues in order to gauge interest, arrange financing, and formulate the program. The sound advice of Robin Boadway and Pierre Pestieau were particularly valuable, as always. Richard Bird and Dieter Bös were most supportive and helpful in their capacities as ISPE Executive Committee chairmen.

Hiromitsu Ishi, a member of the ISPE Executive Committee, played a critical role in helping to secure funding from the Nihon Hosei Gakkai; without this basic support, the conference would never have materialized. I also drew upon financial resources from Vanderbilt University, including faculty research funds and special assistance from the College of Arts and Sciences, the Graduate School, and the Department of Economics. Several participants were able to arrange for their expenses to be funded from other sources, which helped substantially in easing the financial burden. The staff of the Department of Economics provided much-needed administrative and secretarial assistance. Much of my own work on the book was completed during a year spent at the Public Economics Division of the Policy Research Department of the World Bank. I am most grateful to my colleagues at the World Bank for their hospitality and support.

A number of the papers published here have previously appeared in a special issue (Volume 3, No. 2) of *International Tax and Public Finance,* published by Kluwer Academic Publishers. *ITPF* editors Richard Bird and especially Jack Mintz were most helpful in managing the preparation of the special issue. Part or all of the following papers are reprinted here:

(1) "Introduction: Fiscal Aspects of Evolving Federations," by David E. Wildasin;
(2) "Efficiency and the Optimal Direction of Federal–State Transfers," by Robin Boadway and Michael Keen;
(3) "Interregional Redistribution through Tax Surcharge," by Helmuth Cremer, Maurice Marchand, and Pierre Pestieau;
(4) "Strategic Provision of Local Public Inputs for Oligopolistic Firms in the Presence of Endogenous Location Choice," by Uwe Walz and Dietmar Wellisch;
(5) "The Structure of Urban Governance in South African Cities," by Junaid K. Ahmad;
(6) "Fiscal Federalism and Local Public Finance: A Computable General Equilibrium (CGE) Framework," by Thomas Nechyba.

Several of these papers have been revised or expanded for publication in this book. I am pleased to acknowledge with gratitude Kluwer's permission to use these materials here.

In addition to the anonymous referees who assisted in reviewing the manuscripts for *ITPF,* I called upon still other colleagues to referee chapters in this book, and I am extremely grateful to them for their advice.

The staff of Cambridge University Press has been most helpful. In particular, editor Scott Parris has been supportive, encouraging, and – not least – patient throughout the duration of this project. I very much appreciate his guidance in bringing this work to fruition.

Of course I must thank the conference participants themselves, particularly those who have contributed papers to this volume, for the indispensable role that they have played. It has been my privilege over the years to participate in numerous conferences and workshops at universities and research institutions around the world. I have always appreciated both the intellectual stimulation and the enjoyable collegial interactions afforded by these activities, and have admired the efforts of their organizers. The discussions in Nashville were lively and productive, as gatherings of public economists often seem to be, and I hope that this conference has helped to maintain the tradition of friendly and spirited professional discourse that characterizes so many of the meetings of the international public economics community.

Finally, on a personal note, I would like to take this occasion to thank my family for their unfailing support of this and my other professional undertakings.

Contributors

Junaid K. Ahmad is Deputy Chief and Senior Economist in the South Africa Resident Mission of the World Bank. Dr. Ahmad works on public finance issues in developing countries with particular emphasis on intergovernmental fiscal relations. He previously worked on macroeconomic and trade issues in Eastern Europe and South Asia.

Robin Boadway is Sir Edward Peacock Professor of Economic Theory at Queen's University in Canada. He is the author of numerous books, including *Public Sector Economics* (2nd ed., 1984, with David Wildasin), *Welfare Economics* (1984, with Neil Bruce), and the Canadian edition of *Economics* (Joseph Stiglitz, 1994). Professor Boadway has published numerous articles in journals such as the *American Economic Review*, the *Quarterly Journal of Economics*, the *Economic Journal*, and the *Journal of Public Economics*. He has served as a consultant to the World Bank and the Canadian Department of Finance.

Helmuth Cremer is Professor of Economics at GREQAM and IDEI at the University of Toulouse and Institut Universitaire de France. He is the author of forty papers in journals such as the *Journal of Public Economics, Economic Journal, International Economic Review, European Economic Review*, and *Economica*. His current research interests lie in the areas of the design of redistributive policies, tax evasion and its implications for the properties and design of tax policies, and the impact of European integration on tax and transfer policies.

Claude d'Aspremont is Professor of Economics and Research Director of CORE, Université Catholique de Louvain. Professor d'Aspremont is also an associate editor of the journals *Games and Economic Behavior, Journal of Mathematical Economics*, and *Zeitschrift für Nationalökonomie [Journal of Economics]*. His research interests lie in the areas of social choice and welfare analysis, public economics and mechanism design, game theory and applications to industrial organization, and environmental economics. He won the Francqui Prize in 1995.

Louis-André Gérard-Varet is Director of Studies at the École des Hautes Études en Sciences Sociales in Marseilles and a director of GREQAM, the Research Group in Quantitative Economics at the Universities of Aix-Marseilles II and III. A Fellow of the Econometric Society and member of scientific committees of the CNRS-INSEE, his recent research has focused on imperfect competition, incentives, local public finance, and economics of the art market.

Harry Huizinga is Professor of International Economics at Tilburg University, The Netherlands. He has also taught at Stanford University. Professor Huizinga is coeditor (with Sylvester C. W. Eijffinger) of *Positive Political Economy: Theory and Evidence* (Cambridge University Press, 1997, forthcoming). He was a visiting scholar at the International Monetary Fund in 1990, 1993, and 1996 and served as a consultant to the World Bank in 1988, 1990, and 1992.

Michael Keen is Professor of Economics at the University of Essex. He is the coeditor of *International Tax and Public Finance* and is on the editorial boards of the *European Economic Review* and *Fiscal Studies*. Professor Keen has been a consultant to the IMF, the European Commission, and the World Bank and has contributed articles to the *American Economic Review, Journal of Public Economics,* and *Economic Policy.*

Maurice Marchand is Professor of Economics at CORE, University of Louvain. He is the coordinator of the European Research Network on Fiscal Implications of European Integration and has contributed articles to the *Journal of Public Economics, Economica, Oxford Economic Papers,* and the *European Economic Review.* His research interests lie in the areas of optimal taxation, redistribution policies, and health economics.

Thomas Nechyba is Assistant Professor of Economics at Stanford University. His dissertation won the first-place "outstanding dissertation" award from the Association of Public Policy Analysis and Management. He has contributed articles to the *Journal of Political Economy, Journal of Public Economics,* and *Economic Theory.*

Pierre Pestieau is Professor of Economics at the University of Liège. He has written articles for the *Journal of Public Economics, International Economic Review, Journal of Economic Theory, Economica,* and *Euro-*

pean Economic Review. Professor Pestieau's research interests include intergenerational transfer and optimal taxation. He received the Francqui Prize in 1989.

Jeffrey D. Petchey is a postdoctoral Research Fellow in the Department of Economics, School of Business, Curtin University, Western Australia. Dr. Petchey is the winner of the Best Published Paper Prize in the *Journal of the Australian Economics Society* (the *Economic Record*) for 1994. He is currently writing (with Perry Shapiro) a book on the theory and practice of federations.

Perry Shapiro is Professor of Economics at the University of California, Santa Barbara. He has also taught at both the London School of Economics and the University of Michigan. His research has included work on general models of state tax revenues, the use of voting and survey data to estimate private demands for publicly funded goods, and the analysis of compensation for the taking of private property for public use.

Uwe Walz is Professor of Economics at Ruhr University, Bochum. He is the author of *Oligopolistischer Wettbewerb und Internationaler Handel, Mohr* (Siebeck). Professor Walz's work has also appeared in the *Journal of Public Economics, Regional Science and Urban Economics, International Tax and Public Finance,* and *Economica.*

Dietmar Wellisch is Professor of Economics at Technische Universität Dresden. He is the author of two books on public finance and government policy and has written articles for the *European Economic Review, Journal of Public Economics, Journal of Urban Economics, Regional Science and Urban Economics,* and *International Tax and Public Finance.*

David E. Wildasin is Professor in the Department of Economics and Business Administration at Vanderbilt University. He has also been a visiting professor at numerous universities in Europe and served as a consultant to the Public Economics Division in the Policy Research Department of the World Bank. Professor Wildasin's previous publications include *Public Sector Economics* (2nd ed., written with Robin Boadway) and *Urban Public Finance,* as well as over sixty articles in professional journals and books. In addition, he serves on the editorial boards of *International Tax and Public Finance* (coeditor, Policy Watch Section), *Regional Science and Urban Economics, Journal of Urban Economics,* and *Review of International Economics.*

PART I

Introduction

CHAPTER 1

Introduction

David E. Wildasin

From Africa to the European Union, within the established federations of North America and Australia, in China and India, the two Asian giants of the developing world, in the Russian federation, in the formerly planned economies of Eastern Europe, and throughout Latin America, the functions and financing of local and regional government are major issues in the evolution of economic policy and in broad social and political developments. Reform of the fiscal relations between central and subnational governments is an urgent priority in many countries. Increased economic integration within and among countries means that goods, services, capital, and human resources can flow across political boundaries more easily than ever before, creating a new market environment within which fiscal relations are established among countries and among regions within countries.

Stimulated partly by these rapid political and economic changes and partly by its own internal intellectual dynamics, research on the economics of fiscal federalism has attracted much new attention in recent years. The papers in this book provide a sample of some of the recent work in this field. To differing degrees, each reflects real policy problems that are important in some countries or regions as well as some of the intellectual and analytical challenges that confront serious researchers in the area. These essays also reflect the subject's diversity, and readers of the following pages will find that the contributors examine a wide array of questions from a variety of perspectives, employing a variety of analytical methods. The present chapter is intended to provide a guide to the reader, outlining the organization of the book and briefly introducing each chapter by describing the topics analyzed and indicating some of the principal findings.

Part I of the book, which consists of this and the next chapter, is introductory in nature. In Chapter 2 I describe some of the major policy issues, in different parts of the world, in which problems of intergovernmental fiscal relations and fiscal decentralization are prominent. It is indeed striking that these problems are of such widespread interest. In every major

3

region of the world, the assignment of fiscal responsibilities and resources among different levels of government, the coordination of fiscal policies among governments at the same or different levels, and a host of related political and social issues are matters of intense interest to policy makers. Important policy reforms have been taking place in all of these regions. What are some of these recent and prospective reforms? What are the problems they are meant to address? As will become apparent, the institutional context of intergovernmental fiscal relations differs greatly among countries and regions, and this institutional background – the overall level of economic development, the nature of the legal system, ongoing processes of economic and political reform, the organization of monetary and financial institutions, tensions arising from ethnic, religious, or economic differences – has a crucial effect on the nature of the fiscal issues that concern policy makers and citizens.

This diversity of experience is worth appreciating both for policy ana- lysts and for academic researchers. On the one hand, the analysis and for- mulation of policy can benefit from an awareness of the widely varying experiences of different countries and regions, and these experiences offer much fertile ground for academic investigation. At the same time, incau- tious generalizations from specific institutional contexts are likely to be misleading; policy solutions that work well in one context may be quite in- appropriate in others. Researchers face the challenging tasks of culling im- portant insights from particular cases and of applying these insights in other and possibly quite different circumstances. Much of the academic economic research on fiscal federalism has been motivated by concerns with policy issues in developed countries with relatively mature political institutions. Chapter 2, therefore, devotes considerable attention to some of the rather different questions that seem to be particularly relevant in de- veloping countries and in countries undergoing a transition from planned to more liberal economic regimes. This discussion suggests several pos- sible directions for future academic research on fiscal federalism.

Parts II and III of the book, dealing respectively with "Theoretical Is- sues" and "Policy and Practice," contain a total of eight chapters. The five papers in Part II are theoretical essays that examine vertical and horizon- tal fiscal interactions in a multijurisdictional setting. The three chapters of Part III have a more applied orientation, two of them dealing with issues of fiscal decentralization and intergovernmental fiscal relations in specific countries (South Africa and Australia) and one presenting a model for policy analysis with applications relevant to local public finance in the United States.

The first paper in Part II, by Robin Boadway and Michael Keen, analyzes a problem that arises very frequently in discussions of intergovernmental fiscal relations. Given that both higher- and lower-level governments have their own tax systems and expenditure needs, what determines the optimal magnitude of transfers between levels of government? It is common for central governments to transfer substantial fiscal resources to lower-level governments in order to close a perceived "fiscal gap," that is, a gap between the desired level of expenditures by lower-level governments and the level of revenues that they collect. Boadway and Keen formulate the problem of optimal transfers in a framework where each level of government sets the instruments at its disposal in such a way as to promote its own objectives. They study this question in a deliberately stylized model that abstracts from some of the customary reasons for intergovernmental grants, such as the existence of spillover benefits from local public goods or interregional disparities in wealth. This allows them to focus on the normative implications of the fiscal interactions that arise between higher- and lower-level governments when they share a common tax base. In the Boadway–Keen model, the only sources of primary revenue are taxes on the wage income of workers and on rents accruing to other, inelastically supplied factors of production. Since labor is variable in supply, the earnings tax is distortionary, and the distortions the taxes separately imposed by each level of government are cumulative in nature.

Boadway and Keen show that the fiscal interactions between state and central governments that derive from the sharing of a common tax base can lead these governments to choose policies that are inferior, from a welfare viewpoint, to those that a unified central government would choose. This may not surprise practitioners in the field of fiscal federalism, who have often argued that central government use of a productive revenue source such as an earnings tax can preempt states and leave them with insufficient "room" to raise the revenue needed to finance their expenditures. From this viewpoint, programs of intergovernmental transfers from the center to the states, or (what is virtually the same thing) of sharing central revenues with states, are called for in order to assist states in dealing with what would otherwise be revenue shortfalls. Boadway and Keen find that there may be cases where this practical prescription might indeed be correct, but, rather surprisingly perhaps, they also find that the argument might just as well go the other way: the *central* government may end up with insufficient revenue, and a program of transfers from states to the center may actually be needed to improve the overall efficiency of the public sector (the Chinese model?). They show that the distribution of rents between the central and state governments via the taxation of non-wage income as well as other factors can play an important role in determining whether optimal transfers should flow from the states to the central government. In any event, such a "negative fiscal gap" seems by no means to be an unusual occurrence in this sort of model, casting doubt on the presumption that transfers should generally flow from the center to the states.

In Chapter 4, Helmuth Cremer, Maurice Marchand, and Pierre Pestieau address informational aspects of fiscal federalism. In the informal literature of the subject, it is often asserted that local governments have "better information" than central governments and that fiscal decentralization therefore facilitates efficiency in public-sector activities. Until relatively recently, however, economists had few analytical tools with which to investigate such assertions formally. Cremer et al. present one of the first attempts to model in a rigorous way the informational asymmetries between central and lower-level governments. In their model, localities differ both in terms of their endowments of resources and in terms of their preferences for public goods. They assume that localities can act independently in choosing the amount of local public goods to provide. A central government can use intergovernmental transfers to provide extra resources to poor localities or to try to influence the levels of local public expenditures. The central government is assumed to use its grant policy in order to maximize a utilitarian social welfare function, but it has only imperfect information on the basis of which to conduct its transfer policy. In particular, Cremer et al. assume that the central government is unable to distinguish the precise level of resources available to each locality from its own endowments or its preferences for local public goods, so that its intergovernmental transfers and the tax system that finances them must be incentive-compatible.

The main goal of the analysis in this chapter is to characterize the optimal policy of the central government in its fiscal interactions with lower-level governments. As in the analysis of optimal income taxation, incentive compatibility imposes constraints on the form of the optimal grant schedule. However, in contrast to optimal income tax models in which the principal (the government) is ignorant of only one agent attribute (a household's ability), here the agents (lower-level governments) have two attributes about which the principal is uninformed. Cremer et al. show that it may be optimal to distort the pattern of local public expenditure through matching grants. An example illustrates how the optimal grant-tax policy can vary in quite complex ways, with positive or negative matching rates depending on the parameters of the model, as the center attempts to balance efficiency and equity while operating under the burden of imperfect information. Of course, when information is limited and useful, there is usually an incentive to acquire more of it. The authors thus examine what happens when the central government is able to verify the attributes of lower-level governments through a system of costly auditing.

Chapter 5, by Claude d'Aspremont and Louis-André Gérard-Varet, begins with a review of recent trends in France in the assignment of fiscal responsibilities among levels of government. As they explain, a reform was initiated in 1982 that was intended to decentralize some aspects of public expenditure policy, a move away from the traditionally heavy reliance on the central government that has characterized French fiscal policy since the time of Napoleon. In practice, however, the process of decentralization raises numerous important issues for French policy makers. The optimal assignment of expenditure functions and of revenue instruments to lower-level governments presents one important challenge. Equally important is the structuring of fiscal relations between governments, including both the relations between the central government and regional, municipal, and other lower-level governments (vertical intergovernmental fiscal relations) and the relations among the lower-level governments themselves (horizontal intergovernmental fiscal relations). Of course, these issues are not unique to France but arise quite commonly in federal systems. For d'Aspremont and Gérard-Varet, the French case provides a backdrop for a general theoretical treatment of some of the fundamental problems that arise in the design of optimal mechanisms for the coordination of economic agents. They study a model where each agent (e.g., a local government) takes actions (e.g., expenditure and tax policies) that affect not only their own well-being but also that of other agents (e.g., through spillovers of benefits from local public expenditures). The question arises as to whether and how these agents may be induced to take actions that produce socially desirable outcomes. This obviously requires a framework within which the impacts of any one agent's decisions on others is somehow taken into account.

An omniscient planner would be able to solve this problem directly by simply telling each agent what action to take. However, it is actually difficult or impossible to monitor and control the actions of decentralized agents. This problem of "moral hazard" is captured in the model of d'Aspremont and Gérard-Varet by their assumption that the actions taken by individual agents are not observable by others. Their analysis focuses, therefore, on the design of systems of transfer payments among agents that are conditioned on *observable outcomes*. In the context of intergovernmental fiscal relations, one might think of these transfers as being implemented through a system of grants from higher- to lower-level governments, or perhaps through transfers among the lower-level governments themselves. D'Aspremont and Gérard-Varet first analyze the role of transfers in a static setting, taking into account the mutual interactions of agents in a very general model that incorporates the intrinsic uncertainty of the economic environment as well as the imperfect information that characterizes each agent's knowledge of actions taken by others. The authors establish conditions under which programs of transfers among agents can lead to efficient decision making. They then extend this model to an explicitly dynamic context, in which the agents interact with one another over time, with actions in each period affecting both current outcomes and the environment in which decisions in the next period are to be made. The authors show that even in this explicitly dynamic, stochastic setting, it is possible once again to find a system of transfers among agents, in each period, that induces them to choose actions that are socially efficient.

The next two chapters focus on intergovernmental horizontal fiscal interactions arising from the mobility of factors of production. Chapter 6, by Harry Huizinga, examines some of the fiscal implications of labor mobility when migration itself produces externalities. A basic premise of the Huizinga model is that the productivity of an individual worker depends on the quality of the entire work force within a locality or country. This externality means that migration can affect aggregate and average incomes, and the overall efficiency of resource allocation, in ways that depend not only on the attributes of migrants themselves but also on their interactions with other workers in the origin and destination jurisdictions.

Huizinga then analyzes the effects of fiscal policy in this externality-ridden environment, focusing especially on public expenditures for programs - such as retirement, disability, or unemployment - that reduce labor-force participation. Broadly speaking, these policies tend to distort migration incentives by giving rise to fiscal externalities; they can improve work-force quality by inducing low-productivity workers to leave the labor force; and, by changing community composition and the employment status of the population, they affect the voting behavior that determines the level of social benefits. These effects give rise to an analytically rich modeling environment where public policies have a variety of complex impacts on the distribution of welfare and on labor productivity within and among jurisdictions.

For example, Huizinga shows that there may be a broad consensus in favor of some level of social benefits for nonworking residents. This is so because the positive externalities derived from the withdrawal of the least productive members of the work force may raise overall labor productivity so much that the policy benefits even those taxpayers who must support those who do not work. He shows further that immigration may be harmful to existing residents, even when immigrants work and pay taxes to support social benefits for nonworking natives. An analysis of voting on the level of social benefits shows, as one might expect, that employed households tend to favor less generous benefits than those who do not work. Less obviously, voter preferences about immigration will vary by employment status. For example, the median voter always opposes the immigration of workers who will be unemployed. An unemployed median voter would, however, favor entry by any immigrant who works, while only immigrants whose productivity exceeds a certain threshold would be welcomed by a median voter who is employed. These and other findings show that immigration and transfer policies interact in novel ways when the labor market is characterized by external effects, and that familiar conclusions about the welfare gains and losses from these policies must be reassessed in this context.

One major thrust of recent research in local and international public economics has been the analysis of tax competition for mobile capital. The allocation of both portfolio capital and direct investment among jurisdictions depends, in general, on net-of-tax rates of return, and individual jurisdictions may be able to stimulate local investment through tax concessions or other fiscal incentives. A number of studies have examined the efficiency and distributional implications of interjurisdictional competition for mobile capital, with different branches of literature exploring different assumptions about the nature of this competition. The simplest cases to analyze are those in which both firms and governments are numerous and small. When there are many firms, producers do not interact strategically in output or factor markets, responding atomistically to fiscal incentives and to market conditions. When there are many small governments, individual jurisdictions can set their fiscal instruments without taking strategic interactions with other governments into account. The analysis of fiscal competition when both firms and governments operate under idealized conditions of perfect competition has yielded a body of standard benchmark results.

Our understanding of fiscal competition is incomplete, however, if it ignores the departures from perfect competition that arise when firms, governments, or both are small in number; this is the topic of Chapter 7, by Uwe Walz and Dietmar Wellisch. They study an economy with only two jurisdictions and only two firms. These two firms compete as Cournot duopolists in an external output market; in general, the absence of competition implies that these firms will earn positive profits in equilibrium. As in the strategic trade literature, individual jurisdictions have incentives to use their policy instruments to improve the competitive position of "their" producers in the output market in order to generate additional domestic profits. In the Walz–Wellisch model, localities provide productive public infrastructure (i.e., infrastructure that influences the production costs of private producers), financing their expenditures with taxes on firms. In the strategic trade tradition, it is of interest to examine how

localities use these fiscal incentives to affect the strategic interactions
between firms, and this is one important dimension of the Walz–Wellisch
analysis. However, following the literature on fiscal competition for mobile capital, the authors recognize that fiscal incentives affect not only the
output decisions of firms but also their locational choices. A jurisdiction
that offers a particularly attractive bundle of local public services and
taxes may become an agglomeration point for the industry, inducing both
firms to locate together; whether or not this occurs depends in part on
whether local infrastructure exhibits sufficiently strong public goods characteristics. The policy interactions between localities thus become very
complex: not only do fiscal policies affect *how much* firms will produce
but also *where* the firms will produce. Walz and Wellisch analyze these
interactions in a set-up where infrastructure provision and locational
choices are determined first and then output levels are fixed. As they
show, both output and locational choices may be distorted away from
optimal (joint–profit–maximizing) outcomes, depending on the configura-
tion of production costs, infrastructure technology, and other parameters
of the model.

The first paper in Part III, by Junaid Ahmad, discusses urban governance and finance in South Africa. Under the enforced racial separation
and settlement patterns of the apartheid system, both the private and the
public sectors of the urban economies of South Africa had highly distorted spatial structures. The local public sector in white areas was characterized by high levels of public service provision, effective taxation, and
professional administration; the local public sector in black areas by none
of these. Amelioration of race-based economic inequality is a pressing
task facing South Africa today, and reorganization of the local public sector must inevitably play a major part in that process. As Ahmad explains,
there are several ways that this might be done. The "twinning" of formerly white localities with neighboring formerly black localities - so as
to share local tax bases and administrative resources - is one possibility.
Another is the establishment of geographically comprehensive local governments encompassing entire metropolitan areas. These alternatives, or
variations on them, present complex tradeoffs between redistributive objectives and allocative efficiency, especially in the face of rapid economic
restructuring as the heavy and arbitrary regulatory controls of the apartheid era are relaxed. A governmental structure adapted to the spatial economic organization of the apartheid urban area is likely to become out-
moded as employment centers, housing markets, and transportation
systems are transformed. Yet the legacy of the past, embodied in existing
location patterns, is a fact that cannot be erased instantly. South Africa
must thus attempt to reorganize local governance and local finance in the
midst of a spatial transition.

Changes in the jurisdictional structure of local government will certainly influence the ability of localities to meet demands for infrastructure and urban service provision. Grants from higher-level governments will also play a role in financing these activities. As an alternative or supplement to grants, however, localities might attempt to use debt finance as a source of funds. Under apartheid, markets for residential and commercial property in black areas were poorly developed, in significant part due to government policy. Under such circumstances, it is difficult to establish local finance using property or land taxation, which have been traditional revenue sources for white localities in South Africa. However, the dismantling of apartheid and the prospect of improved economic development in poor areas should strengthen local revenues over time. Under these conditions, the use of borrowing to finance a backlog of urban infrastructure has considerable appeal. However, as Ahmad discusses, there are potential pitfalls in the use of borrowing as an instrument of local finance, and an important task for policy makers in South Africa is to structure local government institutions so that they can reap the benefits of capital market access without undermining local fiscal responsibility. Exposure to capital markets can discipline local policy makers and create incentives for efficient financial and investment strategies, but this requires that the rules of the game governing the fiscal interactions among different units of government and the definition of their responsibilities with respect to capital market obligations be clearly and appropriately defined.

Chapter 9 is by Thomas Nechyba, who reports on a program of research aimed at analyzing the simultaneous interaction of market and political decision making in local public finance through a computable general equilibrium (CGE) model. In Nechyba's model, decisions about local public good provision are made through simple majority voting by residents, with property taxes (or, in some experiments, other fiscal instruments) used to finance local spending. A crucial feature of the model is that the local electorate is endogenously determined: households are free to move among localities in order to find the location that is best for them, taking into account local public good provision, local taxes, and local housing costs. Calibrating his model using data from local school districts in New Jersey, Nechyba is able to compute allocations of resources and prices such that all markets clear and all public policies are majority-voting equilibria.

This framework allows a much more comprehensive analysis of structural changes in local government finance and intergovernmental fiscal relations than is usually possible. For example, Nechyba uses it to show how individual localities – that is, the current, voting residents of individual localities – have incentives to use property taxes rather than income taxes to finance local expenditures. He also describes how the model can be used to study the effects of both explicit and implicit intergovernmental transfers on the overall levels of, and interjurisdictional variation in, public good provision. Previous theoretical research leads one to anticipate that matching grants ought to stimulate local public spending more than equal amounts transfered in the form of lump-sum grants (e.g., through equalizing grants). Theoretical analysis cannot, however, determine the magnitude of the effects of different types of grants. Nor can theory alone predict the quantitative impact of federal income tax deductibility of local taxes, a form of implicit intergovernmental transfer that Nechyba also analyzes. For policy analysis, estimates of empirical magnitudes are of great value, and the CGE approach has much to offer in this respect. At the same time, because general equilibrium modeling requires that behavioral and accounting relations satisfy overall consistency conditions, it imposes a useful discipline on quantitative policy analysis. For instance, Nechyba's model demands that government budgets be balanced; this means that, although a program of grants to local governments may tend to increase local public spending by providing more resources to the local public sector, the effects of the taxes that are used to finance these transfers must also be explicitly taken into account. The CGE model described here is amenable to many additional types of policy analysis, and the model itself could in principle be extended or modified in a variety of ways to reflect institutional or economic factors that might be of special relevance in particular policy contexts.

The final contribution to the volume, by Jeffrey Petchey and Perry Shapiro, discusses fiscal tensions between the states and the central government in Australia. Their paper is motivated by a perennial issue in any federation – namely, the degree of autonomy that lower-level governments should have. This issue is partly conceptual in nature: is it the nation or its individual component jurisdictions that are regarded as the fundamental constitutional units of the polity? As Petchey and Shapiro discuss, this issue was debated in nineteenth-century America by Calhoun and Webster, and by Deakin and others at the founding of the Australian federation; indeed, it is debated today in the context of the European Union. Questions of "nationhood" certainly entail cultural, social, and political dimensions. For economists, however, it is natural to try to find the critical distinctions between a truly "national" system and a more weakly linked "multistate" regime in terms of their fiscal performance, especially with respect to the efficiency and distributional consequences of centralized versus decentralized tax and expenditure policy. In this spirit, Petchey and Shapiro set out an illustrative analysis in which they compare the economic outcomes of three different political–institutional structures, which they designate the "competitive federal," "cooperative federal," and "centralized" systems. (Under cooperative federalism, states can enter into agreements with each other to coordinate policies; in competitive federalism, they act entirely independently.) The authors postulate a society divided into two states, each of which contains some people who place a high value on public services ("high demanders") and some who place a low value on these services ("low demanders"). This simple set-up is enough to bring into play the classic problems of minority and majority interests within states and in the nation as a whole, including the possibility that local majorities may not be national majorities. As Petchey and Shapiro show, the levels of taxes and expenditures chosen in each case will differ because the political constituencies and potential policies in each regime are different, and no one regime unambiguously dominates the others in economic terms. For example, cooperative federalism may be better than competitive federalism from the viewpoint of low demanders in one state, but may hurt high demanders, or perhaps fellow low demanders, in the other state. In other words, the diverse groups will not generally agree about which form of political organization provides the best economic results, and the disagreements among groups may run not only along income or preference dimensions but along spatial lines as well.

This assessment of the ambiguous economic performance of different constitutional regimes may reflect the ambiguous resolution of the tensions between state and central authority that we observe in practice. Petchey and Shapiro discuss in some detail the evolution of state and central fiscal authority in Australia, showing that the taxing powers of state governments have been severely constrained not only by the letter of the constitution but by its interpretation in a series of High Court decisions over the course of the present century. The states retain formal responsibility for many important areas of public expenditure. However, Petchey and Shapiro find that their limited ability to raise revenues means that states have relatively little autonomy in practice. Rather, they rely heavily on grants from the central government to finance their expenditures, and the center has used conditionality of grant assistance to control state expenditure policy. Potential reforms of this system, such as moves toward greater state fiscal autonomy, would likely generate patterns of political support and opposition among diverse constituencies in different states, patterns that reflect not only pure income and preference differentials among groups but also the extent to which these groups would be able to influence fiscal policies within the context of more decentralized political decision making.

CHAPTER 2

Fiscal Aspects of Evolving Federations:
Issues for Policy and Research

David E. Wildasin

1. INTRODUCTION

There has been a resurgence of interest, in many parts of the world, in problems of multilevel government finance. Recent and ongoing political and economic developments raise questions about the role of the national government, subnational governments, and supranational public authorities in the provision and financing of public-sector programs. This chapter provides a selective review of policy issues and recent trends in a number of different countries and regions.

Problems of fiscal centralization and decentralization by their nature tend to have important political and institutional dimensions that vary from one country or region to another. Shifting the locus of fiscal responsibility among levels of government may occur relatively incrementally, as in stable federations like the United States, or they may occur with dramatic speed, as in the disintegration of the Soviet Union or the unification of Germany. In all cases, however, there are specific historical and institutional factors that channel the process of fiscal adjustment within the broader context of overall economic and political change. Widely varying political and economic systems, levels of economic development, and legal, constitutional, and fiscal traditions form the milieu within which the responsibilities of different levels of government are determined. If it is difficult to appreciate fully the importance and interactions of all of

I am grateful to numerous colleagues for comments on this paper and for general discussions of the topics discussed here. These include R. Bird and many World Bank colleagues, especially J. Ahmad, H. Davoodi, S. Devarajan, G. Eskeland, D. Sewell, P. Vieira da Cunha, and H.-F. Zou. Talking with them about fiscal federalism issues throughout the world has been enormously instructive and has greatly reduced the formidable barriers involved in trying to understand the diverse and often complicated fiscal problems encountered in countries undergoing rapid economic and political change. None of these individuals, however, can be held accountable for any errors, omissions, or lapses of judgment. This paper was written while the author was visiting the Public Economics Division of the Policy Research Department of the World Bank, whose hospitality is greatly appreciated.

these factors for any single country, it is probably impossible to do so for many countries taken together. Yet, precisely because each country's fiscal institutions are dependent on local circumstances, analysts and policy makers can potentially benefit greatly from the broader perspective that can be obtained from study of the problems of intergovernmental fiscal relations encountered in other countries and regions. The institutions of fiscal federalism vary widely across the world, and it is worthwhile trying to cull what insights we can from observation and comparison of the divergent experiences of different countries.[1]

The present chapter attempts, within a short space, to highlight a few of the issues of fiscal federalism, intergovernmental fiscal relations, and fiscal decentralization that have emerged throughout the world in recent years. Section 2 discusses the developed countries of Western Europe and North America, regions in which basic economic and political institutions are relatively stable and where policy changes occur in a comparatively orderly fashion. This section draws attention to some of the important fiscal dimensions of economic integration in the European Union and to some of the long-standing tensions in the mature federations of the United States and Canada. Section 3 examines the problems of fiscal federalism in several important developing and "transition" countries. Here the institutional background is much less settled, and the pressing problems of fiscal structure take on a somewhat different character. A survey of recent developments in India, China, Brazil, Argentina, and Russia shows that the public finances of central and subnational governments in each of these countries have undergone significant changes in recent years, and that the ongoing evolution of the fiscal institutions and responsibilities of different levels of government will play a major role in the economic and political development of these countries in the coming decades. Based on the discussion of Sections 2 and 3, Section 4 identifies some topics for future research.

2. FISCAL FEDERALISM: EUROPEAN AND NORTH AMERICAN PERSPECTIVES

The European Union

In Western Europe, the process of economic integration among the countries of the European Union (EU) raises numerous questions of fiscal coordination among member states. The taxation of multinational enterprises and the administration of national value-added taxes in an EU free of fiscal frontiers present immediate practical problems (see e.g. Fehr, Rosenberg, and Wiegarard 1995 and Tanzi 1995, and references therein, for recent discussions of VAT and the taxation of corporations and capital returns in a multinational setting). Furthermore, as labor and capital markets within the EU (and between EU and non-EU countries) become increasingly integrated, fiscal externalities associated with national-level redistributive policies are likely to become more important. Oates (1968) and others have argued that the redistributive functions of the public sector are not within the proper sphere of responsibilities of "lower-level" governments, that is, governments which are open with respect to the markets for labor and capital. Traditionally, the "central" government to which redistributive functions would be assigned is conceived to be a national government. When factors of production become increasingly mobile across international boundaries, however, the government of a single country is no longer a central government in the relevant sense. One must therefore ask whether the extensive national-level redistributive programs that have developed over the course of the present century in the EU (and elsewhere) will remain viable over time. If it is possible to perpetuate them, will it be desirable to do so? Does multinational policy coordination, perhaps through the further development of EU-level institutions, provide an appropriate mechanism through which redistributive and other fiscal policies can be organized?[2]

Although the financing of agricultural subsidies has presented major and at times almost crippling challenges to the EU, its regional development and social fund expenditures have increased over time. At least until recently, it was not difficult to imagine that still more policies of this type might be shifted to the supranational level in the longer term. The Single Market, the Maastricht Treaty, the expansion of EU membership to include Austria, Finland, and Sweden (and the prospective accession of some of the rapidly reforming countries of Eastern Europe) seemed to exemplify a powerful momentum in favor of European policy integration. However, attainment of the Maastricht timetable for harmonization of monetary and fiscal policies now seems to be very unlikely for most EU member states. Notably, it appears that the most stubborn obstacles to *monetary* union, at least as envisaged in the Maastricht treaty, arise from the difficulties that countries will face in meeting the *fiscal* convergence criteria, particularly those restricting the size of government deficits and debt/GDP ratios. For instance, the requirement that national debt not exceed 60% of GDP is certainly out of reach for countries like Belgium (the seat of many EU institutions) and Italy (one of the large EU countries, along with Germany, France, and the UK), countries whose current debt/GDP ratios exceed 100%.

Failure to meet the fiscal convergence criteria set out in the Maastricht Treaty would not appear, however, to present any fundamental obstacle to monetary union. The criteria, after all, are somewhat arbitrary, and it is intrinsically problematic to tie a qualitative event – a country's accession to a monetary union – to a quantitative economic indicator. If the debt/GDP ratio matters at all for monetary stability, it matters in a quantitative way, and there is no economically meaningful critical value around which a country's accession to a monetary union will have qualitatively divergent impacts. Indeed, it is interesting to note in this context that Belgium, with one of the highest debt/GDP ratios in the EU, has long had an effective monetary union with Luxembourg, which has one of the lowest. Flexible interpretation of the fiscal criteria may well allow the monetary union to proceed in any case (as discussed e.g. in Artis 1996). The important lesson to draw from this experience is probably not that monetary union is hard to achieve but rather that individual EU countries find it extremely difficult to impose restraints on social and redistributive policies for the sake of meeting obligations to other EU member states. The problems of monetary union à la Maastricht, in other words, cast doubt on the feasibility (and perhaps the desirability) of harmonization of fiscal policies and the social and distributional objectives that they embody.

Even as the proper role of EU-level fiscal institutions is debated, the organization of fiscal affairs within EU member states is undergoing substantial change. Efforts have been underway in France, Italy, and Spain to decentralize political and fiscal authority (Gérard-Varet 1994; Goodspeed 1994; Owens and Panella 1991). The internal economic integration accompanying German unification, including particularly freedom of labor and capital mobility within the national market, has required a strong central government response, owing to the uneven levels of development between East and West, coupled with a commitment to uniform fiscal treatment under generous programs of social benefits (see Sinn and Sinn 1992 for further discussion). The structure of local government finance in the United Kingdom, and in particular the attempt to reduce local reliance on property taxes by shifting to poll taxes, has been the subject of vigorous controversy (Besley, Preston, and Ridge 1994).

Canada

Whereas issues of fiscal centralization and decentralization are attracting new attention in the EU, they have been of enduring concern in established federations such as the United States and Canada.[3] Equalization of fiscal status has been a long-standing goal of Canada's very substantial programs of grants from the national to the provincial governments, and the need to understand better the equity and efficiency implications of these programs has stimulated a steady stream of research on the economics of

intergovernmental transfers.[4] Of course, the separatist movement in Quebec heightens sensitivity to intergovernmental fiscal relations in Canada
and may yet result in a fundamental political restructuring, or even disintegration, of the Canadian federation – changes that would likely necessitate profound fiscal restructuring as well. The disposition of national
liabilities and assets (e.g., the national debt, the public pension system,
public lands and corporations) and the coordination of health and social
welfare policies among the provinces would present serious challenges to
policy makers in a politically and fiscally fragmented Canada.[5]

The United States

In the United States, shifts in the balance of fiscal authority between the
federal, state, and local governments tend to mirror basic changes in domestic policy. The period since the 1930s has witnessed substantial growth
in federal government involvement in redistributive policies, including
public pensions and transfers to the poor. Although the federal government plays a major role, independently of states and localities, in the provision of retirement income and health care for the elderly, much of its
participation in other redistributive programs – especially those aimed at
providing cash and health benefits for the poor (AFDC and Medicaid) –
has taken the form of matching grants to state governments. These transfers have been accompanied by significant restrictions on the form and
administration of the programs they support, contributing to calls for fundamental reforms that would convert federal support to lump-sum assistance to the states with minimal restrictions on their use. Because federal
matching rates lower the cost to state governments of assisting the poor by
50% or more, such reforms could result in significant reductions in total
redistributive spending. On the other hand, it is possible that decentralization of redistributive programs would result in greater program effectiveness – for example, through better targeting of benefits, gains in
administrative efficiency, or basic program redesign. There is certainly
considerable dissatisfaction with the apparent inability of existing welfare
programs to achieve significant progress in poverty eradication, and it is
possible that the diversity of policies that would likely emerge from a
more decentralized policy regime may uncover useful information about
how to improve policy design and implementation.

The division of fiscal responsibilities between state and local governments has also been the subject of continuing reassessment in the United
States. The provision of primary and secondary education has been a principal function of local governments in the United States throughout the

present century, and the persistence of significant variations in levels of provision among localities testifies to substantial differences in demand for education within the population. A large fraction of the U.S. population lives in metropolitan areas that contain dozens of individual localities within commuting distance of core cities, so that households can obtain quite diverse levels of public education provision through their residential choices.[6] However, since education is an important determinant of lifetime well-being, equity considerations can conflict with the unequal provision of education that allocative efficiency would require.[7] Indeed, courts in many states have held that inequalities in the level of fiscal resources available to different localities for the finance of education violate state (but not federal) constitutional requirements for equal protection or treatment (see e.g. Inman and Rubinfeld 1979). It is one thing to declare a system of finance to be inequitable, however, and something else again to find remedies that are both effective and efficient. As discussed by Nechyba (1994), the complex interactions between underlying economic inequalities, household mobility, housing markets, and voting behavior imply that policy interventions – aimed, for instance, at school finance – are likely to have consequences that are far from obvious.

Whether in response to court mandates or simply as a matter of policy, state government transfers to local school authorities have grown substantially throughout the postwar period. In the eyes of critics, however, state government involvement in local education has contributed to an increase in bureaucratization, the possible capture of education bureaucracies by teachers' unions, and perverse performance and fiscal incentives for local school authorities. In a number of states, parents are being given greater freedom to choose which public schools their children attend. Providing vouchers that could be applied to the cost of either private or public schooling would carry this type of reform a step further. Note that partial or complete privatization of schools, which would constitute a step in the direction of greater *decentralization* in education *provision,* could be accompanied by generous state support for vouchers, which would constitute a step in the direction of greater *centralization* of education *finance.* This shows that education – like many public sector programs – bundles together different public sector functions, such as the provision of certain goods and services and the attainment of an equitable distribution of income. Some of these functions, such as redistribution, may be best suited to higher-level governments, while others, such as school administration or curriculum design, may be best left to local authorities or to the private sector. The bundling of functions in a single program may thus give rise to tensions between fiscal centralization and decentralization and to complex interactions between levels of government in the form of inter-governmental transfers.

3. FISCAL FEDERALISM IN LESS DEVELOPED COUNTRIES AND IN TRANSITION ECONOMIES

Whereas much of the controversy in the United States over the proper roles of different levels of government has revolved around issues of equity and allocative efficiency, recent trends toward fiscal decentralization in many Third World and transition economies have focused new attention on macroeconomic stability. When Musgrave (1959) identified macroeconomic stabilization as one of the three principal branches of the public household (in addition to the allocative and distributive branches), many economists were convinced that fiscal policy could play an important and perhaps decisive role in managing short-run aggregate demand fluctuations so as to achieve both price stability and full employment. From the traditional Keynesian perspective, the conventional wisdom has been that the manipulation of fiscal policy for purposes of short-run demand management should be left to the central government rather than to local governments (see e.g. Oates 1968). This conventional wisdom remains relatively intact, at least insofar as Keynesian views on short-run macroeconomic policy survive at all. Nevertheless, new concern has arisen about the macroeconomic effects of fiscal decentralization, not because of new views about the effects of local or provincial government fiscal policy on the business cycle but rather because of worries that fiscal decentralization may contribute to structural deficits and fiscal imbalance. Even in the absence of moves toward fiscal decentralization, it has proven difficult in many countries to control aggregate public-sector borrowing; in turn, heavy public borrowing has increased the pressure on central banks to engage in inflationary finance. The question is whether fiscal decentralization tends to accentuate or to mitigate these sorts of problems. Where traditions of state/provincial and local government fiscal responsibility are weak, where the institutions of political control and accountability are immature, and where administrative professionalism and control are poorly developed, there may be a risk that lower-level governments may abuse or mismanage their borrowing authority, leading to aggregate fiscal imbalance with accompanying adverse macroeconomic consequences (Bird, Ebel, and Wallich 1995a; Prud'homme 1995; Tanzi 1996). A discussion of some important less developed countries and transition economies will illustrate how fiscal federalism issues have become entangled in problems of overall macroeconomic policy management. The following sections outline some of the policy issues that have arisen recently in several important countries, including India, Argentina, Brazil, China, and Russia.

India

Beginning in the late 1980s, India began serious efforts to limit the growth of government debt. The central government has made substantial progress in this regard, but there are increasing fiscal difficulties at the state government level (World Bank 1995a). India has an established federal system and highly elaborated programs of intergovernmental revenue sharing and fiscal transfers. Both the Planning Commission and the Finance Commission provide extensive grants to state governments in order to promote development and fiscal equalization. This system has come under criticism for creating perverse and conflicting incentives for state governments and for failing to promote equity objectives (Murty and Nayak 1994, Rao and Agarwal 1994). Of late, state government borrowing from the central government has begun to create serious fiscal stress: for a number of states, the cost of debt service now amounts to 15% or more of state government expenditures (World Bank 1995a). In part, this seems to be the consequence of increases in the interest rates at which state governments are allowed to borrow from the central government. Although these rates are no doubt still below the level at which state governments could borrow on external markets, they have been brought closer to market rates, reducing the implicit central government subsidy to state government borrowing. Like any reduction in central government transfers to states, this has the immediate effect of reducing the central government deficit while raising deficits at the state level. As a result, state governments now face new pressures to strengthen their revenues and cut expenditures. One consequence has been a push toward privatization of public enterprise in the electricity, water, and transportation sectors, a move which typically allows these enterprises to restructure employment and other aspects of their operations more freely than could occur in the public sector and which also allows them to raise capital more easily from market sources. It also seems likely that the states will introduce value-added taxes in order to generate additional revenue, a move that raises issues of tax harmonization and coordination rather similar to those faced in the EU context (Burgess, Howes, and Stern 1995).

Raising the interest rates charged to state governments should reduce the incentives for state governments to resort to deficit financing and may help to facilitate liberalization of the financial sector of the economy generally. Reductions in the explicit and implicit subsidies to state governments may also help the central government to control its own borrowing. The states of India, however, continue to face many demands for public expenditures for economic development and poverty reduction. The attempt to meet these demands was a principal motivation for the establishment of the system of grants and loans to the states in the first place. Although many states may be able to strengthen their own-source revenues, substantial disparities among the states will persist. Some states may face fiscal crises as they attempt to undertake expenditures in excess of their revenues, which may prompt fiscal and regulatory interventions by the central government; other states may, in cutting expenditures (e.g., for basic health and education), produce significant political pressures for assistance from the center. In such circumstances, the question arises as to how intergovernmental transfers and borrowing arrangements can be structured so as to provide states with adequate fiscal resources without weakening their incentives for fiscal discipline. A sufficiently high level of transfers from the center to the states would obviate any need for state borrowing, but this might simply shift fiscal imbalances back to the center. The resolution of these and related issues is likely to occupy a prominent place in discussions of overall macroeconomic management, development, and income distribution in India for some time to come.

Latin America

Macroeconomic considerations have also figured prominently in discussions of fiscal federalism in several countries in Latin America. A number of Latin American countries have undergone significant recent changes in the structure of intergovernmental fiscal relations and in the comparative roles of different levels of government. Broadly speaking, one might characterize the region as a whole as moving toward increased reliance on lower-level governments to manage public expenditures; in some cases, this shift has been accompanied by increases in local government revenue capacity, but in other cases the increased spending by lower-level governments has been financed mainly by transfers (either through grants or through shared taxes) from higher-level governments. The experience has been quite varied, as described for instance in a recent report of the Inter-American Development Bank (1994; hereafter IADB), which discusses trends and pitfalls in fiscal decentralization in the region as a whole and presents case studies of Argentina, Colombia, Chile, and Peru.[8]

In Peru, for example, the constitution of 1979 included provisions for the establishment of regional governments, but these provisions were not implemented until 1990 and then were reversed by a constitutional reform in 1993. By contrast, constitutional reforms in Chile that were meant to shift fiscal responsibilities to lower-level governments seem actually to have had a real effect: central government spending as a share of total public spending fell from 95% in 1970 to 87% in 1980, while the expenditure share of local government rose from 5% to 13%. (It is noteworthy, however, that increased local spending has not been accompanied by a corresponding increase in own-source revenue; central government revenues accounted for over 97% of all public-sector revenues both in 1970 and 1980.) Colombia has seen a steadier growth of local fiscal responsibilities over time, with local spending rising from about 10% to about 17% of total public spending between 1980 and 1992, and with local own-source revenues increasing from 5.6% to 7.3% of total government revenues.

Argentina.   In the case of Argentina, problems of fiscal federalism are closely intertwined with the country's problems of macroeconomic and monetary stability. Throughout the 1980s, the central government resorted to deficit financing of public expenditures; the central bank, in monetizing these deficits, increased inflationary pressures to extraordinary levels. Resolution of the fiscal crisis of the central government and the establishment of effective controls on monetary growth have thus been critical issues for recent economic policy in Argentina, and indeed the country has made substantial progress on these problems in the 1990s (World Bank 1993). In this environment of macroeconomic instability, there has been a significant shift of revenue and expenditures to the provincial and local governments. This shift resulted in part from reforms in the late 1980s mandating that a large fraction (over 50%) of the revenues from major central government taxes be passed along to the provinces, while discretionary grants from the center to the provinces were reduced. In 1983, central government expenditures accounted for about 52% of total government spending, but by 1992 this had fallen to about 43%; provincial spending rose from 30% to 37% of government spending, and local spending rose from 5.4% to 8.6% over the same period (IADB). Own-source revenues for each level of government remained roughly steady over this period, reflecting a large increase in central transfers to the provinces.

Improved management of Argentina's fiscal and monetary crises has thus coincided with substantial fiscal decentralization. There is concern, however, that transfers to provincial governments have grown too quickly and that there is insufficient reliance on own-source financing to encourage accountable and responsible spending at the provincial level (World Bank 1993). In addition, provincial government deficits have been financed in part by provincial banks, many of which have gone bankrupt. The central bank's policy of managing these banks and absorbing their losses provided provincial governments with a circuitous mechanism of inflationary finance, weakening incentives for fiscal discipline at the provincial level. Recent reforms of the financial sector and of central bank policy making are designed in part to avoid these pitfalls. Argentina presents an interesting example of a country where financial-sector and monetary reform, central government fiscal adjustment, and the restructuring of intergovernmental fiscal relations have been closely interrelated.

Brazil. Brazil is another country where problems of deficit finance by subnational governments have recently come to the fore. Brazil is a federation in which both state and local governments have traditionally played an important fiscal role. Substantial functional responsibilities are assigned to state and local governments by a 1988 constitution, which also provides for fiscal transfers from the center to the state and local governments (Prud'homme 1989). A significant fiscal role for lower-level governments antedates the new constitution, however: state and local government own-revenues have typically accounted for 40–50% of total government revenue since the late 1950s (Shah 1991, table 5), and a substantial share of central government revenue has been transferred to lower-level governments via grant and revenue-sharing programs throughout this period. Interestingly, state governments in Brazil have utilized a value-added tax as a major source of own-revenue; this tax has yielded revenues of about 5% of GDP in recent years, accounting for around one fourth to one third of total tax revenue collected in the country as a whole.

The recent evolution of fiscal federalism in Brazil cannot be properly assessed, however, without taking into account the relationship between lower-level governments, public enterprise, and the banking sector. Like Argentina, Brazil has experienced extraordinarily high rates of inflation in the recent past. Monthly inflation rates above 10% were commonplace during 1983–85, fell significantly during 1986, and then returned to double-digit levels in 1987. Since then, inflation has frequently exceeded 20% per month (World Bank 1994, Statistical Appendix, table 1). During this highly inflationary period, state governments have owned major commercial banks, and – particularly in major economic centers such as Sao Paulo and Rio de Janeiro – the states have engaged in deficit financing while relying on the state-owned banks to purchase state debt. In 1991, state governments had an outstanding debt of about $57 billion (U.S.) (World Bank 1994, table 11), compared for example to a total external debt of roughly $120 billion. The total indebtedness of the states has since roughly doubled to about $110 billion (World Bank 1995d). Rapid increases in real interest rates have drastically increased the burden of debt service, and some states (e.g. Sao Paulo, whose debt accounts for almost half of all state debt in Brazil) have ceased paying principal and interest to state-owned banks. These banks are important components of the financial sector in Brazil, and they now face a financial crisis since the debts of state governments and public enterprises are their principal assets. Indeed, the fiscal status of the state governments is more precarious than indicated by the official debt figures. For example, state public expenditures are dominated by outlays for payrolls, so public capital expenditures are at correspondingly low levels, which is probably indicative of low or negative net public capital investment in infrastructure. More important, as large as the current wage bill for public employees may be, the states have relied heavily on deferred compensation, giving rise to substantial underfunding of public employee pensions.[9]

In order to forestall a general financial crisis, the central bank has assumed responsibility for the management of some major banks. The central bank, and the central government, may thus absorb the debts incurred by the state governments. This is not an attractive policy option, however, because fiscal discipline is seen as a key element in the effort to help the central bank limit expansion of the monetary base and thus control inflation. It would be undesirable, on this account, for the central bank or the central government to bail out the states and their banks either by having the central bank take over the nonperforming loans of the state banks, or by having the central government raise its own deficit by making special transfers to the states with which they could service their debt. In any case, a shift of state liabilities up to central authorities undermines the incentives for fiscal discipline on the part of the state governments and could encourage further explicit and implicit deficit finance at the state level. If the central authorities force the states and their banks into bankruptcy, however, a general banking crisis may ensue and the provision of key public services in major economic centers may be disrupted. The Brazilian situation seems to exemplify a breakdown of fiscal incentives and constraints in the structure of intergovernmental fiscal relations, arising at least in part from the close connections between lower-level governments and key financial institutions and from the mismanagement of monetary and fiscal policy at the central government level that has contributed to a highly inflationary environment. It appears that the de facto structure of intergovernmental fiscal relations includes the use of state banks, and their relationship to the central bank through the financial regulatory system, to shift implicit liabilities for state deficits to the central bank. This structure distributes resources and alters incentives in ways very different from the de jure structure embodied in established programs of intergovernmental grants and revenue sharing.

China

China presents a fascinating case where overall economic reform, macro-economic and monetary policy, and problems of interregional imbalance interact with intergovernmental fiscal relations. One fundamental aspect of Chinese economic reform has of course been the reduction of the role of state planning and control in the operation of the economy. The fiscal arrangements that evolved during the Mao period proved to be poorly adapted to a more market-oriented economic system. A series of reforms involving changes in tax bases, tax administration, and the division of revenues between lower- and higher-level governments has occurred in the past decade (see e.g. Agarwala 1992 and Bahl and Wallich 1992). Uneven economic development among regions – the consequence, in part, of such deliberate policies of selective economic liberalization as the establishment of "special economic zones" along the southeast coast – have given rise to increases in economic inequality that are problematic in themselves and also make it increasingly difficult for China to control internal population movements among regions and between rural and urban areas. Indeed, the enforcement of the *hukou* system of household registration has depended on state bureaucratic control of grain rations, employment, housing, and health care – controls that are eroding and must, it seems, continue to erode as market reforms continue (Cheng and Selden 1994; Harrold and Lall 1993).

Regional inequalities, uneven regional development, and internal population movements all create demands for regionally differentiated public service provision and redistributive transfers. Because the revenue system at each level of government – as well as the structure of intergovernmental fiscal relations – has been changing rapidly, it is easy to see how regions might press demands for fiscal assistance from the central government that the center would be poorly positioned either to meet or resist. Indeed, the central government has relied in substantial part on lower-level governments to collect taxes and to transfer resources to it, while at the same time attempting to distribute funds to lower-level governments in order to promote central government investment and other programs. Under these conditions, it has been difficult for the center to limit transfers to lower-level governments while simultaneously meeting its policy objectives. The weak revenue base of the center has created pressures on the People's Bank of China (PBC) to offer credit to lower-level governments that can be used to finance expenditures in areas deemed important to the central government. Such "policy lending," however, can prevent the PBC from controlling monetary aggregates in a way that achieves overall macro-economic price stability (Lall and Hofman 1995; Ma 1995; World Bank

1995b). Establishing a structure of tax sharing and intergovernmental fiscal transfers between different levels of government is thus a complex problem (Laffont 1995) but one that appears to be quite important for macroeconomic stability.

The Former Soviet Union and Eastern Europe

China is certainly not the only country undergoing a transition away from a socialist system while simultaneously reforming its fiscal structure, including the assignment of expenditure responsibilities and revenue instruments to different levels of government. The former Warsaw Pact countries of Eastern Europe and the states of the former Soviet Union are currently grappling with these problems as well. The breakup of the Soviet Union was itself perhaps the most dramatic and decisive step toward fiscal decentralization. Though it is not often characterized as such, a practical consequence of the dissolution of the Soviet Union has been that the public finances of Ukraine, Russia, the Baltic Republics, and other newly independent states are no longer part of the centralized Soviet system.[10]

Russia. Since the breakup of the Soviet Union, the public finances of the Russian federation have been very fluid and disorganized. Fiscal chaos is perhaps to be expected in the transition away from a centrally planned economy. In the old regime, government finances were intertwined with the administration of a heavily state-controlled economy with distorted prices, extensive regulation, ill-defined property rights, and incomplete markets. The central elements of economic reform – privatization, decontrol of prices, establishment of legal protection of property rights and contracts, and deregulation – must inevitably have major fiscal consequences. One important aspect of fiscal change in Russia has been a drastic contraction in both public expenditures and taxes; by one recent estimate, public expenditures at all levels of government fell from roughly 65% of GDP in 1992 to about 45% in 1994, while revenues fell from about 45% of GDP to around 35%.[11] Of course, a clearer delineation of public and private responsibilities is a key element of economic reform in Russia, and a substantial reduction in the size of the public sector, together with a refocusing of public-sector activities on core government functions, is an important part of the reform process.

In the midst of this rapid reduction in overall spending and taxation, the assignment of revenues and expenditure functions by level of government and the structure of intergovernmental fiscal relations have likewise been changing rapidly. Federal government revenues and expenditures appear to have fallen substantially while regional government revenues and spending have increased, at least as a share of GDP. Major taxes are collected by regional governments, and specified shares of these taxes are supposed to be passed up to the central government. However, a number of regions have unilaterally withheld all or part of the taxes collected in their territories. The administration and sharing of taxes between the center and many of the regions are managed on an ad hoc basis, with negotiated settlements to determine their respective tax shares and jurisdictions.[12] Meanwhile, the central government has shed many expenditure functions, leaving the regions with significant new functional responsibilities.

The Russian federation is an extremely heterogeneous country, with wide spatial disparities in incomes, resource endowments, and social and ethnic characteristics. These disparities suggest a potentially important role for central government transfers to promote more fiscal uniformity in tax burdens and public service provision among the regions. However, the limited ability of the center to administer and collect taxes and the shifting of expenditure responsibilities to lower-level governments may signal the evolution of a looser federation, one in which the role of the central government in transferring fiscal resources among regions is very constrained and in which the fiscal circumstances of different regions would therefore reflect their underlying heterogeneity. It will not be easy, even if it is deemed desirable, for the central government to reverse recent trends toward regional fiscal autonomy and political decentralization. Indeed, several observers (Bahl and Wallich 1995; McLure, Wallich, and Litvack 1995) have noted that the unwillingness of the constituent republics to share fiscal resources with the center played a major role in the dissolution of the Soviet Union. This process (which, incidentally, is reminiscent of the fiscal problems that faced the United States under the Articles of Confederation) could lead to the further breakup of the Russian federation. It is worth noting that, even if this should occur, problems of intergovernmental fiscal relations would not then disappear. The regions of the Russian federation would undoubtedly continue to interact economically through trade, capital flows, migration, and spillovers from public and environmental goods. However, in the absence of a central government, these economic interactions – and the fiscal issues to which they inevitably give rise – would have to be managed "horizontally," that is, through coordination (or competition) among jurisdictions.

Fiscal Restructuring: Issues on the Horizon

Before concluding this overview of developing and transition economies, let us look briefly at the prospects for future change in political and fiscal institutions.

The breakup of Czechoslovakia and of Yugoslavia, like the dissolution of the Soviet Union, represent cases where fiscal decentralization has occurred in an extreme form – that is, through the demise of the central government. Numerous other countries, including particularly those where ethnic and religious tensions are high, may well follow the path of the Soviet Union, Czechoslovakia, and Yugoslavia. Governmental structures in numerous African countries (e.g., Sudan, Somalia, Rwanda, Burundi, Nigeria) could easily fragment along ethnic and regional lines, as indeed has already happened in Ethiopia. Long-standing ethnic strife in Sri Lanka persists and has led to proposals for constitutional reform that would divest the central government of considerable fiscal authority, allowing greater autonomy for regional governments to serve the Tamil, Sinhalese, and other ethnic groups in the country.

The dissolution of existing jurisdictional structures is a likely prospect in many countries, but there are also important cases where increased economic and fiscal integration appear to be on the horizon. On the Korean peninsula, the division of the country at the close of the Korean War has been followed by nearly a half-century of divergent political and economic development. Growing economic disparities between North and South Korea, and uncertainty about the continuity of political institutions in North Korea, raise questions about the durability of the status quo. The possibility exists that unification, perhaps sudden, will present Koreans with fiscal challenges like those that arose so unexpectedly in Germany. In North America, Canadian fiscal policy has often co-evolved with trends in its large trading partner to the south. The North American Free Trade Agreement brings the United States, Canada, and Mexico into a more closely integrated economic system, which will increase the importance of fiscal interactions among these countries; the same may be true of the Mercosur countries of South America. Immigration policy and labor mobility often raise important fiscal issues for jurisdictions that are economically integrated; this is certainly true for the United States in relation to Latin America and for Israel in relation to the nascent Palestinian authority and the territories occupied by Israel since the 1967 war. In South Africa, constitutional reforms are redefining the roles of central, provincial, and local governments in ways that should facilitate greater economic, political, and social integration of that country's several racial and ethnic populations, presenting substantial challenges for fiscal policy (see Ahmad 1994).

The course that political developments will take in these and other countries is impossible to foresee. Continued change in political structures can be anticipated, however, suggesting that fiscal issues such as those discussed here will be of recurring interest for some time to come.

4. CONCLUSION

The discussion in this chapter has provided a sample of some of the important issues of fiscal federalism in a number of countries and regions of
the world, including the EU, Canada, the United States, India, China,
Russia, Argentina, and Brazil. The economic and demographic signifi-
cance of these cases, and of others that could well have been discussed,
is obvious. Particularly in a world where the basic political organization
of the state is undergoing rapid reform and restructuring, the tensions
and opportunities created by the fiscal interactions among governments
at all levels are of critical concern. The adaptation and effective development of fiscal institutions, including the organization of intergovernmental
fiscal relations, is an ongoing and evolutionary process that requires continuing study and analysis.

Political, social, legal, and economic conditions are generally important for the analysis of fiscal issues, but this is perhaps especially the case
for the analysis of fiscal decentralization, the fiscal interactions among
governments, and other issues of fiscal federalism. These conditions vary
widely throughout the world, however, which provides both opportunities and difficulties for research and policy analysis. Much of the established literature of fiscal federalism has been explicitly or implicitly ori-
ented toward the institutions and policy issues that arise within developed
countries, particularly Canada and the United States. These countries and
their fiscal problems are of interest in themselves and have provided a
context within which many important principles and hypotheses have
been developed and tested. Making due allowance for the differing circumstances of other regions and countries, application of the findings of
this literature can contribute a great deal to the understanding of related
issues throughout the world. At the same time, wide institutional variations mean that rather different policy problems are likely to arise in differing settings, requiring shifts of emphasis in analysis and research, and
opening up new topics for investigation. The preceding discussion suggests several topics for research that have not received as much attention
in the past as they seem to warrant.

One topic that deserves further attention, especially in the context of
developing and transition economies, is the interplay between intergovernmental grants and government borrowing. Debt policy creates a wedge
between a government's (primary) expenditures and its (primary) revenues. Intergovernmental grants do the same: recipient governments, like
governments that borrow, can spend more than they collect in revenue,
whereas the primary expenditures of donor governments are reduced relative to their revenue. In many countries, lower-level governments receive

transfers from those at higher levels, and the higher-level governments engage in borrowing. How is this different from allowing lower-level governments to borrow directly, bypassing the intermediary of the central government? Do fiscal interdependencies between central and lower-level governments, reflected in intergovernmental transfer programs, imply that lower-level government borrowing creates implicit liabilities on the part of central governments? If so, must central governments impose controls on lower-level borrowing, or is it possible to structure intergovernmental fiscal relations in such a way as to allow local borrowing without inducing adverse local incentives? In the absence of independent local access to capital markets, should one view the central government as a financial intermediary or delegated borrower acting on behalf of local governments, obtaining funds through the issuance of debt that can then be transferred to lower-level governments through intergovernmental grants? What are the advantages or disadvantages of this sort of intermediation?

A related question for research concerns the issue of "hard" and "soft" budget constraints for lower-level governments. In China, Russia, Brazil, and elsewhere, central government monetary and fiscal authorities seem to absorb fiscal imbalances incurred by lower-level governments. Why do these countries settle their intergovernmental fiscal transactions on an ad hoc basis, responding to the fiscal distress of lower-level units with a variety of special loans, grants, negotiated tax-sharing agreements, directed credit programs, and other emergency bailouts, rather than establishing firm and transparent rules that would govern the form and extent of fiscal flows between central and subnational fiscal and financial institutions? It is likely that the unsystematic and flexible arrangements found in a number of countries do not provide effective incentives for lower-level governments to manage their expenditure, tax, and other fiscal decisions efficiently or responsibly. Many observers have argued that it is desirable to establish hard budget constraints for lower-level fiscal authorities, which may well be sound normative advice. But what, exactly, are the economic distortions associated with soft budget constraints? What sorts of institutional reforms might help to establish hard budget constraints? A more detailed institutional comparison of different countries might shed some light on these questions. In addition, formal modeling is needed to clarify the nature of the incentives associated with different institutional structures and thus to shed light on the types of institutional change that might facilitate more effective organization of decentralized fiscal systems.

The formation or dissolution of countries is a topic about which modern economics has not had much to say (but see Austin 1996; Berkowitz 1997; Burbidge et al. 1994; Casella 1994; Shapiro and Petchey 1994). Perhaps because of the rigid polarization of the Cold War and the high

potential costs of superpower confrontation, national boundaries in much
of the world, especially the developed world, have been relatively stable
during the past half-century. In historical terms, however, such stability
may be anomalous. Changes in jurisdictional structure may be part of
the normal course of economic events to which we ought to become ac-
customed. In any case, the existence of national units within established
boundaries is now called into question with increased and sometimes un-
settling frequency, and one must similarly question whether the "country"
remains the appropriate unit of analysis for at least some important issues
in economics. What are the fundamental economic forces that shape "natural" economic areas? Are there significant economic benefits or costs
that result from the inclusion of several regions within one jurisdictional
structure? From a normative viewpoint, what are the economic considerations that determine the optimal size of a country, and what are the crucial economic functions of national governments? From a positive viewpoint, to what extent do economic forces drive the political restructuring
that we observe, and where may these forces take us in the future?

Gains from economic association through trade in goods and services
and from free movement of factors of production are certainly crucial
elements of this story. Demographic change, changes in the technology of
communication and transportation, and the development of market institutions may alter the optimal or equilibrium boundaries of political units
over time. Such change invariably raises questions about the organization
of the public sector and the assignment of expenditures and revenues to
different levels of government. The integration of labor and capital markets, for example, can be promoted by political union among governments or through policies such as deregulation of capital markets or relaxation of immigration controls. Such integration must certainly provide
greater opportunities for the efficient deployment of factors of production over space and among industries, but, by affecting factor markets, it
also affects the distribution of income. Perhaps the distributional effects
of factor market integration would create a greater role for government
redistributive policies, for example by cushioning some factors from negative quasirents. Yet, as mentioned already in Section 2, the opening of
factor markets may limit the ability of governments to undertake redistributive policies. Conversely, erecting barriers to factor movements by
political separation may entail efficiency losses while facilitating government policy interventions. The patterns of gains and losses resulting from
the reorganization of jurisdictional structures can thus be quite complex.
To understand them fully requires an appreciation of the economic consequences of changes both in market organization and in policy outcomes
resulting from the reorganization of the public sector. This raises a series

of questions that cuts across many areas of economics, including labor economics, finance, urban and regional economics, and international economics, as well as public economics and political economy.

NOTES

1. See Bird (1994) for insightful discussion of the benefits and limitations of comparative analyses of federal finance; also see McLure et al. (1995), who provide a concise comparative survey of intergovernmental fiscal relations, and Shah (1994) for a general discussion of fiscal federalism issues in developing countries. The following discussion is intended to illustrate some of the diversity of issues relating to fiscal federalism and fiscal decentralization that arise in many parts of the world today and to provide references to some (though only a portion) of the relevant literature for interested readers.
2. For discussion of these issues, see e.g. Wellisch and Wildasin (1996), Wildasin (1991, 1992, 1994, 1997, forthcoming a), and, for surveys and many additional references, Cremer et al. (1995) and Wildasin (forthcoming b).
3. A number of the fiscal issues that arise in another mature federation, Australia, are discussed by Petchey and Shapiro (1994).
4. See e.g. Boadway and Hobson (1993), Courchene (1984), Shah (1995), and references therein.
5. See the contributions to Boadway, Courchene, and Purvis (1991) and Banting, Brown, and Courchene (1994) for further discussion.
6. Revelation of preferences through locational choices offers the prospect that more efficient levels of public good provision can be achieved than otherwise would be the case, a possibility identified by Tiebout (1956) in an influential article.
7. It has proven very difficult to determine exactly what variables under the control of policy makers are able to influence educational outcomes; in particular, per-student educational expenditures do not seem to have the decisive impact on educational output that one might anticipate (see e.g. Hanushek 1986). This greatly complicates the school finance debate, since the true nature of any efficiency–equity tradeoffs remains obscure.
8. See also Campbell, Peterson, and Brakarz (1991), Winkler (1994), and World Bank (1996a) for further discussion of the experience of fiscal federalism in Latin America.
9. Under proper deficit accounting, changes in the real value of public infrastructure assets and in implicit or contingent liabilities such as underfunded pensions should be included in a comprehensive measure of the change in public-sector net worth (see e.g. Boadway and Wildasin 1989; Eisner 1986; Kotlikoff 1992; and references therein). This type of accounting is seldom undertaken, however, which can give rise to perverse incentives. The underfunding of municipal employee pensions in the United States is a long-standing problem; see e.g. Epple and Schipper (1981) and Inman (1980, 1981).
10. See Bird, Ebel, and Wallich (1995b) for discussions of fiscal decentralization and intergovernmental fiscal relations in Hungary, Poland, Bulgaria, Romania, Albania, and Ukraine, in addition to the Russian federation. Problems of

local government finance in Estonia are discussed in World Bank (1995c). See also Bahl (1995) for comparative discussion of China, Russia, and the United States.

11. World Bank (1996b, tables A.1–A.3). This shrinkage in the size of the public sector in relation to GDP is all the more remarkable in view of the fact that GDP itself has fallen by about 40% during the same period (World Bank 1996c, table A3). It must be noted that, in Russia, fiscal and other statistical reporting is incomplete and accounting methods are unstable. Large errors must therefore be expected in fiscal accounts, and figures are unlikely to be properly comparable over time.

12. See e.g. Bahl and Wallich (1995), McLure et al. (1995), and World Bank (1996b, p. 17; 1996c, pp. 44–6). Some (though not all) of these negotiated settlements involve resource-rich regions and the sharing of rents that accrue to resource-intensive industries.

REFERENCES

Agarwala, R. (1992), "China: Reforming Intergovernmental Fiscal Relations," Discussion Paper no. 178, World Bank, Washington, DC.

Ahmad, J. (1994), "The Structure of Urban Governance in South African Cities." [Chapter 8 in this volume]

Artis, M. (1996), "Alternative Transitions to EMU," *Economic Journal* 106: 1005–15.

Austin, D. A. (1996), "The Price of Nationalism: Evidence from the Soviet Union," *Public Choice* 87: 1–18.

Bahl, R. (1995), "Comparative Federalism: Trends and Issues in the United States, China, and Russia," in Roy (1995), pp. 73–102.

Bahl, R., and C. Wallich (1992), "Intergovernmental Fiscal Relations in China," Policy Research Working Paper no. WPS 863, World Bank, Washington, DC.

Bahl, R., and C. Wallich (1995), "Intergovernmental Fiscal Relations in the Russian Federation," in Bird et al. (1995b), pp. 321–78.

Banting, K. G., D. M. Brown, and T. J. Courchene (eds.) (1994), *The Future of Fiscal Federalism.* Kingston, Ontario: Queen's University.

Berkowitz, D. (1997), "Regional Income and Secession," *Regional Science and Urban Economics* 27: 17–46.

Besley, T., I. Preston, and M. Ridge (1994), "Fiscal Anarchy in the UK: Modelling Poll Tax Noncompliance," Paper presented at ISPE Conference on "Fiscal Aspects of Evolving Federations" (August, Nashville, TN); forthcoming in *Journal of Public Economics.*

Bird, R. M. (1994), "A Comparative Perspective on Federal Finance," in Banting et al. (1994), pp. 293–322.

Bird, R. M., R. D. Ebel, and C. I. Wallich (1995a), "Fiscal Decentralization: From Command to Market," in Bird et al. (1995b), pp. 1–68.

Bird, R. M., R. D. Ebel, and C. I. Wallich (eds.) (1995b), *Decentralization of the Socialist State: Intergovernmental Finance in Transition Economies.* Washington, DC: World Bank.

Boadway, R. W., T. J. Courchene, and D. D. Purvis (eds.) (1991), *Economic Dimensions of Constitutional Change.* Kingston, Ontario: John Deutsch Institute for the Study of Economic Policy.

Boadway, R. W., and P. A. R. Hobson (1993), *Intergovernmental Fiscal Relations in Canada.* Toronto: Canadian Tax Foundation.

Boadway, R. W., and D. E. Wildasin (1989), "Long Term Debt Strategy: A Survey," in H. A. A. Verbon and F. A. A. M. van Winden (eds.), *The Political Economy of Government Debt.* Amsterdam: North-Holland, pp. 37-68.

Burbidge, J. B., J. A. DePater, G. M. Myers, and A. Sengupta (1994), "Federation as Coalition Formation," Paper presented at ISPE Conference on "Fiscal Aspects of Evolving Federations" (26-28 August, Nashville, TN).

Burgess, R., S. Howes, and N. Stern (1995), "Value-Added Tax Options for India," *International Tax and Public Finance* 2: 109-41.

Campbell, T., with G. Peterson and J. Brakarz (1991), *Decentralization to Local Government in Latin America and the Caribbean: National Strategies and Local Response in Planning, Spending, and Management* (Latin America and Caribbean Technical Department Regional Studies Program, Report no. 5). Washington, DC: World Bank.

Casella, A. (1994), "The Role of Market Size in Club Formation," Paper presented at ISPE Conference on "Fiscal Aspects of Evolving Federations" (26-28 August, Nashville, TN).

Cheng, T., and M. Selden (1994), "The Origins and Social Consequences of China's *Hukou* System," *China Quarterly* 139: 644-68.

Courchene, T. J. (1984), *Equalization Payments: Past, Present, and Future.* Toronto: Ontario Economic Council.

Cremer, H., V. Fourgeaud, M. L. Monteiro, M. Marchand, and P. Pestieau (1995), "Mobility and Redistribution: A Survey," unpublished manuscript.

Eisner, R. (1986), *How Real Is the Federal Deficit?* New York: Free Press.

Epple, D., and K. Schipper (1981), "Municipal Pension Funding: A Theory and Some Evidence," *Public Choice* 37: 141-78.

Fehr, H., C. Rosenberg, and W. Wiegard (1995), *Welfare Effects of Value-Added Tax Harmonization in Europe.* Berlin: Springer-Verlag.

Gérard-Varet, L.-A. (1994), "Decentralization of Public Policy and Incentives," Paper presented at ISPE Conference on "Fiscal Aspects of Evolving Federations" (26-28 August, Nashville, TN).

Goodspeed, T. J. (1994), "Efficiency and Equity Consequences of Decentralized Government: An Application to Spain," *International Tax and Public Finance* 1: 35-56.

Hanushek, E. (1986), "The Economics of Schooling: Production and Efficiency in the Public Schools," *Journal of Economic Literature* 24: 1141-77.

Harrold, P., and R. Lall (1993), "Reform and Development in 1992-93," Discussion Paper no. 215, China and Mongolia Department, World Bank, Washington, DC.

Inman, R. P. (1980), "Wages, Pensions, and Employment in the Local Public Sector," in P. Mieszkowski and G. E. Peterson (eds.), *Public Sector Labor Markets.* Washington, DC: Urban Institute, pp. 11-57.

Inman, R. P. (1981), "Public Employee Pensions and the Local Labor Budget," *Journal of Public Economics* 19: 49-71.

Inman, R. P., and D. L. Rubinfeld (1979), "The Judicial Pursuit of Local Fiscal Equity," *Harvard Law Review* 92: 1662-1750.

Inter-American Development Bank (1994), *Economic and Social Progress in Latin America: 1994 Report.* Washington, DC: Inter-American Development Bank.

36 DAVID E. WILDASIN

Kotlikoff, L. (1992), *Generational Accounting*. New York: Free Press.
Laffont, J.-J. (1995), "Incentives in China's Federal Tax System," Paper presented at ISPE Conference on "The Distributional Aspects of Fiscal Policy: The Implications of Economic Integration" (June, Colchester, UK).
Lall, R., and B. Hofman (1995), "Decentralization and the Government Deficit in China," in Roy (1995), pp. 195–220.
Ma, J. (1995), "Macroeconomic Management and Intergovernmental Relations in China," Working Paper no. 1408, Policy Research Department, World Bank, Washington, DC.
McLure, C. M., Jr., C. I. Wallich, and J. Litvack (1995), "Special Issues in Russian Federal Finance: Ethnic Separatism and Natural Resources," in Bird et al. (1995b), pp. 379–404.
Musgrave, R. A. (1959), *Theory of Public Finance: A Study in Public Economy.* New York: McGraw-Hill.
Murty, M. N., and P. B. Nayak (1994), "A Normative Approach for Resource Transfers in a Federal State," in A. Bagchi and N. Stern (eds.), *Tax Policy and Planning in Developing Countries.* New Delhi: Oxford University Press, pp. 231–61.
Nechyba, T. (1994), "Computable General Equilibrium in Local Public Finance and Fiscal Federalism: Applications to Local Taxation, Intergovernmental Aid, and Education Vouchers." [Chapter 9 in this volume]
Oates, W. E. (1968), "The Theory of Public Finance in a Federal System." *Canadian Journal of Economics* 1: 37–54.
Owens, J., and G. Panella (eds.) (1991), *Local Government Finance: An International Perspective.* Amsterdam: North-Holland.
Petchey, J., and P. Shapiro (1994), "'One People, One Destiny': Centralization and Conflicts of Interest in Australian Federalism." [Chapter 10 in this volume]
Prud'homme, R. (1989), "State and Local Finance and Public Policy in Brazil," unpublished manuscript, Observatoire de l'Economie et des Institutions Locales, Institut d'Urbanisme de Paris, Université Paris XII.
Prud'homme, R. (1995), "The Dangers of Decentralization," *World Bank Research Observer* 10: 201–20.
Rao, M. G., and V. Agarwal (1994), "Inter-governmental Fiscal Transfers in India: Some Issues of Design and Measurement," in A. Bagchi and N. Stern (eds.), *Tax Policy and Planning in Developing Countries.* New Delhi: Oxford University Press, pp. 195–221.
Roy, J. (ed.) (1995), *Macroeconomic Management and Fiscal Decentralization.* Washington, DC: World Bank.
Shah, A. (1991), "The New Fiscal Federalism in Brazil," Discussion Paper no. 124, World Bank, Washington, DC.
Shah, A. (1994), "The Reform of Intergovernmental Fiscal Relations in Developing and Emerging Market Economies," Policy and Research Series no. 23, World Bank, Washington, DC.
Shah, A. (1995), "Intergovernmental Fiscal Relations in Canada: An Overview," in Roy (1995), pp. 233–55.
Shapiro, P., and J. Petchey (1994), "Secession and the Median Voter," Paper presented at ISPE Conference on "Fiscal Aspects of Evolving Federations" (26–28 August, Nashville, TN).
Sinn, G., and H.-W. Sinn (1992), *Jumpstart.* Cambridge, MA: MIT Press.
Tanzi, V. (1995), *Taxation in an Integrating World.* Washington, DC: Brookings.

Tanzi, V. (1996), "Fiscal Federalism and Decentralization: A Review of Some Efficiency and Macroeconomics Aspects," in M. Bruno and B. Pleskovic (eds.), *Annual World Bank Conference on Development Economics*. Washington, DC: World Bank, pp. 295–316.

Tiebout, C. M. (1956), "A Pure Theory of Local Expenditures," *Journal of Political Economy* 64: 416–24.

Wellisch, D., and D. E. Wildasin (1996), "Decentralized Income Redistribution and Immigration," *European Economic Review* 40: 101–33.

Wildasin, D. E. (1991), "Income Redistribution in a Common Labor Market," *American Economic Review* 81: 757–74.

Wildasin, D. E. (1992), "Relaxation of Barriers to Factor Mobility and Income Redistribution," in P. Pestieau (ed.), *Public Finance in a World of Transition* (suppl. to vol. 47 of *Public Finance/Finances Publiques*). The Hague: Foundation Journal of Public Finance, pp. 216–30.

Wildasin, D. E. (1994), "Income Redistribution and Migration," *Canadian Journal of Economics* 27: 637–56.

Wildasin, D. E. (1997), "Income Distribution and Redistribution within Federations," *Annales d'Economie et de Statistique* 45: 291–313.

Wildasin, D. E. (forthcoming a), "Factor Mobility, Risk, Inequality, and Redistribution," in D. Pines, E. Sadka, and I. Zilcha (eds.), *Topics in Public Economics*. Cambridge University Press. [See also "Factor Mobility, Risk, and Redistribution in the Welfare State," *Scandinavian Journal of Economics* 97: 527–46.]

Wildasin, D. E. (forthcoming b), "Factor Mobility and Redistributive Policy: Local and International Perspectives," in P. B. Sorensen (ed.), *Public Finance in a Changing World*. New York: Macmillan.

Winkler, D. R. (1994), *The Design and Administration of Intergovernmental Transfers: Fiscal Decentralization in Latin America*. Washington, DC: World Bank.

World Bank (1993), *Argentina: From Insolvency to Growth*. Washington, DC: World Bank.

World Bank (1994), *Brazil: An Agenda for Stabilization*. Washington, DC: World Bank.

World Bank (1995a), *Economic Developments in India: Achievements and Challenges*. Washington, DC: World Bank.

World Bank (1995b), *China: Macroeconomic Stability in a Decentralized Economy*. Washington, DC: World Bank.

World Bank (1995c), *Estonia: Financing Local Governments*. Washington, DC: World Bank.

World Bank (1995d), *Brazil State Debt: Crisis and Reform*. Washington, DC: World Bank.

World Bank (1996a), *Colombia: Reforming the Decentralization Law: Incentives for an Effective Delivery of Services*. Washington, DC: World Bank.

World Bank (1996b), *Fiscal Management in Russia*. Washington, DC: World Bank.

World Bank (1996c), *Russian Federation: Toward Medium-Term Viability*. Washington, DC: World Bank.

PART II

Theoretical Issues

CHAPTER 3

Efficiency and the Optimal Direction of Federal–State Transfers

Robin Boadway & Michael Keen

1. INTRODUCTION

A common feature of federations is that higher levels of government collect more revenues than they need for their own expenditure requirements and so transfer funds to lower levels; that is, a positive "fiscal gap" exists.[1] Indeed, this occurs (between the national government and municipalities) even in unitary nations. Yet, despite the extensive literature on the role and structure of intergovernmental grants, there has been very little analysis of the optimal size – or, indeed, sign – of the fiscal gap in federal systems.[2] The purpose of this paper is to take a first step toward a theory of the optimal fiscal gap by analyzing the efficiency arguments for a mismatch between expenditure and revenue-raising responsibilities in a federation.

Standard fiscal federalism principles create a prima facie case that the optimal fiscal gap is typically positive, with the case for decentralizing expenditure responsibilities seen as stronger than that for decentralizing revenue raising.[3] The decentralized provision of public goods and services can improve efficiency by ensuring that public service provision is better suited to local tastes and needs, by inducing greater political accountability, by enhancing cost effectiveness and innovation through interjurisdictional competition, and by reducing administrative and agency costs associated with a central bureaucracy. Devolving taxation responsibilities can also be beneficial in improving fiscal accountability and allowing tax structures to respond to local characteristics. On the other hand, decentralized taxation can detract from the equity and efficiency of the tax system. Equity is compromised to the extent that the central government is no longer able to ensure a common standard of vertical and horizontal

We are grateful for comments by Timothy Besley, Richard Musgrave, and other participants in the ISPE Conference on "Fiscal Aspects of Evolving federations" at Vanderbilt University, by Dan Usher and Horn-chern Lin, and by three referees and the editor of this volume, David Wildasin. Financial support from the Social Sciences and Humanities Research Council of Canada is gratefully acknowledged.

equity across the nation; furthermore, local jurisdictions may "compete away" redistributive elements of their tax systems. Efficiency may be violated to the extent that tax bases are more mobile from the perspective of lower levels of government, deterring them from raising tax rates through the induced loss of tax base. This can lead to wasteful tax competition to attract mobile factors of production, resulting in the non-optimal provision of public goods and services by lower-level jurisdictions. The proposed policy response to all this is typically to retain more taxing responsibility than expenditure responsibility at higher levels of government, implying a positive fiscal gap.

Formal analysis of the fiscal gap requires explicitly modeling the decisions of more than one level of government and the interactions between them; indeed, this is the essence of a federal system of government. However, such models are rare in the federalism literature. One apparent reason for this is that even relatively simple models of this kind rapidly become very complicated. The classic analysis in Gordon (1983), for example, identifies many externalities arising from noncooperative behavior by lower-level governments and discusses possible responses at the federal level; however, that federal layer is not explicitly modeled.[4] Yet by concentrating solely on efficiency aspects and including only a minimal number of budgetary decisions by the different levels of government, we are able in what follows to obtain some insight into the consequences of intergovernmental interaction for the fiscal gap, and to evaluate that part of the conventional wisdom which is concerned with efficiency. As will be seen, incorporating both levels of government brings to light potential vertical externalities between them that have previously been generally neglected. These externalities arise from co-occupancy of a common tax base by federal and state governments: increases in state tax rates are then likely to have effects – often, but not necessarily, adverse – on federal tax revenues that are not taken into account by the states. As a result, the efficiency cost of raising marginal public funds that guides state decisions diverges from the socially relevant one. It emerges that, in order to counter this, optimal federal government policy involves a negative tax rate, and that this can imply a negative fiscal gap in reasonable circumstances.[5]

The model used is a simple one of a federal system with two levels of government: a *federal* level with one government and a *state* level with two or more. Each government provides a public good to the residents of its own jurisdiction, and each obtains tax revenues through a distortionary tax on labor. Intergovernmental transfers may occur between the federal government and the states, and it is on these transfers that we focus.

We assume throughout that states behave as Nash competitors with respect both to one another and to the federal government; that is, they take as given the budgetary decisions taken by other governments. However, the federal government, which sets both its own tax rates and the level of grants to the states, is assumed to act as first mover (or Stackelberg leader), committing to its policies before the states and anticipating their effect on states' decisions. This is an extreme assumption, motivated by the fact that there is always only one federal government but usually several state governments. Given the structure of the problem and the desire to focus solely on efficiency issues, states are assumed to be identical, and only symmetric Nash equilibria among the states are considered.

Our analysis is concerned with the size and, especially, sign of the fiscal gap – that is, the excess of states' expenditures over their revenues from "own" sources – rather than with the role of intergovernmental transfers per se. It is important to recognize the distinction between the two. Many of the most common objectives of intergovernmental transfers require little, if any, fiscal gap; for those that do, the size of the fiscal gap is largely irrelevant. For example, one argument for transfers is to internalize the externality arising from the existence of interjurisdictional spillovers.[6] But it is sufficient for this purpose to implement a pure relative-price incentive on lower levels of government; an income transfer is unnecessary. Another key role of intergovernmental transfers is to correct for fiscal inefficiencies and/or fiscal (horizontal) inequities arising in a decentralized federation when lower-level jurisdictions have different fiscal capacities or needs.[7] For this purpose, purely redistributive transfers from jurisdictions with higher-than-average fiscal capacities to those with lower-than-average fiscal capacities would suffice; no net fiscal gap between the two levels is required. To abstract from such familiar considerations, we exclude from the model both interstate expenditure spillovers and differences in fiscal capacity across states. We also assume all households to be identical. This of course rules out one of the key roles of government, which is to redistribute income. In a federal system, it is often argued that redistribution should be primarily the responsibility of the federal government. Given that the tax system is a major instrument for redistribution, this may give a further reason for having relatively more taxing power than spending responsibility at the federal level. Our purpose in adopting these simplifications is to ensure that any intergovernmental transfers that emerge from the analysis result solely from the need for a fiscal gap on efficiency grounds.

The paper proceeds as follows. Following Section 2's detailing of the model, Section 3 considers the benchmark case of a "unitary" nation in which the federal government is able to choose not only its own tax rate and expenditures but also those of the states. In this case, the issue of transfers does not arise, but the rules for deciding on tax rates and public goods provision at both levels characterize a second-best optimum (given the need to use distorting labor taxes). Section 4 considers the optimal fiscal gap when the population is immobile among states. Though unrealistic, this case is instructive in highlighting the vertical fiscal externality at work and its distinctive implications for the optimal fiscal gap. These, indeed, are the central results of the paper, the remainder of which explores some extensions: Section 5 looks at the case in which households are perfectly mobile, and Section 6 at the implications of interstate competition for the tax base. Section 7 concludes.

2. Structure of the Model

The nation consists of k identical states and nk identical households. In the next two sections, households are assumed to be, respectively, completely immobile and costlessly mobile among states. Mobility is not an important issue for describing the model: we concentrate on symmetric allocations, so that mobility does not affect the allocation of population among states (though it may affect the decision rules followed by the state governments). Given symmetry, subscripts denoting states of residence will typically be omitted and introduced only when necessary. For simplicity, the utility of each household takes the separable form:

$$u(x, l) + b(g) + B(G), \tag{1}$$

where x is a private good (and numeraire), l is labor supplied, g is the state public good, and G is the federal public good. The benefits of state public goods accrue only to residents of the state, while those of the federal public good accrue to all members of the nation regardless of where they reside. The functions $b(g)$ and $B(G)$ are both increasing and concave, whereas $u(x, l)$ is increasing in x, decreasing in l, and quasiconcave. The budget constraint faced by each household is:

$$x = (w - \tau)l, \tag{2}$$

where w is the wage rate and τ the per-unit tax on labor. The latter, in turn, is given by $\tau = t + T$, where t is the state tax and T the federal tax.[8]

The household maximizes utility (1) subject to the budget constraint (2), which yields the following first-order condition:[9]

$$(w - \tau)u_x + u_l = 0. \tag{3}$$

This equation gives labor supply $l(w - \tau)$, which when substituted into (1) yields indirect utility $v(w - \tau) + b(g) + B(G)$. For concreteness of interpretation, we assume that $l'(w - \tau) > 0$. Somewhat surprisingly, however, the central results are independent of the sign of l', a point to which we return later. By the envelope theorem, differentiating the indirect utility function with respect to w yields

$$v' = u_x l. \tag{4}$$

The production side of the economy is similarly simple. Each state is endowed with the same amount of some fixed factor.[10] Output is produced by applying labor services to the fixed factor according to an increasing and strictly concave production function $f(nl)$, where n is the number of workers in the state and $f(0) = 0$. The output can be used interchangeably for the production of x, g, or G; thus, the marginal rates of transformation between public goods of each type and private goods are normalized at unity. The private sector is perfectly competitive, so the market wage is given by the usual marginal productivity condition:

$$w = f'[nl(w - \tau)]. \tag{5}$$

This yields a wage function $w(\tau, n)$, with

$$w_\tau = \frac{-f''nl'}{1 - f''nl'} \in (0, 1); \qquad w_n = -\frac{w_\tau l}{nl'} < 0. \tag{6}$$

All rents are assumed to accrue to the public sector (since they represent an efficient source of tax revenues). A proportion $\theta \in [0, 1]$ accrues to the federal government and the remaining $(1 - \theta)$ accrues to the state in which the rents are generated; θ is taken as given throughout the analysis. The rents generated in the typical state are:

$$r(\tau, n) = f[nl(w(\tau, n) - \tau)] - nl(w(\tau, n) - \tau)f'[nl(w(\tau, n) - \tau)]. \tag{7}$$

Differentiating (7) and using (6) yields

$$r_\tau = (1 - w_\tau)f''n^2l'l = \frac{n^2lf''l'}{1 - f''nl'} < 0; \qquad r_n = -\frac{r_\tau l}{nl'} > 0. \tag{8}$$

Note that, in a symmetric equilibrium with all states pursuing the same policies (the case we focus on), the population n, the wage w, rents r, and government policies will be identical in all states; hence, so too will be the level of utility.

State governments provide the pure local public good[11] g and finance it by the labor tax plus any transfer S that they receive from the federal government. The state budget constraint is thus:

$$g(t, T, S, \theta, n) = ntl[w(\tau, n) - \tau] + S + (1 - \theta)r(\tau, n). \tag{9}$$

The sign of S indicates the direction of federal–state transfers, which is our central concern: $S > 0$, for example, corresponds to a positive fiscal gap, with transfers running from the federal government to the states. For later use, note from (9) that

$$g_t = (w_\tau - 1)ntl' + nl + (1 - \theta)r_\tau, \tag{10}$$

$$g_T = (w_\tau - 1)ntl' + (1 - \theta)r_\tau = g_t - nl, \tag{11}$$

$$g_S = 1, \tag{12}$$

$$g_n = tl + ntl'w_n + (1 - \theta)r_n. \tag{13}$$

The state selects t and g to maximize the per-capita utility of its residents, taking as given the policies of the federal government and all other state governments;[12] the presumption is that there are enough states for each to ignore the effects of its policies on other states, as well as on the federal government. The solution to the state problem is a pair (t, g) that depends upon federal policies (T, G, S), the allocation of rents θ, and, in the immobile population case, state population n. The implications of mobility for state behavior are examined in Sections 5 and 6.

The federal government acts as a first mover, recognizing the effects of its policies on the behavior of the states. We deal with symmetric equilibria, so federal policies, which are uniform across states, will have no effect on the allocation of population. Thus we need not be concerned with analyzing any migration response to federal policies. The federal budget constraint is

$$G(T, t, S, \theta, n) = knTl[w(\tau, n) - \tau] - kS + k\theta r(\tau, n). \tag{14}$$

Again for later use, note that

$$G_T = (w_\tau - 1)knTl' + knl + k\theta r_\tau, \tag{15}$$

$$G_t = (w_\tau - 1)knTl' + k\theta r_\tau = G_T - knl, \tag{16}$$

$$G_S = -k. \tag{17}$$

The federal government chooses its policies (T, G, S), taking as given its share of the rents θ and bearing in mind the implications for (t, g), to maximize per-capita utility.

3. Optimal Policies in the Unitary Nation

As noted at the outset, the usual argument for a positive fiscal gap is that it is necessary to avoid outcomes resulting from state government behavior that, while optimal from the state's perspective, are inefficient from a national perspective. For exactly this reason, this section considers the benchmark case in which states are given no taxing or spending powers. We do this by consolidating the budget constraints (9) and (14) - thereby eliminating intergovernmental transfers S and the rent-sharing parameter

θ – and by allowing the federal government to choose the total tax τ on labor along with g and G.

One feature of our model is that there is indeed no welfare loss from adopting a unitary government structure, since all of the familiar potential gains from decentralization outlined in Section 1 have been suppressed. An implication is that the decentralized outcomes with which we are ultimately concerned cannot be welfare-superior to the best unitary one; the best decentralized regime will be that which mimics most closely the unitary optimum. It may seem strange (though it is certainly not unusual) to analyze issues of fiscal federalism in a model with this feature. But our purpose is to model not the *reasons* for decentralizing fiscal responsibilities to the states but only the *consequences* of doing so. For this purpose, the intrinsic superiority of the unitary form provides a useful clarity of focus.

Consider then the unitary optimum. Assuming it to be symmetric, this optimum will involve all states having the same numbers of residents. Thus we can suppress n from the problem, which can consequently be written as follows:

$$\max_{\{\tau, g, G\}} \{v[w(\tau) - \tau] + b(g) + B(G)\} \tag{18}$$

subject to

$$G + kg = kn\tau l[w(\tau) - \tau] + kr(\tau). \tag{19}$$

Using (4) and (8), the first-order conditions for this readily reduce to

$$\frac{nb'(g)}{u_x} = \frac{knB'(G)}{u_x} = \frac{1}{1 - \tau l'/l}. \tag{20}$$

Equations (20), together with the budget constraint (19), characterize the second-best optimum, denoted by (τ^*, g^*, G^*).

The unitary government, it should be noted, will deploy the distorting labor tax only if the federation is underpopulated in the sense that aggregate rents $kr(0, n)$ are insufficient to finance the first-best level of aggregate expenditure. In particular – and this is a special case that we shall utilize in the sequel – it is straightforward to show that, if n is optimal, rents exactly suffice to finance first-best levels of public expenditure.[13]

Equations (20) are standard optimality conditions for public goods supply in a distorted economy; they are simplified versions of the well-known Atkinson and Stern (1974) rule.[14] They indicate that both the sum of the marginal rates of substitution of each state public good g for the private good x (across the typical state's population) and the sum (across the federation) of the marginal rates of substitution of G for x should be equal to $1/(1 - \tau l'/l)$. We refer to this term as the *marginal cost of public funds* (MCPF). As long as the federation is underpopulated, so that $\tau^* > 0$, the MCPF is greater than unity (given our assumption that $l' > 0$).

4. OPTIMAL POLICIES WITH IMMOBILE HOUSEHOLDS

We now reintroduce state governments and consider optimal federal policies when households are completely immobile among states; issues arising from mobility are taken up in subsequent sections. As discussed before, we assume that the federal government is a Stackelberg leader, moving first and committing itself to its tax, expenditure, and transfer policies. The states move second, taking federal policies as given. Because the federal government anticipates the effects of its actions on state behavior, we analyze decisions in reverse order.

4.1. The Representative State's Problem

State governments choose t and g to maximize the per-capita utility of their residents, taking as given the state population n, federal policy variables (T, G, S), and their share $(1-\theta)$ of rents, and subject to the state budget constraint (9). The first-order condition is simply:

$$(w_\tau - 1)v' + b'g_t = 0. \tag{21}$$

Substituting for g_t from (10), and then from (4) for v', from (8) for r_τ, and from (6) for w_τ, we obtain our first proposition.

Proposition 1. *With households immobile across states, the MCPF of the state government is given by*

$$\frac{nb'}{u_x} = \frac{1}{1 - tl'/l - \theta f''nl'}. \tag{22}$$

Together with the state budget constraint, this yields the state policy variables as functions $t(T, S; \theta, n)$ and $g(T, S; \theta, n)$.[15] To interpret the rule in Proposition 1, note that the denominator on the right can be written as:

$$1 - \frac{tl'}{l} - \theta f''nl' = 1 - \frac{\tau l'}{l} + \left(\frac{Tl'}{l} - \theta f''nl'\right) \tag{23}$$

$$= 1 - \frac{\tau l'}{l} + \frac{G_t}{(w_\tau - 1)knl}, \tag{24}$$

where the second equality follows from (16) and (8). Comparing equation (23) – to which we turn in a moment – with (20) shows that the MCPF at the state level differs from the second-best optimal decision rule for g by two terms; (24) then shows that the sign of this divergence depends simply on that of the impact on federal revenues of an increase in state taxation. If this externality is negative, then (recalling from (6) that $w_\tau <$ 1) the state MCPF is lower than that corresponding to the unitary rule: state taxes, loosely speaking, would then be expected to be higher than in the unitary second-best case, and state expenditures correspondingly also higher.[16]

The two components of the external effect on the right-hand side of (23) have straightforward interpretations. First, the state government neglects the effect on federal tax revenues of the labor supply response to its tax decisions. Given our assumption that $l' > 0$, this labor supply effect will diminish federal revenues so long as $T > 0$.

The second term in the external effect in (23), $-\theta f'' n l'$, reflects the change in the federal government's receipt of rents as a result of the induced response of labor supply (and wage rate) to changes in the state tax. From the social point of view, this change in rents is a pure transfer and so does not appear in the second-best MCPF expression for the unitary nation, (20). From the state's perspective, however, it represents a redistribution of income between residents of the state and the federal government, and the state cares only about the first of these. Again, given $l' > 0$, since $f'' < 0$ this term is positive for $\theta > 0$; an increase in the state tax rate reduces labor supply, causing a reduction in rents – a proportion θ of which is at the expense of the federal government (and hence not recognized by the state). This second effect, like the first, tends to reduce the magnitude of the right-hand side of (22) and so causes the state MCPF to be lower than the second-best optimal value.

Before turning to federal policies, it will prove useful to consider the way in which federal decisions affect the state's choice of tax rate $t(T, S; \theta, n)$. Differentiating (21), the slope of a state's reaction function with respect to the federal tax rate is found to be:[17]

$$t_T = -1 + \frac{(w_\tau - 1)[(b')^2 l' - b'' v' l]}{b'[(w_\tau - 1)^2 v'' + v' w_{\tau\tau} + b' g_{tt} + b'' g_t^2]}. \tag{25}$$

The denominator of the second term is negative (by the second-order condition on the states' problem), as is the numerator (recalling (6)). Thus t_T can in general have either sign.[18] Note though that, given $l' > 0$, (25) implies $1 + t_T > 0$: the state tax may fall in response to an increase in the federal tax, but not by so much that the combined rate $\tau = t + T$ also falls. For the effect of the intergovernmental transfer, one finds:

$$t_S = -\left(\frac{b'' g_t}{(w_\tau - 1)^2 v'' + v' w_{\tau\tau} + b' g_{tt} + b'' g_t^2}\right) \le 0. \tag{26}$$

As one would expect, an increase in the transfer S received by the state can only reduce the state tax rate. The state tax is unaffected by the transfer if and only if $b(\cdot)$ is linear, so that income effects are concentrated entirely on the state public good.

4.2. The Federal Government's Problem

Consider now the optimal policy of the federal government, given the behavior of the states just described. Its problem is then to maximize

$$V(T, S; \theta) \equiv v[w(\tau) - \tau] + b[g(t, T, S, \theta)] + B[G(T, t, S, \theta)] \qquad (27)$$

subject to $t = t(T, S; \theta, n)$, as given by the solution to the state's problem.

For the reason noted previously, the federal government will seek to replicate as closely as possible – given its lack of direct control over the states' decisions – the second-best optimal allocation of resources in the unitary nation, characterized in Section 3: because its decision problem is seemingly more constrained than that of the unitary government, it can certainly do no better than the unitary optimum. And it is easily verified that, when it moves first, the federal government is able to replicate the unitary second-best exactly. To see this heuristically, note that it has three policy instruments (T, S, G) with which to achieve the three second-best policy variables (τ^*, G^*, g^*), given the state responses $t(T, S)$ and $g(T, S)$. Setting $G = G^*$, it can then also induce the optimal values for τ and g by choosing T and S such that $\tau^* = T + t(T, S)$ and $g^* = g(T, S)$. Thus we have the following result.

Proposition 2. *With households immobile across states, the federal government acting as a first mover with respect to the states can achieve the second-best optimum.*

Taking θ as given is clearly no real restriction in this context (assuming there are no other restrictions on federal policy variables, such as non-negativity requirements); it would be a redundant policy instrument. This is not to say, however, that the value of θ is irrelevant to the federal government's choice of policy variables. As will be seen shortly, the optimal values of both T and S depend upon the federal government's share of rents θ.

The next step is to characterize explicitly how the federal government must choose T and S so as to implement the second-best optimum. Consider first the choice of T in the constrained maximization of (27). The necessary condition is

$$(w_\tau - 1)(1 + t_T)v' + (g_t t_T + g_T)b' + (G_t t_T + G_T)B' = 0. \qquad (28)$$

Using the first-order condition for the state problem together with (11) and (16), the MCPFs at the state and federal levels are related as follows:

$$\frac{knB'}{u_x} = \frac{nb'}{u_x}\left(\frac{1}{1+(1+t_T)G_t/(knl)}\right). \tag{29}$$

Recalling that $1+t_T > 0$, the MCPF for the federal government thus exceeds that of the state governments if and only if an increase in the state tax rate reduces federal revenues. The explanation for this is straightforward. For whilst the federal government takes full account of the impact of its policies on the revenues of the state governments, the latter ignore their effect on federal revenues. If $G_t < 0$ – for which (from (16)) it is sufficient that the federal tax rate T be strictly positive – this asymmetry reduces the MCPF perceived at the state level relative to that at the federal level.

Consider now the federal government's choice of transfer S. Differentiating (27) and using (12), (17), and (21), one finds the welfare effect of a small change in S to be

$$\left(\frac{dV}{dS}\right)\frac{n}{u_x} = \left(\frac{nb'}{u_x} - \frac{knB'}{u_x}\right) + \left(\frac{nB'}{u_x}\right)G_t t_S. \tag{30}$$

There are thus two considerations in determining the optimal intergovernmental transfer. One, captured in the first term on the right of (30), is a gain from transferring funds from whichever jurisdiction has the lower MCPF to whichever has the higher. For example, if $G_t < 0$ then it will be desirable, on this account, to transfer funds *away* from the states and toward the center: the exact opposite, that is, of the usual presumption. This, however, is not the end of the story. Though appealing, the simple policy prescription – that transfers should go from whichever level of government has the lower MCPF to whichever has the higher – is not, in general, correct. The reason for this, captured by the second term of (30), is that the transfer itself will typically affect the tax set by the states and hence also affect the extent of the vertical externality operating between levels of government. Specifically, a transfer toward the states, inducing a reduction in the excessively high state tax rate, will be desirable so long as [19] $G_t < 0$. These two considerations thus point in opposite directions, and will do so for any value of $G_t \neq 0$. With $G_t < 0$, for example, the states set too high a tax rate; although this suggests transferring some revenue away from them to finance the federal government, such a transfer will induce them to set an even higher tax rate, intensifying the vertical externality. In one special case, however, (30) gives a very sharp result. If the federal tax rate is positive and $b(\cdot)$ is linear (so that transfers have no effect on the state tax), then welfare is increased by a small transfer toward the level of government with the higher MCPF.

At an optimum, of course, the transfer S will be chosen so that dV/dS equals zero. Combining this with the condition (29) characterizing the optimal federal tax, we have $G_t = 0$. Thus, as one would expect, federal and state MCPFs are equated; from (24), their common value is then exactly as given by the second-best rule for the unitary state. By (16) and (8), the federal tax rate that satisfies $G_t = 0$ at the second-best optimum, T^*, is given by:

$$T^* = \theta f''[nl(w(\tau^*, n) - \tau^*)]nl(w(\tau^*, n) - \tau^*) \leq 0. \qquad (31)$$

Note that, because $f'' < 0$, we have $T^* < 0$ for $\theta > 0$. That is, the federal government should subsidize labor. We may summarize as follows.

Proposition 3. *If households are immobile across states then, in order to achieve the second-best optimum, the federal government acting as first mover must subsidize labor at the rate* $T^* = \theta f'' nl \leq 0$.

The obvious intuition for this result is that a federal subsidy is needed in order to offset the tendency of states – as they neglect the adverse effect that their tax increases have on federal government revenues – to set their tax rates too high. This, however, is a little too glib. For note that the result in Proposition 3 is independent of the sign of l': even if the labor supply curve were downward-sloping, so that an increase in the state tax conveyed a beneficial vertical externality on federal revenues (pointing to state taxes being too low, not too high), the optimal federal tax would still be negative. Rather, the intuition behind Proposition 3 is that the federal government should arrange matters so that, at the margin, state taxes have no effect on federal revenues, ensuring that the states will fully internalize the social costs of their revenue raising. This in turn requires that the effect on federal receipts from labor taxation induced by a small increase (say) in labor supply nl, which is simply T, exactly offset the induced increase in its receipt of rents, $\theta f'' nl$. It is the internalization of the vertical externality, not excessively high state taxes, that calls for a federal subsidy.

Proposition 3 leaves the sign of the optimal intergovernmental transfer S – the sign, that is, of the optimal fiscal gap – ambiguous. Recalling the federal budget constraint (14), it is clear that this will generally depend on, inter alia, the strength of preferences toward the federal public good and the size and distribution of rents. To fix ideas, it is useful to consider three special cases.

Case 1: $\theta = 0$. Suppose that all rents are allocated to the states. In this case, Proposition 3 implies that $T^* = 0$. The federal government then has no receipts of its own, so that federal expenditure on G must be financed entirely by transfers from the states. Thus $S^* < 0$ and, contrary to the usual presumption, the optimal fiscal gap is negative.[20] Note, moreover, that if θ is thought of as a choice variable, this case points to a particularly simple recipe for replicating the unitary second-best outcome: Allocate all rents and tax powers to the states, and finance federal expenditures by transfers to the center.

Case 2: Optimal National Population. A second instructive special case is that in which the total population of the federation is optimal, so that rents exactly suffice to finance first-best levels of expenditure. Suppose, too, that θ happens to be such that each level of government receives exactly enough rents to finance its first-best expenditure. This situation might seem a happy one, with no need for either level to deploy distorting taxes, and no need for transfers between them. Noncooperative behavior, however, prevents this outcome. For, as we have just discussed, the states will still perceive a gain from taxing labor as a device for transferring rents from the central government, which again calls for offsetting behavior by the federal government. As a consequence of needing to subsidize labor while still providing the national public good, the federal government will find itself having to extract revenues from the state governments. That is, the optimal fiscal gap is again negative.

Case 3: $G^* = 0$. Finally, take the extreme case in which federal expenditure is worthless. One might expect to reach the orthodox conclusion that transfers should go from the center to the states. But even in this case the optimal fiscal gap may be negative. For Proposition 3 implies that the federal government will still need to finance a labor subsidy if $\theta > 0$, and its revenue from rents may not be sufficient for it to do so. To see this, note that setting $G = 0$ in the federal budget constraint and using (31) yields $S = \theta r(1 - E_r)$, where $E_r \equiv -f''(nl)^2/r > 0$ denotes the elasticity of rents with respect to employment nl. If that elasticity exceeds unity, the optimal fiscal gap is thus negative even when there is no need for any public expenditure at the federal level (and hence, note, it will certainly be negative when there *is* such a need): intuitively, a high responsiveness of rents implies that the reduction in rents consequent upon the states' taxation of labor has a powerful effect in diminishing the federal government's ability to finance the corrective subsidy from its own resources. And it is indeed perfectly possible that $E_r > 1$, a sufficient condition being that $f''' \leq 0$. Thus when $f(\cdot)$ is quadratic, for example, the optimal fiscal gap is certainly negative. Moreover, with CES production it can be shown to be sufficient – but not necessary – for an optimally negative fiscal gap that the elasticity of substitution between labor and the immobile factor be less than 0.5.

One can certainly construct examples in which the optimal fiscal gap is positive, as conventional wisdom has it: from the condition in the preceding paragraph, for example, it can be seen that this will be so if there is no federal public good and production is Cobb–Douglas. There seem to be few useful general results on the sign of the optimal fiscal gap.[21] The preceding examples suffice to show, however, that the optimal fiscal gap can be negative in quite reasonable circumstances.

It may be useful to summarize the somewhat unfamiliar arguments of this section. At their heart is an effect arising from co-occupancy of a common tax base by federal and state governments: a vertical externality imposed by state tax-rate changes on federal government revenues. This externality will tend to cause the MCPF perceived by the states to differ from the true marginal cost of raising state revenues. To correct for this, the federal government must eliminate the impact of state taxes on federal revenues by imposing a negative tax rate on the common base. If the federal receipt of rents is low enough relative to the subsidy required and its own expenditure needs, which may plausibly be the case, then the federal government will have to obtain transfers from the states; that is, the optimal fiscal gap will be negative.

5. The Implications of Perfect Mobility

Suppose now that households can relocate costlessly among states and therefore do so until utilities are equalized. State governments are fully aware of this and take account of the effects of their own actions on the allocation of population among states. In all other respects, the model remains unchanged. It is convenient to consider the special case in which there are only two[22] states (identical, as before), indexed A and B.

In order to determine the effect of state policies on population allocation, we need to characterize the migration equilibrium. Denoting by $\bar{n}$ the total population, of whom n_A reside in state A and the remaining $\bar{n} - n_A$ in state B, free mobility implies that, in equilibrium,

$$v[w(\tau_A, n_A) - \tau_A] + b(g_A) = v[w(\tau_B, \bar{n} - n_A) - \tau_B] + b(g_B). \quad (32)$$

This determines n_A as a function of the tax rates and public expenditures of the two states, $n_A(\tau_A, \tau_B, g_A, g_B)$. We assume that it yields a unique and stable symmetric equilibrium.[23]

The representative state government is again assumed to maximize the per-capita utility of its residents, but now taking account of migration responses. Writing the typical state's population function as $n(\tau, g)$ (suppressing arguments referring to the other state), per-capita utility is

$$v[w(\tau, n(\tau, g)) - \tau] + b(g) + B(G), \tag{33}$$

and the state budget constraint can be written as

$$g = n(\tau, g)tl[w(\tau, n(\tau, g)) - \tau] + S + (1 - \theta)r(\tau, n(\tau, g)). \tag{34}$$

The state's problem is thus to choose t and g to maximize (33) subject to equation (34).

It is straightforward to show that the first-order conditions for this problem, evaluated at a symmetric equilibrium, reduce to exactly the condition (21) found previously for the case in which individuals are immobile.[24] Thus we have our next proposition.

Proposition 4. *Optimal federal and state policies are the same when workers are perfectly mobile as when they are completely immobile.*

Thus, in particular, the prescription of Proposition 3 and the force of the examples that followed it continue to apply.

This result – that state behavior is essentially unaffected by migration of households – has its counterpart in the literature. A standard result in existing models of federalism is that, in a world with perfect labor mobility and nondistorting taxes, if state governments maximize per-capita utilities while taking into account migration responses to their own policy actions and taking the policies of other states as fixed, then their behavior will be perfectly efficient in the sense that it will follow first-best (Samuelson) rules for expenditures and taxation.[25] Proposition 4 shows that the conclusion that mobility has no effect on policy continues to apply even with distortionary taxation. The reason for this is that with states maximizing the per-capita utility of their own residents and with these constrained by migration equilibrium to be the same across states, they are effectively maximizing per-capita utility across the federation; Myers (1990) refers to this as "incentive equivalence."[26]

The critical implication of Proposition 4 for present purposes is that the efficiency argument for a fiscal gap is independent of the degree of mobility of labor and derives instead from the distortionary nature of taxation. To see this, consider the special case in which the labor supply is completely inelastic ($l' = 0$). In this case, with or without population mobility, state behavior follows the Samuelson rule for g by (22). Moreover, since then $G_t = 0$, the federal government will also follow the Samuelson rule for G (by (29)). Therefore (from (30)), $dV/dS = 0$ at any value of S; that is, the size of the fiscal gap is completely irrelevant. Thus, at least for the case of labor taxation, mobility in itself is entirely irrelevant to the sign of the optimal fiscal gap.

6. Tax Competition

We have assumed so far that mobility applies to households. Although this captures whatever interstate competition for population may exist, it does not capture the other form of interstate competition that has been prominent in the literature: competition for factors of production. Although previous analyses have typically treated this as competition for capital, we analyze the case of mobility of labor; the two are much the same.[27]

Suppose then that while households are free to work in any state, they remain resident in their initial location. They receive the going wage in the state in which they work, and pay labor taxes there as well, but they benefit from public expenditure g in their state of residency. As before, we treat the special case in which there are just two states, A and B. To maintain symmetry, the number of residents in each state is fixed at $\bar{n}/2$. Given free mobility of labor, equilibrium now requires that the after-tax wage rate be equated across the two states:

$$w(\tau_A, n_A) - \tau_A = w(\tau_B, \bar{n} - n_A) - \tau_B. \tag{35}$$

This yields a worker allocation function $n_A(\tau_A, \tau_B)$; expenditures of the state governments no longer enter the mobility condition, because workers benefit from g in their home state.

The analysis again proceeds backwards, starting with the state's problem: the choice of t to maximize $v[w(\tau, n(\tau)) - \tau] + b[g(t, T, n(\tau), S, \theta)]$. Routine manipulation of the necessary conditions for this demonstrate[28] that the state MCPF is greater than that given by (22) – pointing, loosely speaking, toward lower state taxes – if and only if $tl > \theta(\partial r/\partial n)|_l$. The implication is that, for arbitrary federal policies, the effect on the level of state taxes of this kind of labor mobility is ambiguous. To see why, note that attracting an additional worker affects both the level and the distribution of income within the state. Output rises by wl, the gross wage paid to that worker, of which the state captures tl in taxes. At the same time, the reduction in the gross wage leads to a redistribution from labor to the fixed factor; with $\theta > 0$, this redistribution has the undesirable effect, from the state's perspective, of transferring income to the federal government. A state will thus wish to attract additional workers only if the first effect dominates the latter.

Consider now the problem of the federal government. Since the two states will respond identically to a change in the federal tax, such a change will have no effect on the allocation of workers. The federal problem thus has exactly the same structure as in Section 4 (though the precise form of the states' response t_T will generally be different). Once again, by choosing T and S appropriately, the federal government has enough policy instruments to replicate the unitary second-best outcome. Note, however, that the size and sign of the fiscal gap required may be very different from that needed when households are fully mobile. Suppose, for instance, that $\theta = 0$, so that all rents go to the states. In the cases analyzed in Sections 4 and 5, where residency and place of work coincide, it is then optimal for the federal government to set $T = 0$ and finance itself by a negative fiscal gap. In the present case, however, a positive federal tax would be needed to stymie the downward pressure on tax rates from interstate competition for workers. Thus, as the traditional arguments cited in Section 1 would lead one to expect, it seems more likely that transfers should go from the center to the states. In fact, it is straightforward to establish the following.

Proposition 5. *When the federal government moves first, competition for workers (whose residency is fixed) increases both the optimal federal tax rate and the optimal transfer to the states.*[29]

Proof. See the Appendix.

This proposition tends to confirm the conventional wisdom, outlined in Section 1, that interstate competition for mobile factors provides an argument for increasing the fiscal gap; the optimal fiscal gap may still be negative – since the considerations identified earlier continue to apply – but interstate tax competition makes it more likely to be positive.

7. Concluding Remarks

It is a surprising feature of the literature on fiscal federalism that the interaction between the decisions of higher and lower levels of government has rarely been modeled explicitly. This paper has set out a model that does so, and turned it to the analysis of a key issue in federal relations: the optimal size and sign of the fiscal gap. To this end, we have assumed away all reasons for a fiscal gap other than those arising from pure efficiency considerations. In this simple framework, some striking results emerge. In particular, we have shown that, contrary to conventional wisdom, efficiency arguments call for a *negative* fiscal gap in perfectly reasonable circumstances.

Underlying these results is a vertical fiscal externality between levels of governments that arises from their co-occupancy of a common tax base, with state tax decisions consequently affecting the federal tax base. Two aspects of this effect deserve emphasis. First, the central results derived here do not depend on whether that externality is beneficial or harmful. They derive simply from the need to eliminate it. In the model used here, this requires subsidizing labor so as to offset any increase in income from rents that the federal government may receive when changes in state taxation induce a change in labor supply. Second, the force of the arguments depends on the extent of effective rather than formal co-occupancy by distinct levels of government. Suppose, for example, that the federal government is allocated a uniform wage tax and the states a general sales tax; in a formal sense, there is no co-occupancy. Under familiar conditions, however, the two taxes are entirely equivalent: effective co-occupancy – of the kind modeled here – would then be complete. In a more complex setting, with the possibility of differentiated indirect taxation, this exact correspondence will fail. Clearly, though, interactions of the kind analyzed here will still be very much at work. Indeed, the analysis may then have implications for the appropriate assignment of instruments to levels of government: the federal government may be unable to achieve the second-best optimum, for example, if indirect taxation is reserved for the states. For present purposes, however, the critical point is that federal systems are likely to be characterized by considerable effective co-occupancy.

Attention has been restricted here to simple forms of strategic behavior by the federal government and the states, with the former acting as Stackelberg leader. Other types of interaction may be equally or more plausible. The federal government might also play Nash.[30] State and federal governments in some federations may better be modeled as choosing policies in a bargaining framework (particularly in relation to transfers) or as playing a repeated game. It remains to be seen what role for the fiscal gap might emerge in such contexts.

APPENDIX

PROOF OF PROPOSITION 5

Noting that the migration equilibrium condition implies, in symmetric equilibrium, that

$$n_\tau = \frac{1-w_\tau}{2w_n}, \tag{A.1}$$

the first-order condition for the state's problem can be written as

$$\frac{b'}{v'} = \left(\frac{2g_l}{1-w_\tau} + \frac{g_n}{w_n}\right)^{-1}. \tag{A.2}$$

Noting from (10) and (11) (using (7) and (8)) that $g_t = nl - (g_n nl'/l)$, this becomes

$$\frac{b'}{v'} = \left(\frac{g_l}{1-w_\tau} + \frac{g_n + nlw_n}{w_n(1-w_\tau)}\right)^{-1} \tag{A.3}$$

and hence, using (10), (8), and (6), we have

$$\frac{nb'}{u_x} = \left(1 - \frac{tl'}{l} - \theta f''nl' + \frac{g_n + nlw_n}{nlw_n(1 - w_\tau)}\right)^{-1}. \tag{A.4}$$

From (13), (6), and (8),

$$g_n + nlw_n = (1 - w_\tau)(tl + \theta f''nl^2), \tag{A.5}$$

so that (A.4) becomes

$$\frac{nb'}{u_x} = \left[1 - \left(\frac{1 + w_\tau}{w_\tau}\right)\left(\frac{tl'}{l} + \theta f''nl'\right)\right]^{-1}. \tag{A.6}$$

Comparing (A.6) with (20), the value of T needed to achieve the second-best outcome is given by

$$T = T^* + \frac{\tau^*}{(1 + w_\tau)} > T^*, \tag{A.7}$$

where $T^* = \theta f''nl$ is the federal tax rate when households are fully mobile.

Since τ^* and total revenue are again at their second-best levels, it follows from the federal budget constraint and from the increase in T just established that S will now be higher than in the circumstances of Sections 4 and 5. ◻

NOTES

1. Notable exceptions include China, as well as the United States under the original articles of federation. Looser organizations of sovereign nations, such as the European Union and the United Nations, also usually finance their central budgets principally by transfers from member states.
2. An exception is Brennan and Pincus (1996), who develop a theory of conditional grants based on considerations similar to ours (that is, differences in the excess burden of raising revenues at two levels of government) and use it primarily to evaluate the positive effects of grants (such as the "flypaper" effect). However, in their model the marginal costs of public funds at the two levels of government are independent of one another, whereas in our analysis their interdependence is crucial.
3. Most of the arguments cited here may be found in the classic treatise by Oates (1972), and some go back to Musgrave (1959).
4. See also Wildasin (1986) for a comprehensive analysis of decision making in a federation.
5. A paper by Dahlby (1994) also recognizes some of the same forces as in our paper, especially differences in the perceived efficiency costs of raising revenues at different levels of government using concurrent revenue sources.
6. See Oates (1972), who develops the classic arguments of Musgrave (1959).
7. See Boadway and Wildasin (1984). Indeed, in the case of inefficiencies arising from fiscal externalities, voluntary transfers among the states would suffice, as Myers (1990) has shown.
8. Deductibility of state taxes against federal taxes complicates matters without yielding substantive additional insights.

9. For functions of several variables, derivatives are indicated by subscripts; for functions of a single variable, differentiation is indicated by a prime.
10. We give them equal endowments of the fixed factor to avoid the possibility of grants being used for horizontal redistribution.
11. It would make no significant difference to the results if – reflecting, perhaps, congestion costs – the benefits accruing to state residents from g depended upon state population, or even if g were a publicly provided private good.
12. The assumption that states maximize per-capita rather than total utility is one of substance: it is well known that the two criteria can give different results (Wildasin 1986). Note too that the assumption that states take as given the policy variables of other jurisdictions implies that they ignore the requirement that budgets of other jurisdictions be balanced.
13. These claims, which are simple variants of the usual Henry George theorem (Hartwick 1980; Wildasin 1986), are established by introducing the tax on rents as a choice variable and varying n (holding k fixed).
14. The Atkinson–Stern rule includes an additional term in the numerator, involving the effect of changes in g on tax revenues. This is absent from (20) as a consequence of additively separable utility.
15. Separability removes effects through G.
16. The fact that the MCPF for state governments within a federation tends to be lower than the second-best optimal value was first noted by Dahlby (1994), who goes on to suggest that this is also true of the federal MCPF. This implicitly assumes that the federal government also behaves as a Nash competitor; see note 30.
17. The derivation here uses (10), the relationship between g_{tT} and g_{tt} it implies, and the first-order condition (21).
18. See Keen and Kotsogiannis (1995) for a discussion of an analogous ambiguity in the context of capital taxation.
19. Recall from (26) that t_S is nonpositive.
20. It should be emphasized that this negative fiscal gap is not an inevitable consequence of the states having all the rents: the federal government might have chosen to finance its expenditures by its own labor tax T rather than by a transfer from the states. What Proposition 3 shows is that the federal government would never use $T > 0$ to raise revenues, regardless of the value of θ.
21. However, note that, since $G \geq 0$, it follows from the discussion of Case 3 that it is sufficient for the optimal fiscal gap to be negative that $f''' \leq 0$.
22. This restriction is inessential to the results.
23. In fact, federal models of this sort are particularly prone to problems of instability and multiple equilibria (see Stiglitz 1977). In local public goods models with no federal public good, stability of equilibrium requires that the population of the nation as a whole be at least as large as the sum of the "optimal" population levels (those that maximize per-capita utilities) in all states (Boadway and Flatters 1982); that is, the nation must be "over-populated." In the present model, with both federal and state public goods, matters are not quite so simple. For given federal policies, the level of utility achieved in a symmetric equilibrium when states are maximizing the per-capita utilities of their residents can be denoted $V(n, S, T, \theta)$, where n is each state's population. Stability requires $V_n < 0$, which can be shown to be equivalent to:

$$\theta f'' + \frac{g - S - (1-\theta)r}{n^2} < 0.$$

On the other hand, for there to be positive labor taxation τ^* at the second-best optimum, we require – by the Henry George result mentioned in note 13 – that the nation be underpopulated in the sense that rents are insufficient to finance first-best levels of spending on g and G. Clearly, underpopulation in the sense required for $\tau^* > 0$ is consistent with overpopulation in the sense required for stability.

24. This follows from the first-order conditions for this problem, using expressions derived for n_τ and n_g obtained from differentiating the migration equilibrium condition (32).

25. See Boadway (1982), Wildasin (1986), and Krelove (1992). Note that this result is again contingent on states maximizing per-capita rather than total utilities.

26. Myers and Papageorgiou (1993) and Wellisch (1994) have shown that – in a model with several local jurisdictions, each of which uses nondistorting taxes to provide a public good that can have spillover effects on other jurisdictions, and in which labor is perfectly mobile – voluntary intergovernmental transfers will serve both to internalize the external effect of public good spillovers and to ensure that migration is efficient. Lin (1995), in a model similar to ours but with heterogeneous states and $\theta = 0$, shows that voluntary contributions by the states to the financing of a national public good generate a second-best optimum. Thus, not only is the fiscal gap negative, but there is no apparent need for a federal government at all.

27. A standard model of capital tax competition is that of Zodrow and Mieszkowski (1986), which considers local public goods economies with fixed immobile populations and a given stock of capital that is perfectly mobile across local jurisdictions. Our model, in which capital has been suppressed as a factor of production, could be interpreted as applying to the case where the nation as a whole is small in the world economy and faces a fixed rate of return on capital. In such a model, adding capital would be of no consequence; taxing capital would be analogous to taxing local factors of production. Some aspects of capital income taxation within a federation are analyzed by Keen and Kotsogiannis (1995).

28. See (A.5) of the Appendix.

29. The resolution between the ambiguity of (a) whether the state MCPF is above or below that of (22) and (b) the certainty that the federal tax rate is higher here than in previous sections is that, whereas the former holds for arbitrary federal policies, optimization by the federal government implies that tl will indeed exceed $\theta(\partial r/\partial n)|_l$ when T and S are set so as to implement the second-best optimum. See Boadway and Keen (1994).

30. An earlier version of this paper (Boadway and Keen 1994) considers the case in which the federal government plays Nash relative to the states, with transfers between federal and state governments set by an independent "grants commission." In this case, the second-best optimum cannot be sustained in equilibrium. No simple results on the sign of S emerge. However, once again – and for the same reason as discussed before Proposition 3 – it is not necessarily the case that transfers should go from whichever level of government

62   ROBIN BOADWAY & MICHAEL KEEN

has the lower MCPF to whichever has the higher. Indeed, in this case it is not necessarily optimal for these transfers to be set so as to equate MCPFs between federal and state governments.

REFERENCES

Atkinson, A. B., and N. H. Stern (1974), "Pigou, Taxation and Public Goods," *Review of Economic Studies* 41: 119–28.
Boadway, R. W. (1982), "On the Method of Taxation and the Provision of Local Public Goods: Comment," *American Economic Review* 72: 846–51.
Boadway, R. W., and F. R. Flatters (1982), "Efficiency and Equalization Payments in a Federal System of Government: A Synthesis and Extension of Recent Results," *Canadian Journal of Economics* 15: 613–33.
Boadway, R. W., and M. Keen (1994), "Efficiency and the Fiscal Gap in Federal Systems," Discussion Paper no. 915, Queen's University, Kingston, Ontario.
Boadway, R. W., and D. E. Wildasin (1984), *Public Sector Economics*. Boston: Little, Brown.
Brennan, G., and J. J. Pincus (1996), "A Minimalist Model of Federal Grants and Flypaper Effects," *Journal of Public Economics* 61: 229–46.
Dahlby, B. (1994), "The Distortionary Effect of Rising Taxes," Mimeo, University of Alberta, Edmonton.
Gordon, R. H. (1983), "An Optimal Taxation Approach to Fiscal Federalism," *Quarterly Journal of Economics* 98: 567–86.
Hartwick, J. M. (1980), "The Henry George Rule, Optimal Population, and Interregional Equity," *Canadian Journal of Economics* 13: 695–700.
Keen, M., and C. Kotsogiannis (1995), "Federalism and Tax Competition," Mimeo, University of Essex, Colchester, UK.
Krelove, R. (1992), "Efficient Tax Exporting," *Canadian Journal of Economics* 25: 145–55.
Lin, H.-C. (1995), "Public Goods, Heterogeneous Jurisdictions and Perfect Household Mobility," Mimeo, Queen's University, Kingston, Ontario.
Musgrave, R. A. (1959), *The Theory of Public Finance*. New York: McGraw-Hill.
Myers, G. M. (1990), "Optimality, Free Mobility, and the Regional Authority in a Federation," *Journal of Public Economics* 43: 107–21.
Myers, G. M., and Y. Y. Papageorgiou (1993), "Fiscal Equivalence, Incentive Equivalence and Pareto Efficiency in a Decentralized Urban Context," *Journal of Urban Economics* 33: 29–47.
Oates, W. E. (1972), *Fiscal Federalism*. New York: Harcourt Brace Jovanovich.
Stiglitz, J. E. (1977), "The Theory of Local Public Goods," in M. S. Feldstein and R. P. Inman (eds.), *The Economics of Public Services*. New York: Macmillan.
Wellisch, D. (1994), "Interregional Spillovers in the Presence of Perfect and Imperfect Household Mobility," *Journal of Public Economics* 55: 167–84.
Wildasin, D. E. (1986), *Urban Public Finance*. Chur, Switzerland: Harwood.
Zodrow, R. G., and P. Mieszkowski (1986), "Pigou, Tiebout Property Taxation and the Underprovision of Local Public Goods," *Journal of Urban Economics* 19: 356–70.

CHAPTER 4

Interregional Redistribution through Tax Surcharge

Helmuth Cremer, Maurice Marchand, & Pierre Pestieau

1. INTRODUCTION

In most federal systems, the central government is expected to have a redistributive tax policy, or at least to finance its expenditures in an equitable way. Yet it is not impossible that the regions or the states making up the federation resist such redistribution policy by hiding characteristics that would be needed to achieve a first-best outcome. For instance, if the income of a region (or one of its components) is not observable, then the central government cannot base its redistributive policy directly on actual income levels. It can request the regions to report their income level, but incomes will be revealed correctly only if the regions have the proper incentives to do so. To put it another way, the redistributive policy must be *incentive-compatible,* and this requirement restricts the opportunity set of the central government. Alternatively, it is possible that the region income levels are observable in principle but only at the expense of some costly verification process. The central government may then have the option of directly discovering the actual income level of all the regions; however, this may be (and, as will be shown here, in general actually is) too costly. As a consequence, incentive compatibility restricts redistributive policies under costly information very much as it does under total unobservability.

Assuming regional incomes that are not perfectly observable might raise some objections. In a federal setting such as the United States, it is not conceivable that individual states could hide information pertaining to their production or income. In a confederal setting such as that of the European Union (EU), the national accounts figures of each member state are also well known. Such figures seem to be rather reliable, with the exception of the manner in which informal activities are accounted for. Yet

The authors acknowledge the financial support of the European Commission through the HCM Research Network "Fiscal Implications of European Integration." They thank M. Keen, D. Wildasin, D. Wellisch, and two referees for their comments.

one could argue that this perfect observability will last only as long as those national accounts figures are not used to assess the amount of revenue each nation is expected to supply to the confederal authority. Quite clearly, it will always be difficult to underassess salaried incomes in reported figures, whereas the importance of incomes from self-employment and underground activities can easily be understated.

The analogy between nations and households can be helpful in clarifying this argument. If there were no personal income or wealth taxes, collecting data on the income and the wealth of households would be quite easy. What makes a tax base unobservable (or observable at some cost) is, precisely, taxation. We imply in this paper that if authorities of a confederal government such as the European Union were to raise a nonnegligible amount of revenue based on national production or income of its member states, then it would very probably have to set up a costly confederal tax administration. It should also be pointed out that what we refer to as "income" is not necessarily just national (or regional) income. Rather, it is meant to represent some parameter characterizing a region's ability to pay. For instance, it can be thought of as "discretionary" income available to a region once it has satisfied the minimal subsistence of the poor (or sick) among its population (the number of which may be unobservable to the central government). With this interpretation, the central government observes overall regional income but not the part of it that is devoted to welfare. Hence, what we define here as income is actually income after deduction of the welfare payment.

Admittedly, such problems of asymmetric information are more likely to occur in less cohesive federations than in federal states with a strong sense of national unity.[1] Current history shows that the first case is not that unrealistic. Here we have in mind mainly a confederation of states such as the EU. However, to keep in line with the literature, we will use throughout our analysis the example of a federal country consisting of a number of regions. In this two-level federal system, each region provides its residents with a public good, the level of which is chosen by a benevolent regional government. The central government is responsible for the provision of federal public goods and for interregional redistribution. The representative resident of each region has preferences over a composite private good and the regional public good. Regions differ in income and preferences. Accordingly, a region is characterized by its income level, taken as exogenous, and by a parameter reflecting the taste of its residents for the regional public good.

The central government does not observe the income of the region, or of any of its components, nor the taste parameter. It can, however, observe the levels of expenditure on the regional public good and hence the amount of taxes collected to finance these expenditures. Thus, the central government is forced to allow financing of the federal public good to rely on the only observable variable: each region's public good expenditures. To put it another way, it will finance the federal public good and redistribute income by imposing a possibly nonlinear surcharge on regional taxes. Alternatively, one could say that the central government is going to offer matching grants on local public spending, grants that are nonlinear and possibly negative.

We want to characterize the optimal redistributive policy of the central government in such a setting of asymmetric information. We focus on the properties of the marginal tax rate. As one can expect at the outset, the federal tax structure will depend on the distribution of the two characteristics – income level and taste parameter – across regions. It is clear that the central government might try to acquire more information on those parameters and in particular on the level of income in each region. This can be accomplished with costly audits, the feasibility of which depends not only on their cost but also on the possibility of collusion between regional governments and auditors.

To maintain the household analogy, our model could be applied to individual income taxation; tax liability would be based on a conspicuous consumption good, with taxpayers concealing both their actual income and their preferences for that good. Our paper is in the tradition of optimal income taxation such as that developed by Stiglitz (1982)[2] – with, however, an important difference. Unlike Stiglitz's and most models of this kind, we assume not one but rather two characteristics (adverse selection parameters) to be unobservable by the principal. In standard models of optimal income taxation, individuals differ only in their labor productivity, which is unknown to tax authorities; here, regions differ in their income and in their preferences for the local public good.

Our paper can be viewed as one of the potential applications of the agency approach to fiscal federalism and economic decentralization. With few exceptions, such an approach has not yet been used in this field. This is rather surprising because informational problems are probably the most compelling reason for the existence of decentralized federal systems. In the absence of asymmetric information, most fiscal federalism problems would essentially disappear as a centralized system would dominate all alternative arrangements. The traditional literature has acknowledged this fact through its implicit bias in favor of decentralization. However, it has not explicitly modeled the underlying information structure and the incentive problems that may arise because of asymmetric information. Even in federal states such as Canada and the United States, where the central governments are known to have the best statistical data (which they use for many purposes, including intergovernmental transfers), there is an increasing feeling that local governments have better information on matters relevant for redistribution. In Cremer and Pestieau (1996) it is thus assumed that the central government cannot observe the number of poor but only the aggregate redistributive effort of regional governments; in Schroder (1995), the central authority cannot sort out the "deserving" poor from those who are not.[3] One can think of many other potential sources of asymmetric information – the needs of the poor, local preferences, the real cost of living and hence that of welfare – which are likely to receive increasing attention in future research.

The paper is organized as follows. In the next section, we introduce the model and provide the first-best solution. In Section 3 we characterize the optimal direct mechanism and derive the implementing tax function. The possibility of audits is considered in Section 4.

2. The Model

2.1. The Framework

Consider a federation consisting of four types of regions. Each region is characterized by a benevolent government and a representative resident. These residents, and hence these regions, differ in two respects: the level of income, y, and the preferences for the regional public good, g. Preferences in region i can be described by an additive utility function:

$$u_i(g_i, c_i) = \alpha_i v(g_i) + u(c_i) + h(G),$$

where α_i is the taste parameter, g_i the level of the regional public good, c_i the consumption of the composite good, and G the level of the federal public good. By assumption, $v(\cdot)$, $u(\cdot)$, and $h(\cdot)$ have the usual strict concavity property. We assume that c_i is the numeraire and that both G and g_i are produced with a linear technology; without loss of generality, their unit cost in terms of c_i is 1. The representative resident of region i has an exogenous income of y_i.

Throughout the paper, we assume that α_i can take two values (0 or $\alpha > 0$) and that y can also take two values, y_1 and y_2, with $y_2 > y_1$. We thus have four types of regions. Using n_i to denote the number of regions i, and normalizing it so that $\sum n_i = 1$, we can represent the pattern of regions by Table 1, where $i = 10, 1\alpha, 20, 2\alpha$.

In this paper, for simplicity we use a utilitarian social welfare function. Admittedly, such a specification is hard to defend in a setting where preferences differ across individuals. Alternatively, we could have adopted a more general perspective and characterized the set of Pareto-efficient

Table 1. *Four types of regions*

Income	Taste $\alpha_i =$	
$y_i =$	0	α
y_1	n_{10}	$n_{1\alpha}$
y_2	n_{20}	$n_{2\alpha}$

allocations (first-best and incentive-constrained). Formally, this is equivalent to maximizing a weighted sum of utilities. It is readily verified that all our qualitative results remain valid in this alternative (and yet more general) framework, as long as the weights given to the rich (type-2) communities are not too high – in which case "reverse" redistribution would become optimal and the downward incentive constraints would no longer be binding.

2.2. Full-Information Optimum

The first-best optimal policy is a useful benchmark. In this case, the central government observes not only g_i and of course G but also α_i, y_i, and thus c_i. The first-best problem can be expressed as follows.

Problem 1.

$$\max_{g_i, c_i}\{n_{1\alpha}[u(c_{1\alpha}) + \alpha v(g_{1\alpha})] + n_{2\alpha}[u(c_{2\alpha}) + \alpha v(g_{2\alpha})]$$
$$+ n_{10}u(c_{10}) + n_{20}u(c_{20}) + h(G)\}$$

subject to

$$n_{1\alpha}(c_{1\alpha} + g_{1\alpha} - y_1) + n_{2\alpha}(c_{2\alpha} + g_{2\alpha} - y_2)$$
$$+ n_{10}(c_{10} - y_1) + n_{20}(c_{20} - y_2) + G = 0.$$

One obtains the following first-order conditions:

$$u'(c_{1\alpha}) = \alpha v'(g_{1\alpha}) = u'(c_{2\alpha}) = \alpha v'(g_{2\alpha})$$
$$= u'(c_{10}) = u'(c_{20}) = h'(G) = \varphi, \qquad (1)$$

where φ is the Lagrange multiplier associated with the resource constraint. The marginal rate of substitution between the local public good and the private good ($\text{MRS}_i = dc_{i\alpha}/dg_{i\alpha}$) is here equal to unity, and income is redistributed across regions so as to equate the marginal utilities of private consumption. Furthermore, the Samuelson condition that here amounts to

$$\sum \frac{n_i h'(G)}{u'(c_i)} = 1 \qquad (2)$$

is verified. If, as assumed here, $u(\cdot)$ and $v(\cdot)$ are identical across regions, then one has

$$c_{1\alpha} = c_{2\alpha} = c_{10} = c_{20} \quad \text{and} \quad g_{1\alpha} = g_{2\alpha}.$$

Not surprisingly, with a utilitarian welfare function, regions with positive preferences for the local public good will consume more resources than the others. This allocation is, of course, not achievable if α_i and y_i are not observable. Some regions will try to mimic the others in order to conceal their true characteristics and thereby avoid detrimental redistributive taxation.

3. Optimal Policy under Asymmetric Information

3.1. Optimal Mechanism

Determination of the central government's policy under asymmetric information follows directly from the design of a direct revelation mechanism. The central government is modeled as if it could directly control the levels of regional taxes t_i, of regional public goods (if any) g_i, and, of course, that of the federal public good G. By introducing a gap (positive or negative) between t_i and g_i, we imply that the central government uses the net tax revenue T_i ($\equiv t_i - g_i$) for financing the federal public good and for redistributive reasons. We adopt the accounting convention that g_i is directly paid for by the *central* government. Accordingly, the central government's budget constraint requires $\sum n_i(t_i - g_i) - G = 0$, and region i's consumption of the numeraire good is $y_i - t_i$. This convention has no impact on the results.[4] The implementation of such a mechanism through a nonlinear tax on g_i will be discussed in what follows. When choosing g_i, t_i, and G, the central government is subject to a budget constraint and to the relevant self-selection constraints.

Following Stiglitz (1982), it is useful to represent each region's utility function in terms of the variables that the central government can actually observe or control – that is, g and t. In Figure 1, we represent the indifference curves of the four regions' representative residents going through the same point. Given our assumption, the indifference curves of 10 and 20 are vertical lines and those of 1α and 2α have the usual upward sloping shape, with that of 1α steeper than that of 2α.[5]

The problem at hand has some similarities with the standard nonlinear income tax problem with two ability types. In order to achieve some redistribution, one must ensure that the rich regions do not want to mimic

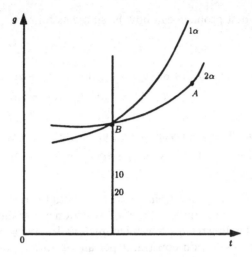

Figure 1. Indifference curves.

the poor regions. At the same time, the taste parameter difference adds a new dimension. Regions of types 20 and 10 will always choose the bundle with the lowest tax; they cannot be distinguished, which implies that $t_{20} = t_{10}$. Regions of type 20 thus benefit from redistribution toward regions of type 10. Subsidizing g makes it possible to partially avoid this undesirable effect, but this will interfere with the traditional self-selection constraint. With full information, some of these regions would have benefited from and some others would have paid for redistribution. It will be seen that, because of the impossibility of sorting out these regions, the optimal tax policy to be adopted by the central government will be different from the traditional optimal income tax function.

Because types 10 and 20 are indistinguishable, two self-selection constraints must be formally introduced in the second-best problem. The first constraint must ensure that high income regions of type 2α do not find it beneficial to mimic low-income regions of type 1α;[6] the second must ensure that a region of type 10 does not want to mimic a region of type 1α. In the latter case, a region of type 10 would spend $g_{1\alpha}$ for which it has no use but would pay a lower tax; the self-selection constraint then amounts to $t_{1\alpha} \geq t_{10}$. The rather simple structure of this problem is due to our assumption that one of the α_i is zero. Also, one can easily show that g_{10} and g_{20} are zero at the optimum: nothing can be gained from setting them at a positive level. On the basis of these considerations, we shall simplify notation in the remainder of this section by substituting t_{10} for t_{20} and by using $g_1 \equiv g_{1\alpha}$, $g_2 \equiv g_{2\alpha}$, and $t_2 \equiv t_{2\alpha}$.

The second-best problem can now be stated as follows.

Problem 2.

$$\max\{n_{1\alpha}[u(y_1-t_{1\alpha})+\alpha v(g_1)]+n_{2\alpha}[u(y_2-t_2)+\alpha v(g_2)]$$
$$+n_{10}u(y_1-t_{10})+n_{20}u(y_2-t_{10})+h(G)\}$$

subject to

(φ) $n_{1\alpha}t_{1\alpha}+n_{2\alpha}t_2+(n_{10}+n_{20})t_{10}-n_{1\alpha}g_1-n_{2\alpha}g_2-G=0,$

(λ) $u(y_2-t_1)+\alpha v(g_2)-u(y_2-t_{1\alpha})-\alpha v(g_1)\geq 0,$

(ψ) $t_{1\alpha}-t_{10}\geq 0,$

where φ is the Lagrange multiplier associated with the revenue constraint ($\varphi>0$), $\lambda\geq 0$ is the multiplier of the self-selection constraint that ensures 2α is as well off telling the truth as by mimicking 1α, and $\psi\geq 0$ is the multiplier of the self-selection constraint pertaining to the possibility of 10 mimicking 1α.[7]

The first-order conditions for Problem 2 are given by

g_1: $(n_{1\alpha}-\lambda)\alpha v'(g_1)-\varphi n_{1\alpha}=0,$ (3)

$t_{1\alpha}$: $-n_{1\alpha}u'(y_1-t_{1\alpha})+\lambda u'(y_2-t_{1\alpha})+\varphi n_{1\alpha}+\psi=0,$ (4)

t_{10}: $-n_{10}u'(y_1-t_{10})-n_{20}u'(y_2-t_{10})+\varphi(n_{10}+n_{20})-\psi=0,$ (5)

g_2: $(n_{2\alpha}+\lambda)\alpha v'(g_2)-\varphi n_{2\alpha}=0,$ (6)

t_2: $-(n_{2\alpha}+\lambda)u'(y_2-t_2)+\varphi n_{2\alpha}=0,$ (7)

G: $h'(G)=\varphi.$ (8)

First, let us interpret the condition of the federal public good. Conditions (3)–(8) imply that

$$\frac{n_{1\alpha}h'(G)}{u'(y_1-t_{1\alpha})}+\frac{n_{10}h'(G)}{u'(y_1-t_{10})}+\frac{n_{2\alpha}h'(G)}{u'(y_2-t_2)}+\frac{n_{20}h'(G)}{u'(y_2-t_{10})}\gtrless 1. \quad (9)$$

Comparing this expression to (2), the Samuelson condition obtained in the first-best setting, it follows that (unless further restrictions are imposed) one can have either an over- or an undersupply of the national public good. This result does not come as a surprise.

Turning to the remaining conditions, one can rather easily show that $\lambda>0$: the constraint ensuring that 2α does not mimic 1α is binding. As to the multiplier ψ, it can be either greater than zero, whence $t_{1\alpha}=t_{10}$, or equal to zero, whence $t_{1\alpha}>t_{10}$. We will consider these two cases in turn.

Case 1: $t_{1\alpha}=t_{10}=t_1$. Combining (6) and (7) yields the marginal rate of substitution between g and c for regions of type 2α:

$$\frac{\alpha v'(g_2)}{u'(y_2 - t_2)} = 1. \tag{10}$$

This is the standard "no distortion at the top" property for type-2α regions, and corresponds to first-best condition (1). Nothing can be gained by distorting the choice of g_2.

We now turn to equations (3), (4), and (5), which combined give us the marginal rate of substitution between g_1 and c_1 for type-1α regions:

$$\frac{\alpha v'(g_1)}{u'(y_1 - t_1)} = \frac{n_{1\alpha} + n_1}{1 - n_{2\alpha}} \frac{n_{1\alpha}}{n_{1\alpha} - \lambda} + R \frac{n_{20} - \lambda}{1 - n_{2\alpha}} \frac{n_{1\alpha}}{n_{1\alpha} - \lambda}, \tag{11}$$

where $R \equiv u'(y_2 - t_1)/u'(y_1 - t_1) < 1$.

To interpret (10) and (11), let us now consider the implementation of the allocation it implies by means of a tax schedule. Accordingly, we define

$$T_i' = \frac{\alpha v'(g_i)}{u'(y_i - t_i)} - 1, \quad i = 1\alpha, 2\alpha,$$

as the marginal tax rate of region i. From (10) we obtain

$$T_{2\alpha}' = 0. \tag{12}$$

In other words, type-2α regions face a zero marginal tax, although their average tax is clearly positive. This corresponds to allocation A in Figure 1.

As for the type-1α regions, their marginal tax rate is given by

$$T_{1\alpha}' = \frac{1}{(1 - n_{2\alpha})(n_{1\alpha} - \lambda)} [n_{1\alpha}(R - 1)(n_{20} - \lambda) + \lambda(n_{10} + n_{20})], \tag{13}$$

where the denominator is positive by (3) while the term $(n_{20} - \lambda)$ cannot be signed. Consequently, the sign of the marginal tax rate is ambiguous. This result is at odds with standard optimal tax models – where the low ability type *always* faces a positive marginal tax rate – and arises because there are two unobservable characteristics in our setting. Intuitively this can be understood as follows. Consider an allocation which implies that $dc_1/dg_1 = -1$ (zero marginal tax rate). If taste were observable (implying that all terms with n_{10} and n_{20} could be deleted from (13)), then a small decrease in g_1 along with a decrease in t_1 ($dt_1 = dg_1 < 0$, resulting in a positive marginal tax rate) would necessarily be welfare-improving. Utility of a 1α region is unaffected and so is the central government's budget constraint. However, it is easily seen that the self-selection constraint is relaxed.[8] Now, if taste is not observable, so that regions of type 20 cannot be distinguished from those of type 1α, then the considered variation also has a negative impact: it results in additional redistribution toward type-20 regions, which tends to reduce social welfare. Depending on which of these two effects dominates, a positive or negative marginal tax rate on type-1α regions will be desirable.

Note that this discussion also illustrates the role played by g in the redistributive policy. Subsidizing g_1 (negative marginal tax rate) is a way of targeting redistribution toward regions of type 1α; cash transfers also benefit regions of type 20.

One can show that Case 1 prevails when the size of all regions is about equal. However, if the sizes are unequal then Case 2 can emerge, as we now see.

Case 2: $t_{1\alpha} > t_{10}$ ($\psi = 0$). Combining (4) and (5) yields

$$u'(y_1 - t_{1\alpha}) - \frac{\lambda}{n_{1\alpha}} u'(y_2 - t_{1\alpha}) = \frac{n_{10}}{n_{10} + n_{20}} u'(y_1 - t_{10})$$

$$+ \frac{n_{20}}{n_{10} + n_{20}} u'(y_2 - t_{10}). \quad (14)$$

This expression states that the social cost of raising revenue through $t_{1\alpha}$ or t_{10} must be equalized. Note that $u'(y_1 - t_{1\alpha})$ is higher than the RHS of (14); hence, if $\lambda = 1$ then we would never want to choose $t_{1\alpha} > t_{10}$. However, with $\lambda > 0$, increasing $t_{1\alpha}$ has the desirable effect of relaxing the self-selection constraint pertaining to 2α's mimicking 1α; that is, it makes it possible to tax type-2α regions more heavily and to redistribute resources toward type-10 regions. In so doing, however, we cannot avoid also helping type-20 regions.

This intuitive explanation gives us some hints as to the occurrence of Case 2. It is likely to prevail if $n_{1\alpha}$ is small and/or if n_{20} is small. If $n_{1\alpha}$ is small, it may be beneficial to sacrifice this group so as to increase redistribution toward type-10 regions. If n_{20} is small then the perverse effect of redistribution toward this well-off group is minimized. One can indeed prove that for $n_{1\alpha} = 0$ and/or $n_{20} = 0$, Case 2 prevails. This proof can readily be extended for sufficiently small $n_{1\alpha}$ or n_{20}.

Let us now look at the properties of the marginal tax rate T_i'. One can easily check that (12) holds, that is, $T_{2\alpha}' = 0$. As to $T_{1\alpha}'$, one can prove that $T_{1\alpha}' > 0$ when $t_{1\alpha} > t_{10}$. Combining (3) and (4) for $\psi = 0$ yields

$$(n_{1\alpha} - \lambda)\alpha v'(g_1) = n_{1\alpha} u'(y_1 - t_{1\alpha}) + \lambda u'(y_2 - t_{1\alpha})$$

or

$$\frac{\alpha v'(g_1)}{u'(y_1 - t_{1\alpha})} = \frac{n_{1\alpha}}{n_{1\alpha} - \lambda} - \frac{\lambda}{n_{1\alpha} - \lambda} \frac{u'(y_2 - t_{1\alpha})}{u'(y_1 - t_{1\alpha})}.$$

Hence

$$T_{1\alpha}' = \frac{\lambda}{n_{1\alpha} - \lambda} [1 - R] > 0.$$

In Case 2 one thus obtains the traditional result of a positive marginal tax rate for the region with the lowest income level. This is not surprising because in Case 2 we do not have the previous situation that led to a negative tax rate. Here, a reduction in $t_{1\alpha}$ does not imply a simultaneous reduction in t_{10} or, rather, in the taxes paid by type-20 regions.

Let us finally provide an example of an implementing tax function. It is readily verified that the following function implements the optimal mechanism:

$$T(g) = \begin{cases} t_{10}^* & \text{if } g = 0, \\ t_{1\alpha}^* - g & \text{if } 0 < g < g_1^*, \\ t_2^* - g_2^* & \text{otherwise}, \end{cases}$$

where t_{10}^*, $t_{1\alpha}^*$, t_2^*, g_1^*, and g_2^* are the solutions to Problem 2. This function applies both to Case 1 and Case 2.

In words, the central government completely subsidizes the regional public good up to the level g_1^*. Regions that choose a higher level of g pay a flat fee of $t_2^* - g_2^*$ and are entirely responsible for their local expenditures (no tax or subsidy at the margin).[9]

To further illustrate the working of this model, we now turn to a numerical example in which we analyze the effect of different sizes of our four groups and different levels of y_2 relative to y_1.

3.2. Numerical Example

We posit $y_1 = 1$, $\alpha = 0.5$, $u(c) = \log c$, and $v(g) = \log g$; also, for simplicity we assume away G. Table 2 gives the values of g_1, g_2, t_1, t_2, $T_{1\alpha}'$, and $T_{2\alpha}$; the last term denotes the amount of taxes paid by 2α to the central government ($T_{2\alpha} = t_2 - g_2$).

In the first five examples, each group is equally represented and the higher income y_2 increases relative to the lower income y_1. Note that while $y_2 - y_1$ increases, the taste difference given by $\alpha = 0.5$ remains constant. As y_2 increases, the type-2α regions contribute more and more to interregional redistribution (tax increases from an initial negative value). At the same time, the marginal rate of taxation on g_1, which is negative at first, turns positive and increases rapidly. Not surprisingly, type-20 regions are the big winners from the increase in unobservable income. Their consumption goes from 0.9 to 4.07 while their income goes from 1 to 4.

There are two unobservable characteristics in our model. When the taste characteristic differential is relatively higher than that of the income characteristic (e.g., example A), optimal taxation is such that $T_{2\alpha} < T_{20} (= t_1)$; in the opposite case (e.g., example E), one has $T_{2\alpha} > T_{20}$. This is again fairly intuitive.

Table 2. *Optimal levels of taxation and public good*

	\multicolumn{9}{c}{Examples}								
	A	B	C	D	E	F	G	H	I
y_2	1.1	1.5	2	3	4	2	2	2	2
$n_{1\alpha}$	1/4	1/4	1/4	1/4	1/4	1/10	1/20	1/100	3/10
n_{10}	1/4	1/4	1/4	1/4	1/4	3/10	7/20	39/100	3/10
$n_{2\alpha}$	1/4	1/4	1/4	1/4	1/4	3/10	6/20	30/100	3/10
n_{20}	1/4	1/4	1/4	1/4	1/4	3/10	6/20	30/100	1/10
g_1	0.40	0.40	0.39	0.37	0.36	0.36	0.33	0.30	0.34
g_2	0.43	0.56	0.69	0.93	1.14	0.69	0.68	0.66	0.66
$t_{1\alpha}$	0.20	0.19	0.16	0.05	−0.07	0.086	0.0397	0.05	0.148
t_{10}	0.20	0.19	0.16	0.05	−0.07	0.086	0.0389	−0.01	0.133
t_2	0.23	0.39	0.61	1.14	1.71	0.61	0.64	0.68	0.68
$T'_{1\alpha}$	−0.01	−0.002	0.08	0.27	0.47	0.26	0.47	0.60	0.28
$T_{2\alpha}$	−0.2	−0.17	−0.08	0.21	0.57	−0.07	−0.02	0.04	0.02

In the last four examples, region sizes are no longer equal. We adopt patterns with small values for either $n_{1\alpha}$ or n_{20} that have been shown to lead to Case 2 and then to $t_{1\alpha} > t_{10}$. In this example, $y_2 = 2$ (for higher values of y_2 and the same patterns, Case 1 prevails), and the marginal rate of taxation $T'_{1\alpha}$ is positive and quite high. To sum up, this exercise illustrates two points: $T'_{1\alpha} \gtrless 0$ in Case 1, and Cases 1 and 2 can both prevail.

This numerical example – and, to some extent, the model it illustrates – is particular. Recall that our setting allows for only two values for each of the two characteristics, income and taste. Furthermore, we have set one of the possible values of the taste parameter at zero. It is clear that any departure from this setting would lead to untractable complexities without much gain in terms of insights and results.

The main results obtained so far can be summarized as follows. First, with two characteristics, standard optimal taxation findings do not necessarily hold. Second, with two unobservable characteristics, redistribution is made more difficult than with just one. Third, the results depend very much on the distribution of characteristics across the regions considered.

4. Auditing

Until now, we have assumed that the central government had no information on the level of regions' income or on preferences for the regional public good. Let us now consider the possibility that the central government hires tax controllers whose role is to reduce the asymmetry of information at some cost. One easily checks that if income is known, the first-best allocation is achievable even though the taste parameter is unknown. This particular result is due to our assumption that one of the values of that taste parameter is zero. Then, perfect redistribution from 02 and $\alpha2$ to 01 and $\alpha1$, and from 01 and 02 to $\alpha1$ and $\alpha2$, is possible.

However, to obtain full information on income and thus the first-best income, we must pay a cost that can be prohibitive. The optimal audit policy considered here is the result of a tradeoff between departure from a first-best allocation and audit cost.

We consider the case in which the central government hires a controller who is both truthful and costly. Depending on this cost and on the penalty assessed on regions found to conceal the true value of their income, one obtains an allocation that is between that of the first-best and that derived in Section 3.1. Finally, we allow for some collusion between controllers and regions. In this scenario, the central government must buy its controller's honesty by offering more than the bribe the regional government is ready to give.

Suppose that, by paying an income z, the central government can obtain a truthful report from a controller who observes the actual level of income. If the controller indicates that the region has underreported its income (i.e., has declared y_1 instead of y_2), then the central government can impose a penalty that is endogenous but bounded. It is easily seen that the principle of maximum deterrence would hold here:[10] the maximum penalty is imposed on any region that is detected misreporting. We assume that the maximum penalty amounts to reducing the level of u to a floor level $\bar{u}$, here normalized to zero. We denote by γ the probability of conducting controls. We allow γ to be dependent on whether or not regions supply local public goods: γ_α or γ_0, respectively.

A high-income region knows that understating its true income will result in a probability γ that this will be detected and thus incur a penalty. This possibility will affect the self-selection constraints of the new problem. Not only could 2α mimic 1α, but now it is also possible for 20 to mimic 10 or 1α. Further, one must ensure that regions with a preference for the local public good pay at least as much as regions without such a preference; otherwise, the latter could mimic the former. Finally, by assuming that $v(0) = -\infty$, the reverse will never occur; that is, type-α regions never find it beneficial to mimic type-0 regions.

We can now state the new problem, which amounts to maximizing social welfare subject to a revenue constraint and five self-selection constraints.

Problem 3.

$$\max\{n_{1\alpha}[u(y_1-t_{1\alpha})+\alpha v(g_1)]+n_{2\alpha}[u(y_2-t_{2\alpha})+\alpha v(g_2)]$$
$$+n_{10}u(y_1-t_{10})+n_{20}u(y_2-t_{20})+h(G)\}$$

subject to

(φ) $n_{1\alpha}t_{1\alpha}+n_{2\alpha}t_{2\alpha}+n_{10}t_{10}+n_{20}t_{20}-n_{1\alpha}g_1-n_{2\alpha}g_2$
$$-(n_{1\alpha}\gamma_\alpha+n_{10}\gamma_0)z-G=0, \qquad (15)$$

(λ) $u(y_2-t_{2\alpha})+\alpha v(g_2)-(1-\gamma_\alpha)u(y_2-t_{1\alpha})-\alpha v(g_1)\geq 0,$ $\qquad(16)$

(μ) $u(y_2-t_{20})-(1-\gamma_0)u(y_2-t_{10})\geq 0,$ $\qquad(17)$

(η) $u(y_2-t_{20})-(1-\gamma_\alpha)u(y_2-t_{1\alpha})\geq 0,$ $\qquad(18)$

(ψ_1) $t_{1\alpha}-t_{10}\geq 0,$ $\qquad(19)$

(ψ_2) $t_{2\alpha}-t_{20}\geq 0.$ $\qquad(20)$

All the Lagrange multipliers are nonnegative and, since the budget constraint is binding, $\varphi>0$. Further, we assume an interior solution for γ_0 and γ_α. In fact, $\gamma_0=1$ or $\gamma_\alpha=1$ can never be optimal: the incentive constraints would then be satisfied with strict inequality and so it would be feasible to reduce the audit probabilities and thus lower costs. However, $\gamma_0=0$ or $\gamma_\alpha=0$ cannot be ruled out, and indeed is likely for high audit costs.

Turning to the first-order conditions, one obtains:

$t_{1\alpha}$: $-n_{1\alpha}u'(y_1-t_{1\alpha})+\lambda(1-\gamma_\alpha)-\eta(1-\gamma_\alpha)u'(y_2-t_{1\alpha})$
$$+\varphi n_{1\alpha}+\psi_1=0, \qquad(21)$$

t_{10}: $-n_{10}u'(y_1-t_{10})+\mu(1-\gamma_0)u'(y_2-t_{10})+\varphi n_{10}-\psi_1=0,$ $\qquad(22)$

$t_{2\alpha}$: $-n_{2\alpha}u'(y_2-t_{2\alpha})-\lambda u'(y_2-t_{2\alpha})+\varphi n_{2\alpha}+\psi_2=0,$ $\qquad(23)$

t_{20}: $-n_{20}u'(y_2-t_{20})-\mu u'(y_2-t_{20})-\eta u'(y_2-t_{20})$
$$+\varphi n_{20}-\psi_2=0, \qquad(24)$$

g_1: $\alpha n_{1\alpha}v'(g_1)-\lambda\alpha v'(g_1)-\varphi n_{1\alpha}=0,$ $\qquad(25)$

g_2: $\alpha n_{2\alpha}v'(g_2)+\lambda\alpha v'(g_2)-\varphi n_{2\alpha}=0,$ $\qquad(26)$

γ_α: $(\lambda+\eta)u(y_2-t_{1\alpha})-n_{1\alpha}z\varphi=0,$ $\qquad(27)$

γ_0: $\mu u(y_2-t_{10})-nz\varphi=0,$ $\qquad(28)$

G: $h'(G)-\varphi=0.$ $\qquad(29)$

To interpret these conditions, one must check whether or not constraints (16)–(20) are binding. This is done in the Appendix, where we show that constraints (16) and (17) are always binding; hence $\lambda > 0$ and $\mu > 0$. We also show that constraint (20) is never binding: $\psi_2 = 0$ and $t_{2\alpha} > t_{20}$. Two cases can then be distinguished.

Case 1: $\eta = 0$. In this case one can have either $\psi_1 = 0$ and hence $t_{1\alpha} > t_{10}$ or $\psi_1 > 0$ and hence $t_{1\alpha} = t_{10}$. The latter solution is shown to occur when $n_{1\alpha}/n_{10} \geq n_{2\alpha}/n_{20}$. Why would we have $t_{1\alpha} > t_{10}$? – only because of the indirect effect of $t_{1\alpha}$ and t_{10} on $t_{2\alpha}$ relative to t_{20} through constraints (16) and (17). This will be more desirable the larger the number of high-income regions with positive preferences for local public spending. Note that in this case $\gamma_\alpha > \gamma_0$; regions that report a positive taste parameter are audited with a higher probability than regions that declare they have no preference for the regional public good (and thus accept a consumption bundle with $g = 0$).

Case 2: $\eta > 0$. In this case, $\psi_1 = 0$ and $t_{1\alpha} > t_{10}$. The possibility of $t_{1\alpha} = t_{10}$ cannot be ruled out as resulting by coincidence from an interior solution. Again, this is fairly intuitive. In Case 2, constraints (16)–(18) are all binding. By increasing $t_{1\alpha}$ relative to t_{10}, one relaxes these self-selection constraints. Note that here one has $\gamma_\alpha \leq \gamma_0$ resulting from (17) and (18).[11]

In both cases, one obtains the standard result that $T_{2\alpha}' = 0$. The sign of $T_{1\alpha}'$ is ambiguous whenever the solution implies $t_{1\alpha} = t_{10}$. However, when $t_{1\alpha} > t_{10}$ one can show that $T_{1\alpha}' > 0$. Considering the discussion in the previous section, this should not come as a surprise. When groups 1α and 10 are separated, the standard argument (in optimal taxation with two groups) applies and group 1α necessarily faces a positive marginal tax rate.

So far, we have assumed an auditor who is both truthful and costly. If the audit cost is too high then one returns to Problem 2 with no information on income. Let us now assume that the controller is costless but still capable of colluding with the regional government. This is not impossible in the present setting, where a tax controller may belong to the region targeted for audit.

The problem is the same as Problem 3 with a new constraint – namely, the coalition incentive-compatibility constraint. To induce truth telling when the auditor has evidence of income concealment that would result in the punishment of the concerned region, the central government must pay the controller at least as much as the regional government would pay to have the report changed; see Tirole (1991).

Solving Problem 3 with this additional constraint yields the same solution, in which the central government promises to give the controller any penalty imposed on regions concealing their true income. As shown by Kofman and Lawarrée (1993), this equivalence arises because here audits are 100% error-proof. Introducing the possibility of imperfect audits would necessitate distinguishing between external and internal audits.

Quite clearly, the solution to Problem 3 is midway between the first-best solution and the solution to Problem 2. Auditing allows the separation of individuals of types 1α, 20, and 10 that before could not be distinguished by the tax system. In particular, auditing allows redistribution from higher- to lower-income regions and from regions without preference for the public good to regions with such preference.

APPENDIX

In this appendix we restrict the number of alternative cases through a series of properties.

Property A1. $\mu > 0$; *namely,* (17) *is binding.*

Proof. If (17) is not binding then one can reduce γ_0, and hence audit costs, without violating any of the constraints. Since $\varphi > 0$, this reduction in audit costs increases welfare. □

Property A2. $\lambda = 0$ *and* $\eta = 0$ *are not simultaneously possible; namely, at least one of the constraints* (16) *or* (18) *must be binding.*

Proof. Same as for Property A1, except now it is γ_α that can be reduced. □

Property A3. $\lambda = 0$ *is not possible.*

Proof. From Property A2, $\lambda = 0$ implies that (18) is binding. Next, observe that from (25)-(26), $\lambda = 0$ implies also $g_1 = g_2$. With (18) binding, $t_{2\alpha} > t_{20}$ would then violate (16). Hence, one must have $t_{2\alpha} = t_{20}$. Dividing (23) by $n_{2\alpha}$ and subtracting (21) divided by n_{20}, and using $\lambda = 0$ and $t_{2\alpha} = t_{20}$ to simplify, yields

$$\left(\frac{\mu + \eta}{n_{20}}\right)u'(y_2 - t_{20}) + \frac{\psi_2}{n_{2\alpha}} + \frac{\psi_2}{n_{20}} = 0,$$

which is impossible (the first term is strictly positive and the second term is non-negative). □

To sum up, we are left with two possible cases as far as constraints (16)-(18) are concerned.

Case 1: $\lambda > 0, \mu > 0, \eta = 0$.
Case 2: $\lambda > 0, \mu > 0, \eta > 0$, and all three constraints are binding.

Property A4. $t_{2\alpha} = t_{20}$ *is not possible.*

Proof. Observe that with $\lambda > 0$, (25) and (26) imply that $g_2 > g_1$. Hence if (16) is binding then one must have

$$u(y_2 - t_{2\alpha}) < (1 - \gamma_\alpha)u(y_2 - t_{1\alpha}),$$

but with $t_{2\alpha} = t_{20}$ this implies that (18) is violated.   □

Let us now examine the two cases listed following the proof of Property A3. For Case 2, the solution can only be interior. For Case 1, two types of solutions can arise depending on whether or not (19) is binding:

 (i) interior solution with $\psi_1 = 0$ and $t_{1\alpha} \geq t_{10}$; or
(ii) $\psi_1 > 0$ and $t_{1\alpha} = 0$.

Recall that in either situation we have $t_{2\alpha} > t_{20}$. For a class of parameter values, in particular if $n_{1\alpha} = n_{10} = n_{2\alpha} = n_{20}$, only (ii) is possible. This follows from Property A5.

Property A5. *Assume that $\eta = 0$; if $n_{1\alpha}/n_{10} \geq n_{2\alpha}/n_{20}$ then the solution necessarily implies that $\psi_1 > 0$ (and hence that $t_{1\alpha} < t_{10}$).*

Proof. We show that with $\psi_1 = \psi_2 = 0$ and $n_{1\alpha}/n_{10} > n_{2\alpha}/n_{20}$, $t_{1\alpha} > t_{10}$ would imply $t_{20} > t_{2\alpha}$, a contradiction. First, it follows from (27) and (28) that with $t_{1\alpha} > t_{10}$ one has

$$\frac{\lambda}{n_{1\alpha}} > \frac{\mu}{n_{10}}. \tag{A.1}$$

Combining (23) and (24) and using $\psi_2 = 0$ yields

$$\frac{n_{2\alpha} + \lambda}{n_{2\alpha}} u'(y_2 - t_{2\alpha}) = \frac{n_{20} + \mu}{n_{20}} u'(y_2 - t_{20}), \tag{A.2}$$

which can be written as

$$\frac{1 + \lambda/n_{2\alpha}}{1 + \mu/n_{20}} = \frac{u'(y_2 - t_{20})}{u'(y_2 - t_{2\alpha})}. \tag{A.3}$$

If the RHS of (A.3) exceeds unity then we have $t_{20} > t_{2\alpha}$. Hence,

$$\frac{\lambda}{n_{2\alpha}} > \frac{\mu}{n_{20}} \text{ implies } t_{20} > t_{2\alpha}.$$

Note that $\lambda/n_{2\alpha} > \mu/n_{20}$ can be written as $\lambda > \mu(n_{2\alpha}/n_{20})$, which is implied by (A.1) if $n_{1\alpha}/n_{10} > n_{2\alpha}/n_{20}$.   □

To sum up, if $n_{1\alpha}/n_{10} \geq n_{2\alpha}/n_{20}$ then the solution necessarily implies $t_{1\alpha} = t_{10}$. Otherwise an interior solution is also *possible*.

Property A6. *If $\eta > 0$, the solution implies $\psi_1 = 0$.*

Proof. If $\psi_1 > 0$ then $t_{10} = t_{1\alpha}$; using (27) and (28) then yields

$$\frac{\lambda + \eta}{n_{1\alpha}} = \frac{\mu}{n_{10}}.$$

Divide (21) by $n_{1\alpha}$, subtract (10) divided by n_{10}, and simplify to obtain

$$\left(\frac{\lambda + \eta}{n_{1\alpha}}\right)(\gamma_\alpha - \gamma_0)u'(y_2 - t_{1\alpha}) = \psi_1\left(\frac{n_{10} + n_{1\alpha}}{n_{1\alpha}n_{10}}\right);$$

hence $\gamma_\alpha > \gamma_0$. But if (17) is satisfied with equality then (18) must hold with strict inequality, which contradicts $\eta > 0$.   □

NOTES

1. However, Laffont (1995) argues that information asymmetries (concerning income levels in particular) play a crucial role in China's recently designed federal system. His model rests on an information structure similar to ours, yet he focuses on enforcement issues rather than on redistributive policies per se.
2. See also Brito et al. (1990) for a more general treatment.
3. See e.g. Gilbert and Picard (1996), Raff and Wilson (1995), and Laffont (1995), in addition to the papers mentioned previously.
4. To see this, note that the case where the g are paid for by *local* governments can be constructed through a simple change of variables. Specifically, one can use net taxes T_i as instruments and eliminate the t_i from the expression by using $T_i = t_i - g_i$ (see also note 6).
5. This is because the higher the net disposable income of a region, the smaller will be the marginal rate of substitution between t and g. (Along an indifference curve of a type-i region, $dg/dt = u'(y_i - t)/v'(g)$.)
6. With a utilitarian welfare function, it is easy to show that the upward incentive constraint $1\alpha \rightarrow 2\alpha$ will not bind at the optimum. If we were instead aiming at Pareto optimality then the constraint could be binding, but this is not an interesting case to study.
7. If the g_i were paid for by local governments (see note 2) then the incentive constraint (λ) would become:

    (λ') $u(y_2 - g_2 - T_2) + \alpha v(g_2) - u(y_2 - g_1 - T_{1\alpha}) - \alpha v(g_1) \geq 0.$

    By posing $T_2 = t_2 - g_2$ it is readily verified that (λ) and (λ') are equivalent. Similar arguments show that none of the other expressions are affected by such a change of variables.
8. Recall that type-2α regions have flatter indifference curves at any given point than type-1α regions. A variation $dt_1 = dg_1 < 0$ thus decreases utility of a mimicking region (i.e., $u(y_2 - t_1) + \alpha v(g_1)$ decreases).
9. With such a tax function, regions of type 1α will choose g_1^* and pay regional taxes of $t_{1\alpha}^* - g_1^* + g_1^* = t_{1\alpha}^*$. Regions of type 10 and 20 choose $g = 0$ and pay t_{10}^*. Finally, regions of type 2α select g_2^* and pay t_2^*.
10. Unlimited penalty would induce truth telling and hence the first-best allocation.
11. If $t_{1\alpha} > t_{10}$ then $\gamma_\alpha < \gamma_0$.

REFERENCES

Brito, D., J. Hamilton, S. Slutsky, and J. Stiglitz (1990), "Pareto Efficient Tax Structures," *Oxford Economic Papers* 42: 61–77.

Cremer, H., and P. Pestieau (1996), "Distributive Implications of European Integration," *European Economic Review* 40: 747–57.

Gilbert, G., and P. Picard (1996), "Incentives and the Optimal Size of Local Jurisdictions," *European Economic Review* 40: 19–42.

Kofman, F., and J. Lawarrée (1993), "Collusion in Hierarchical Agency," *Econometrica* 61: 629–56.

Laffont, J. J. (1995), "Incentives in China's Federal System," Mimeo, IDEI, University of Toulouse, France.

Raff, H., and J. Wilson (1995), "Income Redistribution and Well-Informed Regional Governments," Mimeo, Indiana University, Bloomington.

Schroder, M. (1995), "A Principal–Agent Model of Altruistic Redistribution with Some Implications for Fiscal Federalism," *Economic Design* 1: 217–24.

Stiglitz, J. E. (1982), "Self Selection and Pareto-Efficient Taxation," *Journal of Public Economics* 17: 213–40.

Tirole, J. (1991), "Collusion and the Theory of Organization," in J.-J. Laffont (ed.), *Advances in Economic Theory*. Cambridge University Press, pp. 151–206.

CHAPTER 5

Decentralized Public Decision Making:
The Moral Hazard Problem

Claude d'Aspremont & Louis-André Gérard-Varet

1. INTRODUCTION

The issues involved in designing a system of regional governments have been in recent years at the center of a policy debate all over Europe, not only in countries with strong traditions in favor of centralization – such as France – but also in countries that allowed for some decentralization – such as Germany or (more recently) Belgium. There are many aspects to the debate, such as the perception of national identity or various political strategies and calculations, that do not concern economic issues directly. However, the *assignment issue* in the design of regional government – namely, the allocation of authority for public expenditures among different levels of government – is part of the economics of decentralization. This allocation emphasizes the sharing of responsibility among different self-interested agents involved in a collective decision process. To document this debate with a concrete example, let us start with a brief description of the case for decentralization and regional government in France and the recent reform there.

Since 1982–83 there have been in France substantial changes in the organization of subcentral government. Before that period, public decision making was highly centralized according to principles inherited from the Napoleonic era. All important decisions were made, or at least approved, by bureaus in Paris. At the local level, in each of the 90 *départements,* the main powers were concentrated in the hands of civil servants appointed by the central government – *préfets* (or *recteurs* in the area of education). The *communes* (cities) created at the end of the last century (and now numbering more than 36,000) had elected mayors with greater powers, although still subject to a priori control by the *préfets.* Twenty-two *régions* had been designed in the late 1960s to include an average of four or five *départements.* The regions had indirectly elected assemblies but were run

The support of Commissariat Général du Plan is gratefully acknowledged.

82

by an executive appointed by and accountable to the central government. Although allowed to contribute to the financing of investment projects undertaken by the state or their constituent local authorities, the primary function of the assemblies was to implement regional aspects of the central policy.

The reform, which started in 1982–83 and is still in progress, has introduced five major changes.[1] First, *communes, départements,* and *régions* are now full-scale subcentral jurisdictions, all three endowed with a parliamentary system. In each jurisdiction there is a council elected directly by the citizens and an executive branch elected by the council. The local executive branches can have their own bureaucracy or use, on certain conditions, the central government bureaucracy. Second, these three types of subcentral government are in principle completely independent and, although they may overlap in responsibilities with respect to the same territory, there is no hierarchy among them.

Third, public expenditures have been partly decentralized: *communes* are in charge of urban planning and development, *départements* are responsible for the welfare program and social affairs, and the role of *régions* in development and economic planning has been strengthened. The *régions* have also been given specific responsibility for vocational and professional training and may be required to prepare, in cooperation with the *préfet,* a regional plan for medium-term investment (covering vocational training, research and technology, industrial aid, agricultural development, and communication). In practice, all local governments intervene on economic issues (such as unemployment), and all of them are competent in such areas as culture, tourism, and education. Fourth, the a priori control by the *préfet* has been abolished and replaced by the a posteriori control of a special court.

The fifth change concerns local government finance. Although taxing power is still determined by the central government, resources for the local governments have been increased. Before 1982, *communes* and *départements* shared various direct taxes: a housing tax based on rental income, two property taxes (on developed and nondeveloped land) based on the official market value of land and buildings, and a business tax – *taxe professionnelle* – designed as a tax on value added based on the value of business assets and a fraction of business wage bills. The rates of these taxes were linked by a central formula. The *régions* also received grants from the central government, which they redistributed as specific grants and capital subsidies because their budgetary powers were strictly limited by a centrally set ceiling. The three subnational levels were also allowed to borrow. However, with the 1982 reform, local jurisdictions can now freely choose the rates of the taxes they control. Regions are given the same direct tax bases as the other tiers of local government, and a vehicle registration tax, a vehicle license tax, and a tax on property sales and related registration fees (subject to a ceiling rate) have been transferred from the center to the regions. A new grant scheme has been designed to replace the previous arrangements whereby local and regional authorities received central grants for specific investment projects.

These reforms, introduced in France over a decade ago, have created quite a complicated system of public decision making. The debate over this evolution presently involves two major issues: one concerns the scope and scale of subcentral governments; the other, fiscal implications.

1. *Communes, départements,* and *régions* are competing with regard to how responsibilities should be shared. Should the shape of local and regional jurisdictions be redefined? What sort of contractual arrangements should be promoted among the different tiers of government (in particular, with respect to public investment)?

2. Should subcentral government be allowed to expand or not? How should fiscal responsibilities be shared among jurisdictions (sharing taxes, grants, ...)? What taxes (if any) should be allocated[2] to the different local jurisdictions? If the regions are wholly dependent on their own resources to pay for their spending, then what should be the scale of the redistribution in the overall burden of taxation? What pattern of grants from central government should be made available to correct major gains or losses?

In this paper we concentrate on a theoretical analysis of one particular aspect of these questions by considering the model of a two-tier government system that allows for "large devolutions" to regions.[3] We concentrate on a notion of *political decentralization,* where regions are independent decision units, in contrast to an *administrative decentralization,* where regions would only be vehicles for the implementation of central government decisions. There is a widely shared view among economists that decentralization of public decision making is only ceteris paribus a good thing. There are limits to the extent of decentralization, owing to inefficiencies and inequities that need to be corrected by the central government. However, a preliminary question is to consider conditions under which there are no "distributive incentives" against cooperative agreement, from the point of view of both regional and central government.

In the two-tier government system that we model, the central government covers the whole nation and regional governments cover predefined regions. The regional jurisdictions are independent levels of democratic decision making that give citizens the power to make regional choice with respect to actions covering public investments, the provision of local public goods, and fiscal policy. Under the constitutional arrangement, taxation powers have already been assigned to regional governments. In particular, there are redistributions across individuals made at the level of each jurisdiction. Thus, decentralization of choice at the regional level reflects regional differences in preferences.

It is well known that, in general, local public expenditures have spillover or "externality" effects that are not taken into account by the regional government, leading to collective inefficiencies nationwide. We consider here a situation where the actions of the regional jurisdictions affect the probability of "shocks" at the national level. It may then be in one region's interest to adopt measures that impose costs or have adverse effects on nonresidents. This is a typical example of the *moral hazard* problem arising when interactions among agents occur with imperfect monitoring.

Similar observations, made for the case of the management of a global common property, traditionally support a pessimistic view on the future of cooperation within decentralized systems.[4] When some individual sovereignty must be respected, even though it is in the interest of all to cooperate, an agreement may well fail: if the cooperation is attained then every single agent could earn higher returns by free riding. These observations are also at the basis of the early literature on "fiscal federalism."[5] Clearly such interjurisdictional externalities are "internalized" by having the concerned functions assigned to the central government,[6] which cannot simply sit back and allow each region to act without any mechanism for inhibiting or monitoring the exercise of regional choice. However, the central government could provide incentives for regional governments to coordinate their actions by promoting contractual arrangements that lead to overall efficiency. For that purpose there are instruments available at the central level, such as grants or fiscal surcharges, that allow interregional redistributions and transfers. When designing a transfer scheme, the central government should take appropriate account of spillovers in order to provide correct incentives to regional governments in their choice of actions supporting collectively efficient outcomes.[7]

A decentralized public policy problem – viewed as a partnership among regional jurisdictions managed by a central authority – can be formalized as a game.[8] Following our previous remarks it must be considered a noncooperative game, where the regional jurisdictions are the players choosing their actions in a self-interested way, given arrangements designed by a central government that cannot perfectly monitor their behavior. The issue here is not that the players retain private information, because the objective functions are common knowledge. Rather, at issue is the lack of natural coordination, which leaves open the possibility of free riding. In game-theoretic terms we have a *noncooperative game with complete but imperfect information*.

The fundamental principle of game theory is that any definite plan that prescribes (or predicts) the behavior of all players in such a situation – if this plan is to be understood by the participants and is not to impute irrational behavior to any of them – must designate a *Nash equilibrium* whereby it is in the interest of every participant to respect the agreement whenever all others do. The possibility of free riding in some public affairs shows that often only a "dismal" equilibrium[9] can be reached, one where the solution is far from the collective optimum. The general response suggested by game theory as a means of circumventing the dismal equilibrium problem – in particular, the moral hazard problem – is to make a "cooperative transformation" of the game: creating a new game where some efficient outcome can be sustained noncooperatively. This can generally be obtained in many ways: by repeating the game; by adding "communication devices"; by modifying the initial payoffs through some sort of contractual procedure. In the circumstances we consider here, one can take advantage of the fact that individual payoffs are measured in money (transferable utilities) and so use monetary transfers (as taxes and subsidies) to achieve the appropriate transformation of the game (regions can be seen as large and long-lived agents with very little risk sensitivity).

Many of the practical situations involved in decentralization of public decision making can hardly be reduced to a static game. This is no doubt the case when we consider local governments deciding upon public investments, all contributing to the capital stock of the overall economy. The stock variable can be very comprehensive. It may include, in particular, the state of the environment (global warming, water pollution, ...). There are intrinsic dynamic features in such situations that cannot be treated simply by repeating the game. Thus, the version of the moral hazard problem used, if one wants to reconsider the assignment issue in a dynamic context, should include a national stock variable, perhaps evolving stochastically, but partly determined by regional investments.

These different situations will be captured by extending a model first analyzed in a static mode to a dynamic framework. We consider (Section 2) a finite set of agents, each influencing the determination of a common observable outcome, possibly stochastic, through the choice of a non-observable action. Each agent behaves on the basis of a transferable payoff. With transfers as the instruments used to modify the game, collectively efficient actions can be enforced in several ways, albeit limited by some feasibility requirement on the transfers. If this feasibility constraint is sufficiently weak then there will be no restriction imposed on the outcome function obtaining the right individual incentives from a collective point of view. Otherwise, some condition on the outcome function is required. Then – and this is the central contribution of our paper – we show that such a condition can be extended to dynamic stochastic games (Section 3): a collectively efficient profile of strategies is enforced by a sequence of transfer schemes. This result is obtained for an intertemporal equilibrium concept having strong properties[10] – namely, the "Markov perfect equilibrium." In the conclusion we stress some neglected features of the assignment issue that are crucial to understanding the decentralization of public policy.

2. THE MORAL HAZARD PROBLEM IN A STATIC FRAMEWORK

We introduce first the moral hazard problem[11] as a *static game*. We have a finite set $N = \{1, ..., i, ..., n\}$ of players – the regional jurisdictions – each having to choose simultaneously an *action* a_i – public spending and local taxation – in a finite set A_i. A vector $\mathbf{a} = (a_1, ..., a_i, ..., a_n) \in A = \times_{i=1}^{n} A_i$ is called a *joint action*. There is a finite set X of public *outcomes,* which can be considered as different levels of some national public good. The individual actions together determine stochastically some outcome in the set. More precisely, we introduce a *stochastic outcome function:* a function associating to each joint action $a \in A$ a probability distribution $p(\cdot \,|\, a)$ on the set X. The players share common beliefs about their individual actions, and this is incorporated in the function p. The deterministic case is not a priori excluded; it amounts to having a degenerate stochastic outcome function with all probabilities equal to 0 or 1. To each player i is associated a utility function $u_i(x, a_i)$ defined[12] on $X \times A_i$, which represents local welfare or willingness to pay. Then the payoff of player i can be computed as the expectation

$$U_i(a) = \sum_{x \in X} u_i(x, a_i) p(x \,|\, a).$$

The players' utility functions are common knowledge; that is, we restrict ourselves to the case of *complete information*.

We assume – and this is the moral hazard problem – that only the outcome, and not the actions, are publicly observable. In this static game a joint action a^* is (collectively) efficient if there is no other joint action a such that, for every i, $U_i(a) \geq U_i(a^*)$, with at least one inequality holding strictly. However, in such a game, an efficient joint action cannot in general be enforced as a noncooperative equilibrium (in the sense that no player could increase his or her payoff by unilateral deviation); hence, the main issue is to design specific mechanisms. Because of the non-observability of actions, such mechanisms cannot be based on the observation (or direct monitoring) of individual actions. Assuming that the utilities are measured in some monetary units and are transferable, we will propose an enforcement mechanism, managed by a central authority, that can be realized via monetary transfers among the players.[13]

The transferability assumption allows the central authority to use, as an instrument in the design of an incentive mechanism, *transfer schemes*. Such schemes are functions of the form $t: X \to \mathbb{R}^n$ that give, for every i and every x, the amount of money $t_i(x)$ that i receives ($t_i(x) \geq 0$) or pays ($t_i(x) \leq 0$) if x is observed. A transfer scheme transforms the basic game into a new game with payoff functions given by

$$\sum_{x \in X} [u_i(x, a_i) + t_i(x)] p(x \mid a);$$

the strategy spaces are still given by $\{A_i\}$.

Transfer schemes must satisfy some feasibility property. The strongest one, ensuring that all the surplus generated is shared among the players, is the *budget-balancing condition*:

$$\forall x, \quad \sum_{i \in N} t_i(x) = 0. \qquad \text{(BB)}$$

This is the condition we shall impose in most of our results. A weaker property is to have only the *budget balanced in expected value for some joint action a^**:

$$\sum_{x \in X} \sum_{i \in N} t_i(x) p(x \mid a^*) = 0. \qquad \text{(EB)}$$

This constraint, in expected terms, is relevant in contexts where the central authority (the national government) can provide essentially costless insurance.

Whether balanced everywhere or balanced in expected value, the transfer scheme will have to provide the right incentives to achieve the assigned joint action $a^* \in A$. For this, let us assume that every agent has an outside option giving a utility level normalized to zero, and that the joint action a^* leads to a *nonnegative surplus*:

$$\sum_{x \in X} \sum_{i \in N} u_i(x, a_i^*) p(x \mid a^*) \geq 0.$$

A first requirement for a^* to be *enforceable* is that every agent be given incentive to participate – that is, the transfer scheme should satisfy *individual rationality* constraints:

$$\forall i \in N, \quad \sum_{x \in X} [u_i(x, a_i^*) + t_i(x)] p(x \mid a^*) \geq 0. \qquad \text{(IR)}$$

A second requirement is that the transfer scheme should satisfy *incentive-compatibility* constraints:

$$\sum_{x \in X} [u_i(x, a_i^*) + t_i(x)] p(x|a^*)$$

$$\geq \sum_{x \in X} [u_i(x, a_i) + t_i(x)] p(x|a_i, a_{-i}^*) \quad \forall i \in N, \ \forall a_i \in A_i, \quad \text{(IC)}$$

with $a_{-i}^* = (a_1^*, ..., a_{i-1}^*, a_{i+1}^*, ..., a_n^*) \in \times_{i \neq j} A_j$. The IC constraints require that the joint action a^* be a Nash equilibrium of the game with strategy spaces given by $\{A_i\}$ and payoff functions given by

$$\sum_{x \in X} [u_i(x, a_i) + t_j(x)] p(x|a).$$

Suppose the objective of the central authority is that the players choose an efficient joint action. With perfect transferability, an efficient joint action a^* is simply defined by the condition

$$a^* \in \text{Arg Max}_{a \in A} \ \sum_{x \in X} p(x|a) \sum_{i \in N} u_i(x, a_i). \quad \text{(PO)}$$

The problem is to design a transfer mechanism, based on the observed outcome x, that induces the partners to choose such an a^*. The transfer scheme should be feasible in the sense that it should satisfy some budget constraint. If one requires only a balanced budget in expected value (the EB constraint), then a positive result can be obtained without further assumptions, as the following theorem shows.

Theorem 1. *For any utility profile $\{u_i\}$, any efficient joint action a^* leading to nonnegative surplus is enforceable (IC) by an individually rational (IR) transfer scheme with budget balanced in expected value (EB).*

Proof. We must solve a system of inequalities and equalities in $t \in \mathbb{R}^{nX}$:

$$\sum_x t_i(x) [p(x|a^*) - p(x|a_i, a_{-i}^*)]$$

$$\geq \sum_x [u_i(x, a_i) p(x|a_i, a_{-i}^*) - u_i(x, a_i^*) p(x|a^*)] \quad \forall i, \ \forall a_i \neq a_i^*;$$

$$\sum_x t_i(x) p(x|a^*) \geq - \sum_x u_i(x, a_i^*) p(x|a^*) \quad \forall i;$$

$$\sum_x \sum_i t_i(x) p(x|a^*) = 0.$$

Consider the following necessary and sufficient conditions, as given by well-known separation arguments (see e.g. Fan 1956). *Either* there is no $\lambda \in \times_{i=1}^n \mathbb{R}_+^{A_i}$, $\mu \in \mathbb{R}$, and $\gamma \in \mathbb{R}_+^N$ such that

$$\sum_{a_i \neq a_i^*} \lambda_i(a_i) [p(x|a^*) - p(x|a_i, a_{-i}^*)] + (\gamma_i - \mu) p(x|a^*) = 0 \quad \forall i, \ \forall x, \quad (1)$$

or we have

$$\sum_i \sum_{a_i \neq a_i^*} \lambda_i(a_i) \sum_x [u_i(x, a_i)p(x|a_i, a_{-i}^*) - u_i(x, a_i^*)p(x|a^*)]$$

$$- \sum_i \gamma_i \sum_x u_i(x, a_i^*)p(x|a^*) \leq 0. \tag{2}$$

But (1) implies (by summation over x) that $\mu = \gamma_i \geq 0$ for all i, so that

$$\sum_{a_i \neq a_i^*} \lambda_i(a_i)[p(x|a^*) - p(x|a_i, a_{-i}^*)] = 0 \quad \forall i, \ \forall x. \tag{3}$$

By efficiency we may write

$$\sum_i \sum_{a_i \neq a_i^*} \lambda_i(a_i) \sum_x [u_i(x, a_i)p(x|a_i, a_{-i}^*) - u_i(x, a_i^*)p(x|a^*)]$$

$$\leq \sum_i \sum_{a_i \neq a_i^*} \lambda_i(a_i) \sum_x \left[\sum_{j \neq i} u_j(x, a_j^*)p(x|a^*) - \sum_{j \neq i} u_j(x, a_j^*)p(x|a_i, a_{-i}^*) \right]$$

$$= \sum_i \sum_x \sum_{j \neq i} u_j(x, a_j^*) \sum_{a_i \neq a_i^*} \lambda_i(a_i)[p(x|a^*) - p(x|a_i, a_{-i}^*)].$$

This last expression is null by (3). Using

$$\sum_i \gamma_i \sum_x u_i(x, a_i^*)p(x|a^*) = \mu \sum_x \sum_i u_i(x, a_i^*)p(x|a^*) \geq 0$$

yields (2). ☐

As well illustrated by the example of Radner et al. (1986), Theorem 1 cannot be strengthened by replacing the feasibility constraint (EB) with budget balancing (BB). In their example, there are two agents each having two possible observable outcomes – "high" or "low" – that have positive probability whatever the agents do. An agent who chooses to "work" does increase the probability of "high" output. The agents decide which output they want. It is collectively efficient, in expected payoff terms, for both agents to "work" but, as in a prisoner's dilemma, it is a dominant strategy for each one of them to "shirk."

To solve this problem we shall introduce a condition inherited from the "compatibility condition" introduced by d'Aspremont and Gérard-Varet (1979) in the design, via balanced transfers, of direct revelation mechanisms for efficient collective decision making. This condition was initially stated in "dual" terms. We shall adopt its "primal" version.[14]

Condition C. For all $a^* \in A$ and all $\rho \in \mathbb{R}^{nX}$ such that $\sum_i t_i(x) = \rho(x)$,

$$\sum_x t_i(x)p(x|a^*) \geq \sum_x t_i(x)p(x|a_i, a_{-i}^*) \quad \forall a_i \in A_i, \ \forall i \in N.$$

This condition states that, for any given budget and the identically zero utility profile, any joint action profile is enforceable by a transfer scheme balancing this budget. It can be used to solve the team moral hazard problem as follows. Pick any utility profile $\{u_i\}$ and any efficient a^*. We can always construct transfers of the Clarke–Groves–Vickrey type by letting

$$t_i^0(\cdot) \equiv \sum_{j \neq i} u_j(\cdot, a_j^*).$$

Every participant is thus paying for the effects of his own action on the welfare expected by others, so that efficiency implies the IC constraint to be satisfied. Clearly, the budget-balancing constraint might be broken. However, we may use Condition C and put $\rho(\cdot) \equiv -\sum_i t_i^0(\cdot)$ in order to obtain a transfer scheme t satisfying all equalities and inequalities listed in the condition. Then, defining $t^* \equiv t^0 + t$, we get budget balancing in the sense of (BB) while preserving incentive compatibility. Finally, to ensure individual rationality, we may apply the construction given by Legros and Matsushima (1991), who directly obtain individual rationality for a given utility profile $\{u_i\}$ and for a joint action a^* leading to a nonnegative surplus, as soon as the joint action is enforceable by a budget-balancing transfer scheme t^*. Indeed, it suffices to construct the new transfer scheme t' such that, for all $i \in N$ and $x \in X$,

$$t_i'(x) \equiv t_i^*(x) - \sum_x [u_i(x, a_i^*) + t_i^*(x)]p(x \mid a^*) + \frac{1}{n} \sum_j \sum_x u_j(x, a_j^*)p(x \mid a^*).$$

By construction, this new transfer scheme is still budget-balancing and maintains incentive compatibility (since it amounts to adding a term constant in a_i). This proves the following theorem.

Theorem 2. *Suppose the stochastic outcome function p satisfies Condition C. Then, for any utility profile $\{u_i\}$ for which a joint action a^* is efficient and leads to nonnegative surplus, this joint action is enforceable by an individually rational and budget-balancing transfer scheme – that is,* (IC), (IR), *and* (BB) *hold.*

Condition C is not as restrictive as it may appear. Indeed, the compatibility condition in revelation mechanisms [15] can be shown to be generic: the set of outcome functions satisfying this condition is an open and dense set in the space of all stochastic outcome functions. This means that, with finitely many outcomes and actions and with transferable utilities, the moral hazard problem is "almost always" solvable.

3. A DYNAMIC EXTENSION

Many moral hazard situations have an important dynamic dimension. Players typically compete to exploit the same stock (replenishable or not) over time, and there is an underlying stochastic evolution equation that is affected by the individual actions at each time period. A frequently used technique to model such situations is given by *stochastic differential games*.[16] We shall take an abstract formulation of such a dynamic model in which the state variable is the capital stock, stochastically influenced by current instruments and the past value of the stock.

Consider a possibly infinite sequence of periods $t = 1, ..., \bar{t}, \bar{t} \le \infty$. To each period corresponds a state of the stock $x_t \in X$ and a finite set of actions A_{it} for every player $i \in N$. The initial state is $x_0 \in X$. The stochastic outcome function is now a function p, which to each joint action $a_t \in A_t = \times_{i=1}^n A_{it}$ and to each publicly observed state $x_{t-1} \in X$ associates the probability $p(x_t | a_t, x_{t-1})$ to obtain $x_t \in X$. At each period t, the utility function of player $i \in N$ is $u_i(x_t, a_{it})$.

At period t, player i has a *history* h_{it} describing the sequence of variables that i has observed through time:

$$h_{it} = (x_0, x_1, a_{i1}, x_2, a_{i2}, ..., x_{t-1}, a_{it-1}).$$

A *strategy* of player i is a finite sequence $(\sigma_{i1}, \sigma_{i2}, ..., \sigma_{i\bar{t}})$, where σ_{it} is a map from the set H_{it} of all histories at date t to A_{it}, $\sigma_{it}(h_{it}) \in A_{it}$. The expected payoff of player $i \in N$ at state t is

$$\sum_{x_t} u_i(x_t, a_{it}) p(x_t | a_t, x_{t-1}).$$

Given a vector of strategies for each player, the total expected payoff over time is

$$U_i(x_0, \sigma) = (1-\delta) \sum_{t=1}^{\bar{t}} \sum_{h_t} \sum_{x_t} \delta^{t-1} u_i(x_t, \sigma_{it}(h_{it})) p(x_t | \sigma_t(h_t), x_{t-1}) q_t(h_t | \sigma),$$

where $\sigma_t(h_t) = (\sigma_1(h_{1t}), ..., \sigma_i(h_{it}), ..., \sigma_n(h_{nt}))$ and $q_t(h_t | \sigma)$ is the probability generated by the outcome function and the joint strategy σ to observe history h_t given the strategy. For equilibrium we restrict the class of strategies to the set of Markov strategies. For every i and t, a *Markov strategy* σ_{it} depends upon the history h_{it} only through x_{t-1}:

$$\sigma_{it}(h_{it}) = \sigma_{it}(x_{t-1}).$$

The sequence $(x_0, x_1, ..., x_{t-1})$ is called a *public history*. In that case, the total expected payoff of any player i can be written as:

$$U_i(x_0, \sigma) = (1-\delta) \sum_{t=1}^{\bar{t}} \delta^{t-1} \sum_{(x_1, ..., x_t)} u_i(x_t, \sigma_{it}(x_{t-1})) p(x_t | \sigma_t(x_{t-1}), x_{t-1})$$
$$\times q_t(x_1, ..., x_{t-1} | \sigma),$$

where

$$q_t(x_1, ..., x_{t-1} | \sigma)$$
$$= p(x_1 | \sigma_1(x_0), x_0) p(x_2 | \sigma_2(x_1), x_1) \cdots p(x_{t-1} | \sigma_{t-1}(x_{t-2}), x_{t-2}).$$

The concept of collective efficiency can also be extended straightfor-wardly. An *efficient joint strategy* σ^* is defined as

$$\sigma^* \in \operatorname{Arg\,Max}_{\sigma} \sum_{i \in N} U_i(x_0, \sigma).$$

As in the static case, Nash equilibrium joint strategies cannot, in general, be shown to be efficient. However, as we now show, by looking at a re-strictive class of equilibria and introducing transfers, efficient equilibria can be found under the same conditions as in the static case.

A *Nash equilibrium* (closed loop) is defined as usual. It is a vector of strategies (or a joint strategy) σ^* such that, for any $i \in N$ and any strat-egy σ_i,

$$U_i(x_0, \sigma^*) \geq U_i(x_0, \sigma_i, \sigma^*_{-i}).$$

A Nash equilibrium within a Markov strategy is called a *Markov perfect equilibrium*. This is because it satisfies the property that, for each t and given any x_{t-1}, the continuation payoffs starting from x_{t-1} are identical regardless of the history that led to that state. Formally, it is a joint strat-egy σ^* such that, for any $i \in N$, any strategy σ_i, any $t_0 \geq 0$, and any x_{t_0-1}:

$$U_i^{t_0}(x_{t_0-1}, \sigma_i, \sigma^*_{-i})$$

$$\equiv (1-\delta) \sum_{t=t_0}^{\bar{t}} \sum_{(x_{t_0}, \ldots, x_t)} \delta^{t-1} u_i(x_t, \sigma_{it}(x_{t-1}))$$

$$\times p(x_t | \sigma_i(x_{t-1}), \sigma^*_{-i}(x_{t-1}), x_{t-1}) q(x_{t_0}, \ldots, x_t | \sigma_i, \sigma^*_{-i})$$

$$\leq U_i^{t_0}(x_{t_0-1}, \sigma^*).$$

A joint (Markov) strategy σ^* is *dynamically enforceable through balanced transfers* if, for every $t \geq 0$, there exists a transfer scheme $T_t(x_{t-1}, \cdot) = (T_{it}(x_{t-1}, \cdot))_{i \in N}$ that is *balanced*. That is, $\sum_{i \in N} T_{it}(x_{t-1}, x_t) = 0$ for any x_t, and σ^* is a Markov perfect equilibrium for the modified game ob-tained by replacing each $u_i(x_t, a_{it})$ by $[u_i(x_t, a_{it}) + T_{it}(x_{t-1}, x_t)]$. Formally: for any $i \in N$, any $t_0 \geq 0$, any x_{t_0-1}, and any σ_i:

$$V_i^{t_0}(x_{t_0-1}, \sigma_i, \sigma^*_{-i}, T_i) \leq V_i^{t_0}(x_{t_0-1}, \sigma^*, T_i)$$

with, for any σ_i,

$$V_i^{t_0}(x_{t_0-1}, \sigma_i, \sigma^*_{-i}, T_i)$$

$$\equiv (1-\delta) \sum_{t=t_0}^{\bar{t}} \sum_{(x_{t_0}, \ldots, x_t)} \delta^{t-1} [u_i(x_t, \sigma_{it}(x_{t-1})) + T_{it}(x_{t-1}, x_t)]$$

$$\times p(x_t | \sigma_i(x_{t-1}), \sigma^*_{-i}(x_{t-1}), x_{t-1}) q(x_{t_0}, \ldots, x_t | \sigma_i, \sigma^*_{-i}).$$

We now show that any efficient joint (Markov) strategy is dynamically enforceable using balanced transfers under an extension of Condition C.

Condition $\vec{C}$. For every $t \geq 0$ and every $x_{t-1} \in X$, $p(\cdot \mid \cdot, x_{t-1})$ satisfies Condition C.

Theorem 3. *Suppose Condition $\vec{C}$ holds. Then, for any profile $\{u_i\}$, any efficient joint (Markov) strategy σ^* will be dynamically enforceable by a budget-balancing (and individually rational) transfer scheme.*

Proof. The proof proceeds in three steps.

(1) By the optimality principle of dynamic programming, since σ^* is an efficient joint strategy, for any x_{t-1} we should have

$$\sigma_t^*(x_{t-1}) \in \operatorname*{Arg\,Max}_{a_t} \sum_{x_t} \sum_i u_i(x_t, a_{it}) p(x_t \mid a_t, x_{t-1}).$$

This means that, at any $t \geq 0$ and for any x_{t-1}, an efficient joint action is selected.

(2) By Theorem 2 we have that, at any $t \geq 0$ and for any x_{t-1}, $\sigma_t^*(x_{t-1})$ is enforceable by a budget-balancing (and individually rational) transfer scheme - that is, there exist balanced transfers $T_t(x_{t-1}, \cdot)$ such that, for any $i \in N$,

$$\sigma_{it}^*(x_{t-1}) \in \operatorname*{Arg\,Max}_{a_{it}} \sum_{x_t} [u_i(x_t, a_{it}) + T_{it}(x_{t-1}, x_t)] p(x_t \mid a_{it}, \sigma_{-it}^*(x_{t-1}), x_{t-1}).$$

(3) By the optimality principle as applied to dynamic games (the "one-stage deviation principle"),[17] this expression implies that σ^* is a Markov perfect equilibrium. □

4. CONCLUSION

We have argued in this paper that, under risk neutrality, it is (in general, and contrary to common belief) possible for a central government to design transfers among regional governments in order to solve the basic decentralization tradeoff between incentives and collective efficiency (under budget balancing). The result holds even in a dynamic environment by restriction to a notion of Markov perfect equilibrium. This conclusion can be contrasted to the one of Coase (1960). Coase's theorem states that, in the absence of wealth effects (or under risk neutrality) and under a principle of efficient bargaining (no possibility for further mutual gain), a first-best outcome will be reached regardless of the distribution costs and benefits; transfers play no incentive role but only a redistributive role. Our conclusion is that, even without wealth effects, *incentive and redistributive considerations cannot be separated.*

We have presented a very simple model. In many situations there are, besides nonverifiable individual actions, other variables that contribute to the outcome. For instance, one could require jurisdictions to choose two actions – one centrally verifiable and the other not – with the former more costly because it cannot be tailored exactly to specific features of each region. Provided that these centrally verifiable actions do not generate too large efficiency losses, our conclusions would remain unchanged.

Another dimension of the problem of decentralizing public expenditures arises when the utility functions of the local governments exhibit *risk aversion*. Actually, a central government may be concerned with risk sharing among subcentral jurisdictions, and decentralization – when creating autonomous local jurisdictions – may entail a loss of welfare through reduced opportunities for risk sharing. The point is made by Drèze (1994), who mentions the "ability of a central government *to organize mutual insurance among regions* under its jurisdiction, so that the idiosyncratic shocks affecting individual regions are partly absorbed through stock-dependent transfers between regions." Clearly, in case of idiosyncratic shocks, mutual insurance can be achieved by the adoption of national uniform rules, but these contradict local differentiation. On the other hand, if the rules are set autonomously at the local level then a moral hazard problem arises, making insurance difficult.[18]

In our framework, where a joint collective outcome is stochastically obtained through the actions of the local jurisdictions, the question does not reduce to mutual insurance against local specific shocks. As soon as the utility functions exhibit risk aversion, a collectively efficient arrangement requires efficient risk sharing as well as an efficient profile of actions implemented by the local jurisdictions. This, in general, cannot be sustained as a Nash equilibrium. However, recent results on repeated games with imperfect monitoring[19] show that, even when exact efficiency is unattainable, repetition can make incentive compatibility consistent with profiles arbitrarily close to collective efficiency, at least for patient agents.

Thus, when some collective arrangement embodies an agreement in a suitable equilibrium, the decentralized players will honor the terms of the arrangement because it is in their interest to do so. By allowing for reciprocity, repeated interactions support self-policing. A drawback is that many less attractive arrangements can also be sustained the same way. An alternative approach is to model the situation as a stochastic differential game by introducing monitoring variables and retaliation schemes. However, in the present state of the art, only numerical examples are available.[20]

We have considered decentralization issues only in terms of pure moral hazard problems. However, it may seem reasonable *not* to assume that each region's welfare is common knowledge. But then we have *incomplete information* and the problem becomes more intricate, especially if we retain the moral hazard aspect.[21]

However, the problem has been well analyzed in the transferable utility case with the moral hazard issue discarded – the "pure adverse selection" case.[22] In this scenario the players' individual utilities depend upon their *types* – any possible specification of all the players' private information relevant to the situation. A "belief structure" specifies the probabilities that each player i could assign to each possible combination of types for the other players, as a function of i's own type. The central authority in charge of achieving collective efficiency needs to collect from the players data about their types. Although their goals may differ, the players care about the collective outcome and so the central authority must provide incentives for truth telling. To do so, the central authority commits to an *incentive scheme* specifying how the outcome is selected on the basis of the reports, and possibly some money payments also depending on these reports. In order to elicit information, the central authority may have to make promises that it might rather not keep once the information comes out, and so the assumption of commitment is essential. Side payments help the center to obtain information about the agents' true willingness to pay for particular outcomes, thus showing which decision is truly efficient. A result parallel to Theorem 2 (see d'Aspremont et al. 1991) states that, for any profile of utilities, it is "in general" possible for the central authority – by making appropriate use of common knowledge about the belief structure – to design a collectively efficient and incentive-compatible mechanism that preserves budget balancing.

Now, when extended to incomplete information but limited to adverse selection, the analysis reduces to what a benevolent central authority can do with respect to its subcentral delegates with suitable incentive schemes. What is the lesson for decentralization? Rather than wholly independent units making decisions about the level and pattern of local public goods, subcentral governments appear more as *vehicles* for the implementation of a centrally designed policy. In principle, administrative decentralization means that, instead of sending all information to the center, decisions are delegated to appropriately knowledgeable lower tiers of government. Yet delegation cannot possibly be helpful, since anything that a local government can do, the central government can do as well. Decentralization then appears as a subset of centralization, and is at best harmless.

Centralization clearly helps when decisions are so independent that they cannot be delegated. But it is not really plausible that centralization always dominate decentralization, even when restricting the analysis to administrative decentralization. The foregoing arguments actually miss major problems. One is that the participants in a collective decision process may not trust the central authority's commitment to an incentive scheme. The second problem is that the central authority may have a limited ability to process information. Both problems suggest that to evaluate decentralization under incomplete information requires a reappraisal of the principle according to which the appropriate point of view for the analysis of incentives is to consider a central agent acting as a mediator who communicates directly and confidentially with each player.[23] The same line of reasoning is also essential to capture the features of such hierarchical structures as those involving economic agents and voters or local, regional, and central governments.[24]

Progress in understanding any interesting decentralization in public policy can only be expected from models that integrate a combination of private information, moral hazard, and voluntary participation. Voluntary participation raises no difficulty when there is moral hazard only. The issue is different under incomplete information, where a notion of political decentralization implies a restriction to mechanisms satisfying the constraint that every player be willing to participate once apprised of his or her own private information. This restriction strongly limits the coercive power of the central government, and moreover is costly to collective efficiency. There is actually a basic tradeoff: the freedom to choose, which is a safeguard against abuses by central authority, may well be a barrier to efficiency.

NOTES

1. See Gilbert and Delcamp (1993) for an account of the major administrative changes in France since 1982. See also Gérard-Varet (1995), a report prepared for Commissariat Général du Plan, Paris.
2. It is widely recognized that the taxes raised by subcentral government in France are distorting, regressive, and inequitable across jurisdictions. If these taxes are allowed to grow then the transfer of taxes currently raised by the central government (income tax or VAT) should probably be reconsidered.
3. In 1993, total local government spending in France was almost half of central government spending, accounting for about 10% of GNP. The regions' share of total local spending remains low, at around 5%, but regional spending has been growing (in real terms) at a rate of more than 50% per year, compared with a figure of 5% for the other tiers of local government. Per-capita spending varies across regions from 700 to 1,200 francs. The main sources of regional government revenue in 1993 were their own tax resources, which constituted 49% of total revenue (direct and indirect taxes accounted for about 60% and 40% of tax revenues, respectively). For the other (nontax) resources, the contributions of grants from central government amount to 25%, while borrowing and "miscellaneous income" contributed 13% and 11% (respectively) to total regional government revenue. Variation in tax rates across regions has grown considerably in recent years, as has the contribution of grant income.
4. See Demsetz (1977) or Olson (1965), who provides a classical statement of the "tragedy of the commons." For more recent developments, see the paper by

Moulin and Watts (1994), which builds on Hardin (1968). See also Moulin (1995, pp. 26–36 and chap. 6).

5. See Oates (1968) or Olson (1969). The literature has identified, besides externalities, other reasons in favor of centralizing policy decisions: mobility of tax bases and policies distorting private competition. We disregard these issues here to concentrate on the appropriate devices and institutional arrangements needed to offset the distortions of regional decisions created by moral hazard.

6. Oates (1968) observes that, when lower-tier levels of government are given responsibility for functions that have significant spillover effects on other areas, the functions must be reassigned to a higher tier that embraces all of those affected by the policy. Olson (1969) suggests that an appropriate assignment reflects equivalence between the geographical scope of the decision-making unit and the geographical area within which policy effects are felt.

7. The model that we consider, with a central and regional governments vertically ordered, is closest to the current situation of the EU – where there is only a system of interstate transfers – than to France (or even the United States), where the national (or federal) government has instruments that enable direct distribution among individuals.

8. See Alchian and Demsetz (1972), Holmström (1982), Radner, Myerson, and Maskin (1986), Radner and Williams (1987), or Legros (1989).

9. The expression, coined by Myerson (1985), is an extension of the well-known "prisoner's dilemma." Another example is the collective inefficiency of Cournot oligopoly equilibria. See also Myerson (1991).

10. See Maskin and Tirole (1989) or Fudenberg and Tirole (1991, chap. 13).

11. For a review of the literature on this problem (and references), see Fudenberg and Tirole (1991, sec. 5.5).

12. Some of our results will apply to the more general case where u_i is defined on $X \times A$.

13. This model can be interpreted in several contexts. For example, the outcome x can be the stock of a common resource (a lake, a forest, a pasture) with individual actions giving the level of its free utilization by every owner of the resource (fishing, wood exploitation, grazing). The moral hazard problem is then the "tragedy of the commons." The collective inefficiency of a "subscription equilibrium" for the production of a public good or service (where the actions are individual contributions) is another instance of such a problem. In the context of cooperation on environmental issues, the outcomes describe the state of the environment, which is affected by individual actions, and the utility is often decomposed into the net cost of actions and the damage associated with every state of the environment. Another example is a partnership production, where each agent supplies an unobservable input to a production process and the output is divided among the partners. In a regional context, every local jurisdiction may contribute (by taking actions) to a total fiscal revenue that is redistributed to their inhabitants. Still another context is a Cournot oligopoly in which each firm's output level is not perfectly observable by the other firms in the industry, and where the market price is a (stochastic) function of total output.

14. This is analyzed in d'Aspremont, Crémer, and Gérard-Varet (1995) for the incomplete information case, and in d'Aspremont and Gérard-Varet (1996) for the present model.
15. See d'Aspremont, Crémer, and Gérard-Varet (1991). See also d'Aspremont and Gérard-Varet (1996).
16. Stochastic differential games have been used to address such environmental issues as competition among fisheries in exploiting the same stock of biomass (Levhari and Mirman 1980; Haurie, Krawczyk, and Roche 1994) and global warming (van der Ploeg and de Zeuw 1992; Germain 1995). For models of this kind in the context of industrial organization, see Maskin and Tirole (1987, 1988a,b).
17. See Fudenberg and Tirole (1991).
18. See Persson and Tabellini (1996) for a discussion of the difficulties in enforcing decentralized insurance systems under fiscal federalism environments with moral hazard.
19. See Fudenberg, Levine, and Maskin (1994) and also d'Aspremont and Gérard-Varet (1996).
20. See Haurie et al. (1994).
21. There have been recent models in the fiscal federalism literature introducing different specifications of adverse selection. See e.g. Cremer, Marchand, and Pestieau (1994).
22. See Green and Laffont (1979) or d'Aspremont and Gérard-Varet (1979).
23. This is the "revelation principle"; see Myerson (1991).
24. Tirole (1994) specifically calls for analyzing "fiscal federalism" and the organization of government along these lines.

REFERENCES

Alchian, A. A., and H. Demsetz (1972), "Production, Information Costs and Economic Organization," *American Economic Review* 62: 777–85.
d'Aspremont, C., J. Crémer, and L.-A. Gérard-Varet (1991), "Incentives and the Existence of Pareto-Optimal Revelation Mechanisms," *Journal of Economic Theory* 51: 233–54.
d'Aspremont, C., J. Crémer, and L.-A. Gérard-Varet (1995), "Correlation, Independence and Bayesian Implementation," Mimeo, GREQAM, Marseilles, France.
d'Aspremont, C., and L.-A. Gérard-Varet (1979), "Incentives and Incomplete Information," *Journal of Public Economics* 11: 25–45.
d'Aspremont, C., and L.-A. Gérard-Varet (1996), "Moral Hazard in Teams with Uncertainty and Transfers or Repetition as Enforcement Mechanisms," Mimeo, CORE, Université Catholique de Louvain, Belgium.
Coase, R. A. (1960), "The Problem of Social Cost," *Journal of Law and Economics* 3: 1–44.
Cremer, H., M. Marchand, and P. Pestieau (1994), "Interregional Redistribution through Tax Surcharge," Discussion Paper no. 9469, CORE, Université Catholique de Louvain, Belgium.
Demsetz, H. (1977), "Towards a Theory of Property Rights," *American Economic Review* 57: 347–59.

Drèze, J. H. (1994), "Regions of Europe: A Feasible Status to Be Discussed." *Economic Policy* 17: 266-307.

Fan, K. (1956), "On Systems of Inequalities," in H. W. Kuhn and A. W. Tucker (eds.), *Linear Inequalities and Related Systems*. Princeton, NJ: Princeton University Press.

Fudenberg, D., D. Levine, and E. Maskin (1994), "The Folk Theorem with Imperfect Public Information," *Econometrica* 62: 997-1039.

Fudenberg, D., and J. Tirole (1991), *Game Theory*. Cambridge, MA: MIT Press.

Gérard-Varet, L.-A. (ed.) (1995), *Enjeux et procédures de la décentralisation* (Report prepared for Commissariat Général du Plan). Paris, 4 volumes.

Germain, M. (1995), "Modèle en boucle ouverte," Mimeo, CORE, Université Catholique de Louvain, Belgium.

Gilbert, G., and A. Delcamp (eds.) (1993), *La décentralisation dix ans après*. Paris: Librairie de Droit et Jurisprudence.

Green, J., and J. J. Laffont (1979), *Incentives in Public Decision Making*. Amsterdam: North-Holland.

Hardin, G. (1968), "The Tragedy of the Commons," *Science* 162: 1243-8.

Haurie, A., J. B. Krawczyk, and M. Roche (1994), "Monitoring Cooperative Equilibria in a Stochastic Differential Game," *Journal of Optimization Theory and Application* 81: 73-95.

Holmström, B. (1982), "Moral Hazard in Teams," *Bell Journal of Economics* 13: 324-40.

Legros, P. (1989), "Efficiency and Stability in Partnerships," Ph.D. Dissertation, California Institute of Technology, Pasadena.

Legros, P., and H. Matsushima (1991), "Efficiency in Partnerships," *Journal of Economic Theory* 55: 296-322.

Levhari, D., and L. J. Mirman (1980), "The Great Fish War: An Example Using a Dynamic Cournot-Nash Solution," *Bell Journal of Economics* 11: 322-34.

Maskin, E., and J. Tirole (1987), "A Theory of Dynamic Oligopoly III. Cournot Competition," *European Economic Review* 31: 947-68.

Maskin, E., and J. Tirole (1988a), "A Theory of Dynamic Oligopoly I. Overview and Quantity Competition with Large Fixed Costs," *Econometrica* 56: 549-70.

Maskin, E., and J. Tirole (1988b), "A Theory of Dynamic Oligopoly II. Price Competition," *Econometrica* 56: 571-600.

Maskin, E., and J. Tirole (1989), "Markov Equilibrium," Mimeo, Department of Economics, Harvard University, Cambridge, MA.

Moulin, H. (1995), *Cooperative Microeconomics*. Princeton, NJ: Princeton University Press.

Moulin, H., and A. Watts (1994), "Two Versions of the Tragedy of the Commons," Mimeo, Department of Economics, Duke University, Durham, NC.

Myerson, R. B. (1985), "Negotiations in Games - A Theoretical Overview," Discussion Paper no. 658, Center for Mathematical Studies in Economics and Management Science, Northwestern University, Evanston, IL.

Myerson, R. B. (1991), *Game Theory*. Cambridge, MA: Harvard University Press.

Oates, W. E. (1968), "The Theory of Public Finance in a Federal System," *Canadian Journal of Economics* 1: 37-56.

Olson, M. (1965), *The Logic of Collective Action. Public Goods and the Theory of Groups*. Cambridge, MA: Harvard University Press (2nd ed., 1971).

Olson, M. (1969), "The Principle of Fiscal Equivalence: The Division of Responsibilities among Different Levels of Government," *American Economic Review* 49: 479–87.

Persson, T., and G. Tabellini (1996), "Federal Fiscal Constitutions: Risk Sharing and Moral Hazard," *Econometrica* 64: 623–46.

Radner, R., R. Myerson, and E. Maskin (1986), "An Example of a Repeated Partnership Game with Discounting and with Uniformly Inefficient Equilibria," *Review of Economic Studies* 53: 59–69.

Radner, R., and S. R. Williams (1987), "Efficiency in Partnership When the Joint Output is Uncertain," Discussion Paper no. 760, Center for Mathematical Studies in Economics and Management Science, Northwestern University, Evanston, IL.

Tirole, J. (1994), "The Internal Organization of Government," *Oxford Economic Papers* 46: 1–29.

van der Ploeg, and A. de Zeuw (1992), "A Differential Game of International Pollution Control," Mimeo, Tilburg University, Netherlands.

CHAPTER 6

Migration and Income Transfers in the Presence of Labor Quality Externalities

Harry Huizinga

1. INTRODUCTION

International migrants generally seek employment in the destination country or, if eligible, they receive unemployment benefits or other income support. These migrants differ widely in their age and education and thus in their ability to find employment. The private gains from migration, therefore, depend importantly on migrants' personal characteristics. The economic impact of immigration on nonmigrants in the source and recipient countries likewise depends on who the migrants are. Migration of a source country's most productive workers represents the greatest loss to this country and at the sime time the greatest gain to the recipient country. Not surprisingly, many countries restrict legal immigration to people with sufficient work experience and education. In practice, however, many international migrants receive some income support in the destination country, and migrants may benefit from publicly provided education, housing, and health care. In recent years, countries in Western Europe have been confronted with rising numbers of immigrants from Eastern Europe and Africa. Germany, for instance, absorbed about 230,000 migrants of German origin from the Soviet Union alone in 1992.[1] Migration toward the European Union (EU) can be explained by a mix of economic factors and conflicts in Yugoslavia, Somalia, and other countries. As a result of increasing migration pressures, EU countries face considerable strains on their public finances. These pressures may ultimately lead to a partial undoing of the social welfare state. Consequently, international migration has become an important political issue.

This paper presents a model of international migration which recognizes that workers are of heterogeneous quality.[2] The model assumes that an individual worker's productivity in a country depends positively on the

I am grateful to Robin Boadway, David Wildasin, an anonymous referee, seminar participants at Copenhagen Business School, and participants of the 1994 ISPE Conference on "Fiscal Aspects of Evolving Federations" at Vanderbilt University for useful comments.

average quality of co-workers in the same country. In this setting, international migration affects the productivity of nonimmigrant workers in the source and the recipient countries if it changes the average quality of workers in these countries. The model displays what can be called "increasing returns to average quality," as a country's aggregate output increases more than linearly with average worker quality.

The paper first considers international migration in the absence of any policy intervention. If two countries have different average worker qualities, then all workers in the country with low average worker quality wish to migrate to the other country. The migration incentive ceases to exist once both countries have equal average worker qualities. This leveling effect subsequent to international migration reduces aggregate world output as a result of the increasing returns to average worker quality. The reduction in average worker quality in the immigration country following free migration provides a rationale for restricting immigration to high-quality foreign workers. Similarly, the country of emigration optimally restricts the emigration of its highest-quality workers. In setting their emigration and immigration restrictions, countries may or may not be interested in the income changes obtained by their migrant population. Only if the emigration country cares about migrants' incomes is it possible for there to be positive migration. Djajić (1989) has also considered qualitative restrictions on international labor migration, but in his paper the high- and low-quality workers differ only in the quantity of homogeneous labor they can supply. Qualitative immigration restrictions are then an alternative method to restrict the effective quantity of immigrant labor. In practice, countries frequently discriminate among prospective immigrants on the basis of their perceived level of skills and education. The United States, for instance, grants H-1 work permits to highly trained foreigners for whom no counterparts are available in the U.S. labor market. In fact, immigration may be regarded somewhat more positively in the United States than in Europe precisely because the United States is relatively successful in screening its immigrant pool, even though Borjas (1990) presents evidence that recent immigrants to the United States are more likely than previous immigrants to be low-skilled.

Sala-i-Martin (1992) has argued that the retirement of older, less productive workers can increase aggregate output in a growth context as a result of labor quality externalities. Along similar lines, Huizinga (1997) examines the political economy of welfare benefits in the presence of labor quality externalities in the work place. This paper extends that analysis to a two-country model in order to analyze international migration and income transfers in the presence of labor quality externalities. The transfer system consists of a fixed benefit to all unemployed workers and is financed by a proportional labor income tax. Previous studies of income redistribution with migration (Brown and Oates 1987; Crane 1992; Epple and Romer 1991; Persson and Tabellini 1992; Wildasin 1991) or without migration (Meltzer and Richards 1981) have not taken into account any labor quality externalities. Following earlier contributions, this paper assumes that the transfer level is determined by popular vote. Interestingly, even if employed, the median voter possibly favors a positive transfer level, as redistribution can yield sufficiently large efficiency gains to offset the income taxes necessary to finance the income transfers. The effect of the immigration of variously qualified individuals on the transfer system in political equilibrium is analyzed. The median voter opposes the immigration of all prospective transfer recipients but, more surprisingly, also of a range of workers who will be employed if admitted. Small inflows of prospective welfare recipients, if they occur, potentially lead to a large downward adjustment in the transfer level.

The paper finally considers how the benefit system is affected by an anticipation of potential immigration flows of benefit recipients (following Brown and Oates 1987; Epple and Romer 1991; and Wildasin 1991). Specifically, the implications for the transfer level, income tax rate, labor participation rate, and distribution of income are considered. A prospective influx of foreign benefit recipients in response to higher benefit levels generally leads to a lower benefit level. The income distributional effects and also the total output effect depend on whether the median voter is employed or unemployed. In the former case, lower benefits generally reduce all agents' net incomes and thus also aggregate income. In the latter case, lower benefits imply that income is redistributed from the unemployed to the employed, while aggregate income increases. The result that higher factor mobility reduces the scope for taxation for purposes of income redistribution is also obtained in Persson and Tabellini (1992), who focus on the implications of higher capital mobility.

The remainder of this paper is organized as follows. Section 2 sets out the basic model of international migration in the absence of income transfers. Section 3 introduces income transfers for an economy without migration. Section 4 focuses on the political economy of income transfers in such an economy. Section 5 examines how (exogenous) migration flows affect the politically determined transfer system. Section 6 considers the adjustment of the transfer system in anticipation of international migration movitated by differences in income transfers. Section 7 concludes.

2. MIGRATION WITHOUT TRANSFERS

The world consists of two countries: home and foreign, with asterisks denoting foreign variables. In each country, there is a population of workers that are heterogeneous in their quality, which can be in part innate and in part the result of education. Let a denote the quality of a domestic worker. The variable a is distributed on the interval $[\underline{a}, \bar{a}]$ with density $f(a)$ and distribution function $F(a)$. The size of the domestic population is denoted S, so that $S = F(\bar{a})$. Of course, the population size S is endogenous to migration flows and, in principle, can take on any value. Let μ be the mean domestic worker quality. The quality distribution and total size of a country's population can be altered through migration. A worker's productivity is assumed to be positively related to his or her own quality a and to the mean quality μ of other workers in the same country owing to peer-group effects in the work force.[3] Peer-group effects may arise as low-skilled workers learn from high-skilled workers, or they may be purely psychological. Henderson, Mieszkowski, and Sauvageau (1978) and Arnott and Rowse (1987) have demonstrated that peer-group effects are important in educational settings. Let us assume, specifically, that a worker's output is equal to the product $a\mu$.[4] National income, denoted Y, is the sum of all agents' individual products:[5]

$$Y = \int_{\underline{a}}^{\bar{a}} a\mu f(a)\, da = \mu^2 S. \tag{1}$$

Equation (1) indicates that national income Y is quadratic in average worker quality μ but linear in work-force size S. The model thus displays *increasing returns to average worker quality,* whereas there are only constant returns to scale.

The two countries generally differ in their distributions of worker quality. In particular, let us assume that domestic workers are, on average, of higher quality than foreign workers – that is, $\mu > \mu^*$. In this instance, all the world's workers potentially have a higher individual productivity in the home country than in the foreign country. Consequently, all foreign workers have an incentive to migrate to the home country if migration is costless. Migration generally affects the productivities of the migrants as well as of nonmigrants. Let all foreign workers in a certain quality bracket migrate to the home country. The variable a^* is now taken to be the upper limit of this quality range. The notation da^* then stands for a change in the top limit of the quality bracket of migrating foreign workers. Let Y_m^* denote the income of these foreign migrants, while Y_{-m} and Y_{-m}^* are the incomes of domestic and foreign nonmigrants. An increase in the range of foreign migrants starting from a quality level a^* affects the income variables Y_m^*, Y_{-m}, and Y_{-m}^* as follows:[6]

$$\frac{dY_m^*}{da^*} = (\mu - \mu^*)a^* f^*(a^*), \tag{2}$$

$$\frac{dY_{-m}}{da^*} = (a^* - \mu)\mu f^*(a^*), \tag{3}$$

$$\frac{dY^*_{-m}}{da^*} = (\mu^* - a^*)\mu^* f^*(a^*). \tag{4}$$

Equation (2) confirms that foreign workers of any quality can increase their private incomes by migrating to the home country if $\mu > \mu^*$. Equation (3) indicates that immigration raises home income levels if immigrant workers are of higher average quality than the average original home-country worker (i.e., if $a^* > \mu$) and vice versa. Similarly, emigration lowers foreign incomes of those staying behind if the average quality of emigrant workers exceeds the average quality of original foreign workers (i.e., if $a^* > \mu^*$) and vice versa.[7]

Worldwide income, denoted Y_w, is the sum of the individual incomes of migrants and of nonmigrants in the two countries. Formally, this means that $Y_w = Y^*_m + Y_{-m} + Y^*_{-m}$. Adding (2)-(4), we see that international migration affects world income as follows:

$$\frac{dY_w}{da^*} = [2a^* - (\mu + \mu^*)](\mu - \mu^*) f^*(a^*). \tag{5}$$

From (5), we see that migration increases world output if $a^* > (\mu + \mu^*)/2$, and vice versa.

The effects of migration on the incomes of nonmigrants suggest that countries have strong incentives to regulate international migration. Equation (3), specifically, implies that the home country optimally admits only foreign workers of quality a^* exceeding the average domestic worker quality μ if it cares only about its original inhabitants.[8] Similarly, from (4), the foreign country allows only workers with $a^* < \mu^*$ to emigrate if it cares only about nonmigrating foreign workers. In this scenario, there will be no migration since $\mu > \mu^*$. Alternatively, we can assume that one of the countries cares about the incomes of migrating workers. If only the foreign country takes into account the income gains achieved by migrants, then it allows the emigration of workers with $a^* < \mu^{*2}/(2\mu^* - \mu)$ if $2\mu^* > \mu$ (from (2) and (4)), whereas no emigration restriction is called for if $2\mu^* \le \mu$. It is straightforward to check that $\mu^{*2}/(2\mu^* - \mu)$ exceeds μ with $\mu > \mu^*$, which implies that there is a nonnegligible quality range of workers that both countries initially allow to migrate. As agents within this range migrate from the foreign to the home country, one of the two countries' migration restrictions at some point becomes binding. Alternatively, if only the home country considers the income gains of migrants, then it allows the immigration of foreign workers with $a^* > \mu^2/(2\mu - \mu^*)$, which exceeds μ^*. This implies that there will be no migration, even though the immigrant country internalizes the migrants' income gains.

To conclude this section, let us consider the implications of completely free international migration. The incentive to migrate ceases to exist once the average worker qualities in the two countries are equal – that is, when $\mu = \mu^*$.[9] It is evident that free migration increases (decreases) the incomes of all original foreign (domestic) workers. Interestingly, world income unambiguously declines. To see this, let μ_0 (μ_0^*) and S_0 (S_0^*) denote, respectively, the premigration average worker quality and population size of the home (foreign) country. Relative postmigration world income, denoted θ, is then calculated as

$$\theta = \frac{(S_0\mu_0 + S_0^*\mu_0^*)^2}{(S_0 + S_0^*)(S_0\mu_0^2 + S_0^*\mu_0^{*2})}.\qquad (6)$$

In (6), relative postmigration income θ is less than unity if $\mu \neq \mu^*$. This result is a direct implication of the increasing returns to average quality that was evident in equation (1).[10] The scope for international migration to increase overall income is obviously larger if we include a nonmobile factor of production such as land in the model.[11]

3. The Introduction of Transfers

The present model implies that a worker's productivity increases if other workers of below-average quality leave the labor force. Such exits from the labor force may lead to higher total output if the quality of exiting workers is sufficiently below the average. However, exits from the labor market are never privately advantageous unless the exiters are provided with an alternative source of income. This section considers income transfer schemes with the aim of retiring low-quality workers from the labor force of a country with a fixed population. As will be shown, such transfers are generally Pareto-improving. Labor quality externalities thus provide a strong rationale for the introduction of welfare benefits on efficiency grounds. Other reasons for welfare benefits, such as altruism or income insurance, are not considered in this paper.

Nonactive individuals are assumed to receive a pretax welfare benefit b. To finance these benefits, authorities impose an income tax at a rate τ on all income (including welfare benefits). At a given benefit level b, individuals below a certain critical quality level (if any) leave the work force. The quality level a_c of the marginal worker who is indifferent between working and receiving welfare benefits is given by

$$a_c = b/\mu. \qquad (7)$$

A higher benefit level b implies a higher critical quality level a_c. With individuals of quality exceeding a_c employed, aggregate income Y is given by

$$Y = \int_{a_c}^{\bar{a}} \mu a f(a) \, da. \tag{8}$$

Government budget balance requires that welfare benefit outlays equal income tax receipts as follows:

$$bF(a_c) = \tau[bF(a_c) + \mu^2(S - F(a_c))]. \tag{9}$$

In (9), a higher benefit level b implies a higher income tax rate τ. To see this, note that a higher benefit level raises the welfare income b relative to the pretax labor income of all working individuals and also raises the share of welfare recipients in the total population. Next, let us consider how a change in the critical quality level a_c (and corresponding changes in the benefit level b and the income tax rate τ) affect aggregate income Y. Differentiating Y in (8) with respect to a_c yields

$$\frac{dY}{da_c} = (\mu - 2a_c)\mu f(a_c). \tag{10}$$

National income Y is highest if $a_c = \mu/2$ as a necessary condition from (10), provided that $2\underline{a} \le \mu$.[12] Using (7), we see that the welfare benefit b_y that maximizes national income Y is given by $\mu^2/2$. Next, let us consider how changes in the income transfer scheme affect the distribution of income. The net incomes of employed and unemployed workers, denoted n_e and n_u, are given by $a\mu(1-\tau)$ and $b(1-\tau)$, respectively. Note that a change in the income transfer scheme affects the net incomes of all employed workers proportionately. After some manipulation, we see that changing the critical quality level a_c affects net income levels n_e and n_u as follows:

$$\frac{dn_e}{da_c} = a\mu \frac{(\mu - 2a_c)f(a_c) - (1-\tau)F(a_c)}{a_c F(a_c) + \mu(S - F(a_c))}, \tag{11}$$

$$\frac{dn_u}{da_c} = \mu \frac{a_c(\mu - 2a_c)f(a_c) + \mu(1-\tau)(S - F(a_c))}{a_c F(a_c) + \mu(S - F(a_c))}. \tag{12}$$

Equations (11) and (12) immediately imply that slightly increasing a_c above $\underline{a}$ increases the net incomes of active as well as nonactive workers if $2\underline{a} < \mu$, since $F(\underline{a}) = 0$. Introducing low-level welfare benefits is thus generally Pareto-improving. This result reflects that, in the present model, an income transfer scheme can increase total income rather than merely redistribute income. Let the benefit levels that are consistent with maximizing n_e and n_u be denoted b_e and b_u, respectively, and assume that they are unique. Equations (11) and (12) now imply that $b_e < b_y < b_u$. These results are summarized as follows.

Proposition 1. *The net incomes of all individuals as employed workers are maximized at the same welfare level b_e, whereas unemployed workers receive a highest net income at a welfare level b_u. We also have $b_e < b_y < b_u$, where b_y is the value of b that maximizes national income.*

Let us assume that the preferences of any worker – employed or unemployed – over different values of b are single-peaked. Because a worker can change employment status, overall preferences over the benefit level b can still be double-peaked. Specifically, preferences are double-peaked for workers who change their employment status for a value of b between b_e and b_u. Equivalently, preferences are single-peaked for workers who choose to be employed at a benefit level b_u or who choose to be unemployed at a benefit level b_e.

4. VOTING ON TRANSFERS

In this section, we examine how the transfer system is determined by the political process. In particular, we will assume that the benefit level b is determined by popular vote. As indicated, the employed and the unemployed have the same preferences over the value of b as groups. The employed and the unemployed thus will act as two voting blocs, with the largest prevailing. Hence, we must see which group the median voter wishes to join. To start, note that the electorate will never set the benefit level either below b_e or above b_u, as in these instances all voters' net incomes can be enhanced by either increasing or decreasing the benefit level, respectively. In other words, voting will yield a value of b within the interval bounded by b_e and b_u. For benefit levels between b_e and b_u, there exists the usual tradeoff between the net incomes of the two classes of workers; not surprisingly, the value of the benefit level b that maximizes Y lies between b_e and b_u. It is now useful to consider voter preferences over values of b within this range separately for three categories of workers: (i) workers who are unemployed at a benefit level b_e, (ii) workers who become unemployed for a value of b between b_e and b_u, and (iii) workers who are employed at a benefit level b_u.

Workers in category (i), who are already unemployed at the low benefit level b_e, see their net incomes rise as b is raised from b_e to b_u. These workers, therefore, will always vote for the higher of two values of b within the interval between b_e and b_u. Next, let us consider the workers with double-peaked preferences who cease to be employed at a critical benefit level, denoted $b_c(a)$, between b_e and b_u. The critical benefit level $b_c(a)$ clearly increases with the quality level a. The net incomes of individuals in this group fall with the benefit level b between b_e and $b_c(a)$, whereas their net incomes rise with b for values of b between $b_c(a)$ and b_u. For these individuals, net income is thus lowest at a benefit level $b_c(a)$, when the individual is indifferent between working and not working. At the same time, net income is highest either at a benefit level b_e for the relatively high-quality workers, or at a level b_u for the relatively low-quality workers in this category. Finally, individuals in category (iii), who are employed even at the high benefit level b_u, see their net incomes fall as b rises from b_e to b_u. In summary, all individuals achieve the highest net income at a value of b equal to either b_e or b_u. In particular, workers of quality lower (higher) than a certain level obtain the highest net income at a benefit level b_u (b_e).

The outcome of the vote will be determined by the median voter, who for convenience is denoted v. The voting outcome will be b_e if, at this benefit level, the median voter v obtains higher net income than at a benefit level b_u, and vice versa. In principle, v can be in any of the three catgories of agents. For example, the median voter can be in category (iii), in which case v will vote for a positive level of welfare benefits b_e even though v is employed at this benefit level. If the median voter is in category (ii), then it is possible that v in fact obtains equal net incomes at benefit levels b_e and b_u. Specifically, v can be indifferent between working at a benefit level b_e and not working at a benefit level b_u, in which case the benefit levels b_e and b_u are both possible voting outcomes. Note that in this instance only the median voter is indifferent between benefit levels b_e and b_u, as workers of higher (lower) quality than v will strictly prefer the benefit level b_e (b_u). A necessary condition for the existence of two possible voting equilibria is clearly that the preferences of the median voter be double-peaked.[13] These results are summarized as follows.

Proposition 2. *The unique voting outcome regarding the benefit level is b_e (b_u) if the median voter prefers to be employed (unemployed) at a benefit level b_e (b_u) to being unemployed (employed) at a benefit level b_u (b_e). If the median voter is indifferent between the two, then both b_e and b_u are voting equilibria.*

5. THE EFFECT OF IMMIGRATION ON TRANSFERS

In this section, we consider the impact of immigration on the income transfer scheme. This immigration is assumed to be independent of the income transfer system. Some international migration may indeed be motivated by, for example, a flight from oppression rather than by differences in international net income levels. Let us assume that immigrants have the same rights and duties as original residents. In particular, they are eligible for welfare benefits and they are required to pay income taxes.[14] As an aside, it is first interesting to consider the benefit level as set by a government interested in maximizing aggregate income Y rather than by the outcome of voting by self-interested agents. In this instance, we know from (7) and (10) that $a_c = \mu/2$ and thus $b = \mu^2/2$. Let us assume that foreign workers with quality level a^* migrate to the home country. If a^* is less than a_c then the immigrant workers will be unemployed in the home country, and vice versa. If the immigrants do not work, then the optimal transfer level b, the critical quality level a_c, and also output Y are not affected by the immigration. To finance additional transfers, however, the income tax rate τ must rise. As a result, the net-of-tax incomes of all original home residents fall. If the immigrants' quality a^* exceeds a_c, then the immigrant workers will be employed in the home country. Unlike in Section 2, immigrant workers now pay income taxes. The effect of immigration on the income of original home residents in (3), therefore, must be replaced by

$$\frac{dY_{-m}}{da^*} = (a^* - \mu + \tau a^*)\mu f^*(a^*). \tag{13}$$

Equation (13) accounts for both the productivity externality and the fiscal externality of immigrant workers.[15] Immigrants of quality a^* exceeding $\mu/(1+\tau)$ will, on balance, increase the aggregate income of original home residents. As before, not all potential immigrant workers who can find employment in the home country increase Y_{-m}. In particular, immigrants of quality a^* between $\mu/2$ and $\mu/(1+\tau)$ will work in the home country, but from (13) we see that they thereby reduce the aggregate income of original home residents. Thus, an immigrant's ability to find privately rewarding employment may not be a good test of his or her contribution to other citizens' incomes, owing to the productivity externality. The immigration of foreign workers of quality a^* exceeding a_c generally leads to a change in the income transfer scheme that maximizes aggregate income Y. Such immigration, in particular, leads to a higher (lower) benefit level and a lower (higher) labor participation rate of the original population, if a^* is greater (less) than μ.

Now let us consider how the income transfer system is affected by immigration when the benefit level is determined by popular vote. At the same time, we consider whether immigration will in fact be favored by the median voter. At a given preimmigration benefit level, there are generally three separate channels by which immigration affects the net incomes of original home-country workers. First, if the immigrants become benefit recipients then the income tax rate must rise to finance these additional benefit payments. Second, if the immigrants accept employment in the

home country, then they can affect the productivities of existing employees by their impact on mean worker quality. Third, a higher employment
generally changes total income, and thus the income tax rate, consistent
with financing the existing transfer system. Generally, immigration also
leads to an adjustment in the benefit level selected by the median voter.
This benefit level adjustment, however, has only a second-order effect on
the median voter's net income, following the envelope theorem. We can
therefore ignore the adjustment in the benefit level if we wish to assess
whether the median voter favors immigration.

To start, let us consider the immigration of workers of quality a^* less
than a_c. At the premigration benefit level, these individuals will receive
benefits in the home country. The type of immigration clearly does not
affect the productivities of employed workers. To pay for the additional
income transfers, however, the income tax rate must increase. Consequently, the immigration of prospective benefit recipients reduces the net
incomes of all original home-country residents. Such immigration will
therefore be opposed by the median voter.

Next, let us consider the immigration of foreign workers of quality a^*
exceeding a_c. At the original benefit level, these individuals choose to
work in the home country. The immigrants increase (decrease) the productivity of already employed workers if a^* exceeds (is less than) μ.[16] At the
same time, total output increases (decreases) and, as a result, the income
tax rate falls (rises) if a^* exceeds (is less than) $\mu/2$.[17] If the median voter
is unemployed, then $a_c > \mu/2$ from (12). The income tax rate thus falls,
and the median voter will favor the immigration. If, however, the median
voter is employed, then $a_c < \mu/2$ from (11). The entry of prospective employees of quality $a^* > \mu$ benefits an employed median voter because such
entry (i) increases pretax income and (ii) reduces the income tax rate. The
entry of workers with $a_c < a^* < \mu/2$, to the contrary, harms an employed
median voter because it (i) reduces pretax income and (ii) increases the income tax rate. For a borderline quality level a^* between $\mu/2$ and μ, the
median voter's net income will not be affected because - by a continuity
argument - the reductions in the pretax income level and in the tax rate are
exactly offsetting. An employed median voter favors the immigration of
only those future employees whose quality exceeds this borderline level.
These results are summarized as follows.

Proposition 3. *Any median voter opposes the immigration of prospective unemployed workers. An unemployed median voter favors the immigration of any prospective employed worker, whereas an employed median voter favors the immigration of prospective employed workers of a
quality beyond a certain threshold level.*

In Section 4, we saw that the median voter may be indifferent between working at a benefit level b_e and not working at a benefit level b_u. Small migration flows potentially eliminate this indifference and lead the median voter to strictly prefer one benefit level to the other. The influence of a country's labor quality distribution on the net incomes of workers as employed and as unemployed individuals is examined in Huizinga (1995). In particular, an increase in the relative number of the unemployed is shown to reduce an unemployed median-quality worker's net-of-tax income with $b = b_u$ relative to that individual's net-of-tax income as an employed worker with $b = b_e$. Thus, at some point, an influx of prospective unemployed workers can cause an unemployed median voter to prefer employment with $b = b_e$ to welfare with $b = b_u$. As the benefit level drops from b_u to b_e, the median voter's net-of-tax income changes continuously while other workers' net-of-tax incomes change discretely. Specifically, the net incomes of people of lower (higher) quality than the median voter jump up (down) when the median voter switches preference from a benefit level b_e to a benefit level b_u.

To conclude this section, let us consider which foreign workers in fact have the incentive to emigrate to the home country if only the home country operates an income transfer system. All foreigners have an incentive to emigrate if $\mu(1 - \tau) > \mu^*$. In this instance, foreign workers of any quality will achieve higher net incomes at home after emigrating, regardless of whether they will work in the home country. If instead $\mu(1 - \tau) < \mu^*$, then only foreigners with $a^* < b(1 - \tau)/\mu^*$ (if any) benefit from emigration. In this instance, all immigrants into the home country will be unemployed.[18]

6. TRANSFER POLICY IN ANTICIPATION OF MIGRATION

So far, we have considered how the income transfer system is adjusted in response to exogenous migration flows. In this section, we recognize that the income transfer system itself influences migration flows. In particular, we consider how the anticipation of potential migration flows influences the determination of the income transfer system. Toward this end, let us assume that the world consists of two symmetric countries that both operate an income transfer scheme. Following Brown and Oates (1987), we will assume that only the poor (i.e., those who choose not to work in their own country) are internationally mobile.[19] Their migration is motivated by the difference in the net transfer level $n = n_u - n_u^*$. Let us assume that the unemployed are heterogeneous in their moving costs. As a result, a share $s(n)$ of the foreign unemployed will migrate to the home country if $n > 0$, and vice versa. We will assume $s(0) = 0$, with $ds/dn > 0$. If $n > 0$, then the aggregate income of home residents is less than home output by an amount equal to the expense of providing foreign immigrants with income transfers. In particular, if $n > 0$ then the aggregate income Y_{-m} accruing to original home residents is given by

$$Y_{-m} = Y - s(n)n_u F(a_c^*), \tag{14}$$

where $F(a_c^*)$ is the volume of foreign unemployed; Y is domestic output as in (8).

The exact impact of potential immigration on the income transfer system depends on how the benefit level is determined. Regardless of how benefits are determined, however, one additional cost of higher benefit levels in the presence of migration will be larger income transfers to foreign benefit recipients. This cost of higher benefits ultimately reduces the benefit level compared to the case of no immigration considered in Sections 2 and 3. To illustrate this, let us consider the benchmark case where the benefit level is set so as to maximize the aggregate income to original home residents in (14). If $n = 0$ then an increase in a_c, and thus in the benefit level b, affects Y_{-m} as follows:

$$\frac{dY_{-m}}{da_c} = \frac{dY}{da_c} - \frac{ds}{dn}\frac{dn}{da_c}n_u F(a_c^*). \tag{15}$$

An optimum requires that dY_{-m}/da_c in (15) be zero. We can now show that a symmetric optimum requires $dn/da_c > 0$ in (15), starting from $n_u = n_u^*$. To see this, note that without migration we have $dn_u/da_c > 0$ in (12) for $a_c \le \mu/2$. With migration, the relationship between n and a_c further reflects the following two effects: (i) immigration into the home country, which increases the number of domestic unemployed and leads to a higher domestic tax rate τ, which in turn reduces the net benefit level n_u; and (ii) emigration from the foreign country reduces the number of foreign unemployed and thus leads to a lower foreign income tax rate τ^*, increasing n_u^* (for a given foreign benefit level b^*). Both of these effects tend to reduce the size of dn/da_c. However, for there to be any migration following an increase in b, we need to have $dn/da_c > 0$. It now follows from (15) that optimally $dY/da_c > 0$. The prospect of the immigration of foreign unemployed workers has thus reduced the optimal domestic benefit level b and, in this instance, also the national output Y. If the reduction in the domestic benefit level is slight, then the net income levels of the (un)employed are higher (lower) than in a world without migration.

The prospect of migration similarly leads to lower benefit levels if the benefit level is determined by popular vote. In particular, the benefit level will be reduced below b_e or below b_u depending on whether the median voter is employed or unemployed. If the reduction in benefit levels is slight, then in the first instance the net incomes of all original domestic residents decline relative to the no-migration case. In this instance, the median voter clearly oppposes migration. In the second instance, the net income levels of the employed and unemployed will increase and decrease, respectively. The unemployed median voter will correspondingly oppose free migration. These results are summarized as follows.

Proposition 4.   *The median voter opposes free migration in a symmetric model where unemployed workers are mobile in response to differences in welfare benefits.*

Several authors – including Oates (1968), Musgrave (1969), and Brown and Oates (1987) – have argued that income redistribution is best carried out by the highest level of government in a federal system because of the potential mobility of benefit recipients among the lower-level jurisdictions. In the present model, a redistributive scheme at an international level is not ambiguously better than independent national schemes, because the mobility of welfare recipients can in fact increase the net income of employed individuals if the median voter is unemployed. Note, however, that in the present model the median voter always loses from the potential mobility of the unemployed. The median voter will therefore unambiguously be in favor of transferring the power to operate a welfare compensation scheme to an international authority.

7. CONCLUSION

This paper starts from the assumption that a worker's productivity depends on his or her own qualifications as well as on those of other, nearby workers. In this setting, migration immediately affects the productivities of workers left behind in the source country and of workers in the recipient country. The model displays increasing returns to average quality: the output of a group of workers increases more than linearly with average worker quality. The migration of particular workers may or may not increase world output. However, free international migration generally reduces world output in this model, where mobile labor is the only factor of production. The model in this paper has been applied to migration between countries, but is also applicable to transfers of individuals between institutions such as companies, universities, or even sports teams.

   A main feature of the model is that a system of internal transfers to low-quality workers – so as to remove them from the labor force – can increase total output. More strongly, retiring low-quality workers from the labor force has the potential to increase the net incomes of benefit recipients and nonrecipients alike. The model could thus potentially rationalize the widespread systems of income transfers in the developed countries on efficiency grounds. That migration has important externalities also implies that countries generally wish to restrict the exit and entry of workers. Most countries in the world do, indeed, have restrictive immigration policies.

Transfer systems generally have the dual role of effecting efficient exits from the labor market and of redistributing income. The political process generally will take both aspects of transfer systems into account. The distribution of the voting population determines whether the transfer system benefits the unemployed at the expense of the employed, or whether it benefits both classes of workers. Interestingly, small changes in the composition of the population can have large effects on the outcome of the voting process. In particular, even a limited inflow of benefit recipients can lead the median voter to prefer a materially different transfer system with lower benefit and income tax levels. Such a discrete change in the benefit level leads to upward or downward jumps in the net income levels of all but the median voter. As a result, individuals at the bottom of the income distribution can be expected to be more concerned about international migration than those in the middle of the income distribution.

NOTES

1. See the introduction to Wellisch and Wildasin (1994) for a discussion of the recent EU experience with immigration.
2. See also Bhagwati and Hamada (1982), Djajič (1989), and Kwok and Leland (1982) for models of migration with workers of heterogeneous quality.
3. The mean, by definition, attaches equal weights to the qualities of all workers. However, one can easily think of activities where the productivities of a group's members depend chiefly on the group's most able members, or rather on its least able members. An army's overall success, for instance, may depend primarily on the brilliance of its general. The productivity of a group of workers along a conveyor belt in a car assembly plant, on the other hand, may be determined by the slowest worker. Several studies in the educational field, including Summers and Wolfe (1977), suggest that the exact distribution of student qualities matters for educational attainment.
4. Qualitatively, the welfare implications of migration for migrants and nonmigrants remain unchanged as long as individual output is positively related to the mean worker quality μ. The result that free migration may reduce overall output will, however, depend on the aggregate producing function in (1) being convex in μ.
5. The aggregate production function in (1) considers all workers in a country to be working together. This paper thus ignores the possibility that the labor force within a country will be stratified into different geographical regions or (say)

firms, where peer-group effects operate only at the local level. Even if such local entities exist, the aggregate production function will be as in (1) if individual wages do not reflect the external effect of a worker's presence on the productivity of other workers. In particular, if the wage of a worker is equal to $a\mu_i$, where μ_i is the mean worker quality of locale i, then μ_i will be equal for all i in an equilibrium with free worker movement between locales. Thus, the number of locales per se does not affect the aggregate production function as long as individual wages, as indicated, fail to reflect a worker's external effect on other workers in a country.

6. In deriving (2)-(4), use is made of the following equalities:

$$\frac{d\mu^*}{da^*} = \frac{\mu^* - a^*}{S^*} f^*(a^*) \quad \text{and} \quad \frac{d\mu}{da^*} = \frac{a^* - \mu}{S} f^*(a^*).$$

7. Rivera-Batiz (1982) has previously shown that emigration lowers the welfare of nonmigrants if the average amount of capital owned and removed from the country by the migrants differs from the aggregate capital/labor ratio. In addition, the welfare of nonmigrants may be affected by remittances, as examined by Djajić (1986).

8. Note that the home country's imposition of its optimal immigration restriction implies that fewer foreigners are allowed to migrate to the home country than is necessary to maximize world income, since $\mu > (\mu + \mu^*)/2$.

9. There are, in fact, many ways of dividing the world population into two groups such that mean worker qualities are equal internationally. Also, note that the presence of all workers in a single country is not an equilibrium, as in this instance all workers of above-average quality have an incentive to depart.

10. The existence of increasing returns to average quality suggests that – if the objective is to maximize world output – then, optimally, workers are stratified by their quality.

11. Perhaps an interesting way to include a fixed factor in the present model is to regard Y in (1) not as national income but rather as the national efficiency equivalent of an internationally mobile labor. In this instance, a country's output would be given by $f(L, Y)$, where L is land and f is a production function with standard properties. The overall output effects of international migration are now ambiguous: world output increases as labor seeks the highest marginal product of efficiency-equivalent labor for equal average labor qualities, while world output is reduced as labor tends to equalize average labor qualities for given equal marginal products of efficiency-equivalent labor. To focus on the labor quality externalities of migration, the present paper in effect assumes that the marginal product of efficiency-equivalent labor is equal to unity in both countries.

12. Note that the equality $a_c = \mu/2$ generally can have more than a single solution for a_c. In the following discussion, however, we exclude this possibility.

13. Stiglitz (1974) similarly shows that voters' preferences over the level of public education are generally double-peaked if voters can switch between the public and private education systems; hence, a unique voting equilibrium regarding the level of public education may not exist.

14. Generally, they also are allowed to vote. Note that whether immigrants have voting rights makes a difference only if it influences which of the two benefit

levels (b_e and b_u) is preferred by the median voter. These two benefit levels themselves generally change with the composition of the population, but preferences between the two by those surrounding the median voter are invariant to small immigration flows, unless the median voter is already close to being indifferent before immigration takes place. In the United States, immigrants obtain voting rights only upon becoming citizens.

15. Fiscal and nonfiscal or congestion externalities are prominent in the analysis of locational efficiency in the field of urban public finance (see Wildasin 1986, chap. 2).

16. To be precise, pretax income $a\mu$ is affected by the immigration of prospective employed workers for a given benefit level as follows:

$$\frac{d(a\mu)}{da^*} = a\left(\frac{a^*-\mu}{S-F(a_c)}\right)f^*(a^*).$$

17. Using (9) and applying (10), we see that the tax rate τ is affected by immigration of prospective employed workers for a given benefit level as follows:

$$\frac{d\tau}{da^*} = \frac{-\tau}{bF(a_c)+Y}(2a^*-\mu)\mu f^*(a^*).$$

18. As before, migration in this setting can have a positive or a negative impact on world output. If the transfer system in the home country is chosen so as to maximize output Y, then equation (5), as before, indicates the effect of migration on world output.

19. See Blank (1988) for evidence on the mobility of welfare recipients in the United States in response to interstate differences in welfare benefits.

REFERENCES

Arnott, Richard, and John Rowse (1987), "Peer Group Effects and Educational Attainment," *Journal of Public Economics* 32: 287-305.

Bhagwati, Jagdish N., and Koichi Hamada (1982), "Tax Policy in the Presence of Emigration," *Journal of Public Economics* 18: 291-317.

Blank, Rebecca M. (1988), "The Effect of Welfare and Wage Levels on the Location Decisions of Female-Headed Households," *Journal of Urban Economics* 24: 186-211.

Borjas, George J. (1990), *Friends or Strangers: The Impact of Immigrants on the U.S. Economy.* New York: Basic Books.

Brown, Charles C., and Wallace E. Oates (1987), "Assistance to the Poor in a Federal System," *Journal of Public Economics* 32: 307-30.

Crane, Randall (1992), "Voluntary Income Redistribution with Migration," *Journal of Urban Economics* 31: 84-98.

Djajič, Slobodan (1986), "International Migration, Remittances and Welfare in a Dependent Economy," *Journal of Development Economics* 21: 229-34.

Djajič, Slobodan (1989), "Skills and the Pattern of Migration: The Role of Qualitative and Quantitative Restrictions on International Labor Mobility," *International Economic Review* 30: 795-809.

Epple, Dennis, and Thomas Romer (1991), "Mobility and Redistribution," *Journal of Political Economy* 99: 828-58.

Henderson, Vernon, Peter Mieszkowski, and Yvon Sauvageau (1978), "Peer Group Effects and Educational Production Functions," *Journal of Public Economics* 10: 97–106.

Huizinga, Harry (1997), "Unemployment Benefits and Redistributive Taxation in the Presence of Labor Quality Externalities," in Sylvester Eijffinger and Harry Huizinga (eds.), *Positive Political Economy: Theory and Evidence.* Cambridge University Press.

Kwok, Viem, and Hayne Leland (1982), "An Economic Analysis of the Brain Drain," *American Economic Review* 72: 91–100.

Oates, Wallace E. (1968), "The Theory of Public Finance in a Federal System," *Canadian Journal of Economics* 1: 37–54.

Persson, Torsten, and Guido Tabellini (1992), "The Politics of 1992: Fiscal Policy and European Integration," *Review of Economic Studies* 59: 689–701.

Meltzer, Allan H., and Scott F. Richards (1981), "A Rational Theory of the Size of Government," *Journal of Political Economy* 89: 814–27.

Musgrave, Richard A. (1969), "Theories of Fiscal Federalism," *Public Finance / Finances Publiques* 24: 521–32.

Rivera-Batiz, F. (1982), "International Migration, Non-traded Goods and Economic Welfare in the Source Country," *Journal of Development Economics* 11: 81–90.

Sala-i-Martin, Xavier (1992), "Transfers," Working Paper no. 4186, National Bureau of Economic Research, Cambridge, MA.

Stiglitz, Joseph E. (1974), "The Demand for Education in Public and Private School Systems," *Journal of Public Economics* 3: 349–85.

Summers, Anita A., and Barbara L. Wolfe (1977), "Do Schools Make a Difference?" *American Economic Review* 67: 639–52.

Wellisch, Dietmar, and David E. Wildasin (1994), "Asylum Policy with a Common Labor Market," Working Paper no. 94-W03, Vanderbilt University, Nashville, TN.

Wildasin, David E. (1986), *Urban Public Finance.* London: Harwood.

Wildasin, David E. (1991), "Income Redistribution in a Common Labor Market," *American Economic Review* 81: 757–74.

CHAPTER 7

Strategic Provision of Local Public Inputs for Oligopolistic Firms in the Presence of Endogenous Location Choice

Uwe Walz & Dietmar Wellisch

1. INTRODUCTION

This paper aims to reconsider the basic question of the tax competition literature in a novel framework. Does competition between regions for mobile firms via provision of local public inputs result in a suboptimal allocation? Unlike such previous contributions as Wildasin (1986), Oates and Schwab (1991), or Richter and Wellisch (1996), we abstain from a world of perfect competition. We model strategic interaction not only between regions but also among private firms.[1] Two regions compete for a mobile oligopolistic firm by taxing the profits of all firms locating within their respective boundaries and using the tax revenues to provide local public inputs. Like Brander and Spencer (1985), Eaton and Grossman (1986), or Helpman and Krugman (1989), we model imperfect competition in the output market. However, unlike these studies, we introduce firm mobility.

Location choices of firms are guided by an interplay of agglomeration advantages and disadvantages. The agglomeration advantage is modeled as the partial nonrivalness of local public inputs, whereas the costs a firm must bear when changing its location constitute the agglomeration disadvantage.

The basic question of the paper is thus to analyze how competing regions take the converging and diverging forces into account when providing public inputs, and whether the competition of regions results in too much (little) agglomeration and too high (low) levels of local public

This is an extended version of our paper for the special issue of *International Tax and Public Finance*. The present version includes a detailed discussion of the mixed strategy equilibrium case. We would like to thank two anonymous referees, Clive Bell, David Pines, and especially David E. Wildasin for very helpful comments and suggestions on earlier versions of the paper. Walz gratefully acknowledges financial support from the German Science Foundation.

inputs as compared to the centralized provision of local public inputs. Addressing this question in an oligopolistic framework is the novel feature of our analysis.

We employ a simple, highly stylized set-up that enables us to concentrate on these questions. Rather than providing a general analysis, we hope our approach highlights the most important forces at work. We analyze the outcome of the decentralized game between two regions for different levels of costs associated with a change in location. These costs are a measure of the agglomeration disadvantage. We compare the decentralized game with a situation in which a regional planner maximizes joint welfare of regions. We refer to the latter outcome as the "interregionally optimal" solution. It turns out that only for small moving costs does the game between regions coincide with the interregionally optimal solution. For high levels of moving costs, the outcome of the decentralized game is an equal distribution of firms across regions. Here, the spatial allocation is interregionally optimal, but regions provide an excessive level of public inputs in order to increase their international market shares. At intermediate levels of moving costs, there is either an interregionally optimal spatial allocation but excessive provision of local public inputs, or there is excessive agglomeration as well as excessive levels of local public inputs.

There are other contributions on endogenous location choices in a world of imperfect competition. Our paper is related to studies by Horstmann and Markusen (1992) and by Markusen, Morey, and Olewiler (1993) analyzing the interdependence between output and location decisions of two oligopolistic firms in a two-stage game of firm behavior. These authors determine conditions for alternative regional market structures. However, neither study analyzes a noncooperative game between regional governments. Markusen, Morey, and Olewiler (1994) analyze the noncooperative game between regions when competing for plants by choosing environmental regulations. However, in this framework only one monopolistic firm decides whether it chooses to serve both regional markets from a plant in only one region, to serve both markets from a plant in each region, or not to produce at all. The authors emphasize the existence of equilibria where the monopolistic firm produces in both regions or decides not to produce at all. In contrast, we model a three-stage game between oligopolistic firms and regional governments where an agglomeration solution plays an important role.

The outline of the paper is as follows. In Section 2 we specify the basic model. In Section 3 we investigate the regional planning solution in which a planner controls location decisions and the level of local public inputs, and compare the outcome with that achieved by a central government controlling only the level of the respective local public inputs in both regions. Section 4 examines the decentralized provision of local public inputs by the regional governments; Section 5 summarizes our main findings.

2. THE BASIC SET-UP

We develop a three-region model in which two firms initially located in region A and B produce a homogenous good for a third market. Residents of each region are the sole owners of the respective firms. Ignoring local consumption of the two firms' output in A and B enables us to concentrate on the impact of governmental provision of local public inputs on firms' behavior.[2]

The two firms face the following inverse demand function in the third market:

$$p = a - b(x_A + x_B), \quad a, b > 0, \tag{1}$$

where x_i ($i = A, B$) stands for the output of the ith firm and p denotes the common price. Firms produce under identical constant marginal costs c ($c < a$). Allowing decreasing marginal costs would leave our qualitative results unchanged but complicates the analysis considerably. Increasing marginal costs would be somewhat at odds with our oligopolistic market structure. With increasing marginal costs, there are strong incentives to split firms into parts (either at the same or at different locations) in order to achieve cost advantages. Local public inputs (z_i) reduce marginal costs of firm i; that is, net marginal costs are $c - z_i$. The assumption of private cost reductions by local public inputs – especially local infrastructure like sewage plants and roads – is in line with empirical research (see e.g. Aschauer 1989).

A firm bears a cost (F^i) if it changes its location and builds a plant in the other region. These moving costs could arise owing to the need to scrap buildings and equipment at the old location and build new ones at the new location. Other potential sources for such costs include the cost of search for new suppliers and new employees, the costs of relocating former employees, and the need to shut down production as the result of a move.

Local public inputs are financed by a tax imposed by regional governments on variable (output-dependent) profits of oligopolistic firms located in the respective region.[3]

We assume that costs associated with location changes are not deductible from the tax base. This is done for reasons of simplicity, since it keeps our model symmetric.[4] The profit function of an oligopolistic firm initially located in region i and producing in m ($m = A, B$) is:

$$G_i^m = \begin{cases} [(a-b(x_A+x_B)-c+z_m)x_i](1-t^m) & \text{if } i = m, \\ [(a-b(x_A+x_B)-c+z_m)x_i](1-t^m)-F^i & \text{if } i \neq m, \end{cases} \tag{2}$$

where t^m denotes the profit tax rate in region m.

Local public inputs are – to a certain extent – nonrival goods. We assume a quadratic cost function for local public inputs, $C_z(z_m) = (z_m)^2$. Costs increase less than proportionally if two firms rather than one are using them:

$$C_z(z_m) = (z_m)^2(2)^\phi. \tag{3}$$

The congestion parameter ϕ ($0 \leq \phi \leq 1$) measures the degree of rivalry in the usage of local public inputs. With $\phi = 0$ ($\phi = 1$), local public inputs are pure public (private) goods.

Regional governments are committed (e.g., by law) to a balanced budget:

$$t^m[\tilde{G}_m^m + \tilde{G}_i^m] = C_z(z_m), \tag{4}$$

where $\tilde{G}_i^m$ is the variable before-tax profit function of firm i located in region m. The essential mechanism of our model is the interaction between an agglomeration advantage and an agglomeration disadvantage. The former is the (partial) public good character of the local public input. The latter is represented by the existence of moving costs associated with the change of a firm's location. Whereas the first force calls for an agglomeration solution with both firms located in one region, say region A (the "(2, 0) solution"), the latter one points in the direction of a spatial separation of firms (the "(1, 1) solution").

The model is organized as a three-stage game. In the first stage, regional governments A and B choose the level of local public input. They use contingent strategies, conditioning their respective choices of public input levels on whether at least one firm will locate in the region or not. That is, they choose two different levels of local public inputs depending on whether at least one firm produces in the region or not. This obviates situations in which a region provides local public inputs while the local firm leaves the region, leading to a loss of tax base and an unbalanced budget. We assume that regional governments can credibly commit themselves to the chosen levels of local public inputs, for example through binding statutes. Allowing for credible commitment of governments is a standard procedure in the strategic trade literature (see e.g. Brander and Spencer 1985).

In the second stage of the game, firms decide on their location while taking the level of local public inputs as given. For the sake of tractability and to limit the possibilities for multiple equilibria, we assume that only one firm, say firm B, is mobile. Our model might depict, for example, a case where a firm in region B is entering a market or expanding capacity in order to compete with an established firm in A. Expansion of capacity or the establishment of a new firm is cheaper at home than abroad. The moving costs ($F \equiv F^B$) are a measure of this difference. The firm in region A is assumed, in effect, to face prohibitively high relocation costs.[5] In the third stage of the game, firms choose their outputs simultaneously. We solve for the subgame-perfect solution.

We address the output game first. Maximizing (2) with respect to output yields, in equilibrium,

$$x_i = \frac{1}{3b}(a - c + 2z_i - z_j) \tag{5}$$

(in the agglomeration case, z_i and z_j are identical). As long as $a > c$, firms will always make positive profits. Costs of changing the location arise as the consequence of a deliberate choice. Since profits in the home country are always positive (see (2) and (5) and note that governments maximize firm profits by providing local inputs), the firm in B will choose to relocate if and only if profits in region A are even higher.

3. THE REGIONAL PLANNING SOLUTION

In this section, we hypothesize a regional planner who maximizes the joint welfare of regions A and B - that is, the joint profits of firms. Comparing the outcome of the decentralized policy game with the regional planning solution enables us to show whether local governments fail to take into account the effects of their policies on the other (exporting) region's welfare.

This planner controls firm location as well as the level of local public inputs in each region, but output choices are left to the firms. This constraint on the planning solution reflects our exclusive interest in the spatial allocation and the level of local public inputs. We refer to the constrained regional planning solution as the *interregionally optimal* outcome.

We derive the regional planning solution in two steps. First, we derive the optimal level of local public inputs for the cases with geographically separated firms and with agglomerated firms. Second, we compare the welfare levels with optimally chosen local public inputs to deduce the interregionally optimal spatial allocation. Inserting the cost function for public inputs, as well as (4) and (5), into (2) gives us the joint welfare function in the agglomeration case:

$$\bar{W}(2, 0) = \frac{2(a - c + z_A)^2}{9b} - F - (z_A)^2 2^\phi; \tag{6}$$

in the case with geographically separated firms,

$$\bar{W}(1,1) = \frac{(a-c+2z_A-z_B)^2}{9b} - (z_A)^2 + \frac{(a-c+2z_B-z_A)^2}{9b} - (z_B)^2. \qquad (7)$$

In the agglomeration solution, the optimal level of local public inputs is derived from the first-order condition $\partial \bar{W}(2,0)/\partial z_A = 0$ as

$$z_A^*(2,0) = \frac{2(a-c)}{9b2^\phi - 2}. \qquad (8)$$

In the separation regime, solving simultaneously the two first-order conditions for a welfare maximum $\partial \bar{W}(1,1)/\partial z_A = \partial \bar{W}(1,1)/\partial z_B = 0$ yields the optimal

$$z_A^*(1,1) = z_B^*(1,1) = \frac{a-c}{9b-1}. \qquad (9)$$

Inserting (8) and (9) in the respective welfare functions (6) and (7) and comparing the results gives us a critical level of relocation costs $(\bar{F})$ where both situations yield the same aggregate welfare:

$$\bar{F} = \frac{2(a-c)^2(2-2^\phi)}{(9b2^\phi - 2)(9b-1)}. \qquad (10)$$

For a given degree of congestion (ϕ) we have the following proposition.[6]

Proposition 1. *For high moving costs $(F > \bar{F})$, the regional planner chooses a dispersed regional location of firms and provides the interregionally optimal level of local public inputs $(z_A^*(1,1) = z_B^*(1,1))$ to geographically separated firms. With low relocation costs $(F \le \bar{F})$, an agglomeration solution with local public input levels of $z_A^*(2,0)$ and $z_B = 0$ is interregionally optimal.*

According to (10), increasing the congestion costs associated with an additional firm in one region makes a solution with geographically separated firms more desirable; that is, $d\bar{F}/d\phi < 0$.

Governments usually cannot interfere directly with location choices of firms. It is therefore interesting to know whether the public sector can induce the interregionally optimal allocation just characterized by controlling only the level of local public inputs. Let us thus suppose now that firm B can choose its location in a profit-maximizing way. Consider first the behavior of firm B in the second stage of the game. Firm B will never produce in both regions, because it would have to pay for local public inputs in region B while bearing the relocation costs associated with the establishment of a plant in region A. Firm B will choose to move to region A if this pays the higher net profits for given levels of local public inputs in regions A and B:

$$G_B^A(2, 0, z_A) \geq G_B^B(1, 1, z_A, z_B). \tag{11}$$

Suppose now that there is a central government that controls only the levels of both public inputs and seeks to maximize the joint welfare of both regions. This yields the following.

Corollary 1. *The central government achieves an interregionally optimal spatial allocation by providing the interregionally optimal levels of local public inputs.*

Proof. See Appendix 1.

In other words, the central government can replicate the planning outcome by choosing the interregionally optimal levels of local public inputs. With low moving costs ($F \leq \bar{F}$), the central government chooses $z_A^*(2, 0)$ and $z_B = 0$. This suffices to induce firm B to move. With high relocation costs ($F > \bar{F}$), the choice $z_A^*(1, 1) = z_B^*(1, 1)$ is sufficient for firm B not to move. Corollary 1 thus shows that direct control of the location of firm B is a superfluous instrument for a joint welfare maximizer who also controls public input levels.

4. THE DECENTRALIZED SOLUTION

We now analyze the decentralized solution that emerges as the equilibrium outcome of the first stage of the game and compare it to the interregionally optimal solution derived in the preceding section. Regional governments decide simultaneously on their levels of local public inputs. With both firms agglomerated in region A, regional welfare can be written as[7]

$$W_A(2, 0) = \frac{(a-c+z_A)^2}{9b} - \frac{2^\phi}{2}(z_A)^2,$$

$$W_B(2, 0) = \frac{(a-c+z_A)^2}{9b} - \frac{2^\phi}{2}(z_A)^2 - F. \tag{12}$$

Note that firm B must bear the burden of the relocation costs F. If both firms are geographically separated, regional governments maximize

$$W_i(1, 1) = \frac{(a-c+2z_i-z_j)^2}{9b} - (z_i)^2, \quad i = A, B. \tag{13}$$

We proceed as follows. First, we derive the noncooperative equilibrium of the first stage for given locations of firms. This serves as a reference point for subsequent analysis. Second, we look at the case of small moving costs, where government A can attract firm B to region A simply by providing its optimal level of local public inputs in the agglomeration solution. Third, we contrast this with the other extreme case of large relocation costs, where it is not feasible for government A to induce the movement of firm B. Finally, we look at the case of intermediate moving costs in which government A might be able to attract firm B by deviating from its optimal level of local public inputs in the agglomeration solution. In this last step, the novel feature of our analysis is revealed most clearly. Noncooperative competition for the oligopolistic firm leads to excessive agglomeration and to an excessive provision of local public inputs.

Let us first derive the noncooperative provision of local public inputs for *given* firm location. With an agglomeration solution it is optimal for region B to choose $z_B = 0$, since positive levels of local public inputs would imply costs but no productivity gain. Note that an agglomeration solution with concentration of firms in region B never arises. Because, with an agglomeration solution, the variable part of the welfare function is symmetric for both regions, $z_A^*(2, 0)$ maximizes (12). Maximizing (13) yields the following response functions for the regional governments in the case of spatially separated firms:

$$z_i(z_j) = \frac{2(a - c - z_j)}{9b - 4}.$$ (14)

The inequality $(\partial^2 W_i(1, 1)/\partial (z_i)^2)^2 > (\partial^2 W_i(1, 1)/\partial z_i \partial z_j)^2$ must hold in order to ensure stability in our symmetric model (see Dixit 1986). This is true for $b > 2/3$, which is assumed to hold. Solving (14) simultaneously gives us the noncooperative local public input levels for the separation case:

$$z_i^{nc} = \frac{2(a - c)}{9b - 2}.$$ (15)

4.1. Small Moving Costs

We can now look at situations where local public input levels of $z_A^*(2, 0)$ and $z_B = 0$ for the agglomeration solution constitute a Nash equilibrium of the first stage of the game and an agglomeration solution emerges in the second stage. If moving costs are sufficiently small ($F \le F^1$), region A's government chooses $z_A^*(2, 0)$ in the first stage. In stage 2, firm B will move to region A. The critical value F^1 is implicitly defined by the requirement that firm B must be indifferent between locating in either region for $z_A^*(2, 0)$. Formally, the profit differential function for firm B,

$$\Pi_B(z_A) \equiv G_B^B(1, 1, z_A, z_B(z_A)) - G_B^A(2, 0, z_A),$$ (16)

must take on a value of zero for $z_A = z_A^*(2, 0)$; that is, $\Pi_B(z_A^*(2, 0)) = 0$, where $\Pi_B(z_A)$ denotes the profit differential for firm B in the separation and the agglomeration cases as a function of z_A, given that government B reacts optimally to z_A. Inserting (8) and (14) into Π_B yields

$$F^1 = \frac{(a-c)^2}{(9b2^\phi - 2)^2(9b-4)}[18b2^\phi(3-2^{\phi+1})+8(2^\phi-2)]. \qquad (17)$$

Whenever $F \le F^1$, firm B will move to region A if the latter provides $z_A^*(2,0)$ – even when government B responds optimally to $z_A^*(2,0)$. The choice $z_B(z_A^*(2,0))$ maximizes firm B's profits for $z_A = z_A^*(2,0)$. For $z_B \ne z_B(z_A^*(2,0))$, firm B has an even larger incentive to move. Anticipating this result, the optimal response of region A's government to any z_B is $z_A^*(2,0)$. The subgame perfect equilibrium is unique. It is worth noting that, for a high level of the crowding cost parameter ϕ (e.g. $\phi = 0.6$), the critical moving cost level F^1 becomes negative. With sufficiently large crowding costs the agglomeration advantage is so weak that A's government can never attract firm B with $z_A^*(2,0)$ in the noncooperative equilibrium, even with zero relocation costs.

By comparing F^1 with the critical moving cost level in the planning solution $\bar{F}$, we find that the difference $\bar{F} - F^1$ is increasing in ϕ.[8] There exists a critical value of the congestion parameter, ϕ^*, for which $\bar{F} = F^1$. With rather large congestion effects ($\phi \ge \phi^*$) and $F \le F^1$, the noncooperative equilibrium leads to an interregionally optimal spatial allocation and an optimal provision of local public inputs. If congestion effects are sufficiently small ($\phi < \phi^*$), a level of relocation costs in the interval $\bar{F} < F \le F^1$ implies excessive agglomeration in the noncooperative equilibrium.

The intuition behind this result involves two opposing forces. From the perspective of the regional planner, an agglomeration solution is preferable if joint profits of the firms are larger. In the noncooperative equilibrium, however, each region is interested in its own welfare. Region A must compensate firm B for its moving costs in order to induce a movement. This effect calls for more agglomeration in the planning than in the noncooperative solution. For given moving costs, agglomeration yields higher joint profits, whereas from region B's perspective a solution with spatially separated firms might pay higher profits.

However, a second effect points in the opposite direction. The regional planner compares the agglomeration situation with $z_A^*(2,0)$ and the separation situation with $z_i^*(1,1)$. In contrast, regional governments look at noncooperative local public inputs levels (z_i^{nc}). In the noncooperative equilibrium, the solution with separated firms leads to a lower payoff as compared to the interregionally optimal solution. For agglomeration with $z_A^*(2,0)$, the planning and the noncooperative solutions yield identical payoffs. Hence, this effect calls for excessive agglomeration in the noncooperative equilibrium. With small (large) congestion costs, the latter (former) effect dominates. As we will show in Section 4.3, if moving cost levels satisfy $F^1 < F \leq \bar{F}$ then an agglomeration solution with $z_A^*(2,0)$ would be interregionally optimal. However, owing to the first effect, it is not possible to attract firm B by choosing $z_A^*(2,0)$. This leads to an excessive provision of local public inputs.

We can now establish the following claim.

Proposition 2. *If local public inputs are subject to sufficiently strong congestion costs ($\phi \geq \phi^*$) and if firm relocation costs are sufficiently low ($F \leq F^1$), then the unique decentralized equilibrium ensures an interregionally optimal spatial allocation of firms and an interregionally optimal level of local public inputs. For small congestion costs ($\phi < \phi^*$) and for moving costs that satisfy $\bar{F} < F \leq F^1$, the competition of regional governments leads to excessive agglomeration.*

With small congestion costs, the level of local public inputs is – in a constrained manner – interregionally optimal. If one accepts the interregionally suboptimal spatial allocation then $z_A^*(2,0)$ is interregionally optimal for the agglomeration solution. However, comparing the decentralized outcome with the interregionally overall optimal solution (i.e., a solution with spatially separated firms and $z_A^*(1,1) = z_B^*(1,1)$) reveals an excessive provision of local public inputs (see (8) and (9)).

4.2. High Moving Costs

Now we examine the other extreme of the parameter range of relocation costs. These costs imply a solution with geographically separated firms and the noncooperative levels of local public inputs for the "separation" case ($z_A^{nc} = z_B^{nc}$). Proposition 3 is established for a relocation cost level of

$$F^3 = \frac{4(a-c)^2(2-2^\phi)}{2^\phi(9b-2)^2}. \tag{18}$$

Proposition 3. *A solution with spatially separated firms and a pure strategy equilibrium in the first stage results if and only if the relocation cost level is $F > F^3$. Local governments supply the noncooperative levels of local public inputs z_A^{nc} and z_B^{nc}. This combination is the unique solution. The spatial allocation is interregionally optimal, although regional governments provide local public inputs excessively.*

Proof. See Appendix 2.

With $F > F^3$, the disagglomerative force is sufficiently pronounced that firm B cannot be attracted to region A – the same result as with immobile firms. That $z_i^{nc} > z_i^*(1, 1)$ reflects a profit-shifting argument à la Brander and Spencer (1985).

4.3. Intermediate Moving Costs

Let us now address the first-stage solution for the case where relocation costs are in the intermediate range ($F^1 < F \le F^3$). The crucial question arises of whether region A can induce firm B to relocate by deviating from its optimal level of local public inputs $z_A^*(2, 0)$. We define the public good level $\bar{z}_A$ as the minimal z_A for which firm B will move to region A, given the optimal response of region B's government to $\bar{z}_A$ (i.e., $\Pi_B(\bar{z}_A) = 0$). The provision of $\bar{z}_A$ displays the strategic behavior of region A's government's attempt to change firm B's location. Section 4.1 has demonstrated that, for moving cost levels of $F > F^1$, $\Pi_B(z_A^*(2, 0)) > 0$ must hold. Because $\partial \Pi_B / \partial z_A < 0$ for $z_A < \bar{z}_A$ (see Appendix 3), it follows that $\bar{z}_A > z_A^*(2, 0)$. This implies that region A will never choose $z_A > \bar{z}_A$, as choosing such a z_A would be to move further away from the optimal $z_A^*(2, 0)$. For a level of moving costs of

$$F^2 = \frac{4(a-c)^2(2-2^\phi)}{8+2^\phi(9b-4)9b},$$ (19)

the following lemma is proved in Appendix 3.

Lemma 1. *In a first interval of intermediate moving costs ($F^1 < F \le F^2$), region A's government can attract firm B by providing local public inputs excessively, relative to the optimal level in the agglomeration case ($\bar{z}_A > z_A^*(2, 0)$).*

It remains to study whether the situation described in Lemma 1 is an equilibrium. Local input levels $z_A = \bar{z}_A$, together with the contingent strategies of $z_B = z_B(\bar{z}_A)$ for the case with geographically separated firms and $z_B = 0$ for the agglomeration case, constitute the unique Nash equilibrium in pure strategies if neither region has an incentive to deviate. Neither a solution with geographically separated firms nor an agglomeration solution with $z_A^*(2, 0)$ constitutes a Nash equilibrium in the parameter range under consideration (see Propositions 2 and 3). Deviating from $z_B(\bar{z}_A)$ in the case of geographically separated firms and from $z_B = 0$ for the agglomeration case does not (by definition) pay for region B. We prove in Appendix 4 that for $\bar{z}_A \le z_A^{nc}$ it is also optimal for region A to choose $\bar{z}_A$ as a best response to $z_B(\bar{z}_A)$. By deriving in Appendix 4 a critical level of relocation costs of

$$\hat{F} = \frac{2(2-2^{\phi})(a-c)^2}{(9b-2)^2} \tag{20}$$

for which firm B is just willing to move for $\bar{z}_A = z_A^{nc}$, we can establish our next claim.

Proposition 4. *For a level of moving costs satisfying $F^1 < F \le \hat{F}$, region A's government will induce a concentration of firms in its region by providing a level of public inputs of $\bar{z}_A > z_A^*(2,0)$. This allocation is the unique subgame perfect equilibrium. With $F \in]\max(F^1, \bar{F}), \hat{F}]$, this constitutes a spatially suboptimal interregional allocation and an excessive provision of local public inputs. For $F^1 < F \le \bar{F}$, the spatial allocation is interregionally optimal but local public inputs are provided excessively.*

Proof. See Appendix 4.

By using z_A strategically, region A's government can worsen the separation solution for firm B so much that firm B will prefer to move to region A. Since region B's moving costs are only indirectly taken into account by region A, and since – because of the profit-shifting incentive – the decentralized solution with spatially separated firms always pays less than the planning solution with the same spatial allocation, we have excessive agglomeration for $F \in]\bar{F}, \hat{F}]$.

For the relocation cost interval $\hat{F} < F \le F^2$, the triple $\bar{z}_A, z_B(\bar{z}_A)$ (for the separation solution), and $z_B = 0$ (if firm B moves) is the only candidate for a Nash equilibrium in pure strategies. If region A has no incentive to deviate from the triple $\{\bar{z}_A, z_B(\bar{z}_A), z_B = 0\}$ then this triple, together with an agglomeration solution arising in the second stage of the game, is the unique subgame perfect equilibrium. The decentralized solution brings about excessive concentration of firms ($\hat{F} > \bar{F}$) and an excessive level of local public inputs ($\bar{z}_A > z_A^*(2,0)$).

Finally, we consider moving cost levels of F close to F^2. For F sufficiently close to (but *less* than) F^2, region A will deviate from $\bar{z}_A$ and choose $z_A(z_B(\bar{z}_A))$. If, on the other hand, F is *greater* than F^2 but less than F^3, then no value of $\bar{z}_A$ satisfying $\Pi_B(\bar{z}_A)$ exists. Hence, with relocation costs close to F^2, an equilibrium in pure strategies does not exist. Yet there does exist a mixed-strategy equilibrium in which a $(1,1)$ as well as a $(2,0)$ solution takes place with positive probability (see Appendix 5). The mixed strategy equilibrium is characterized by overprovision of local inputs.

Figure 1 summarizes the outcome of our analysis for the entire spectrum of moving costs and compares the decentralized equilibrium with

132   UWE WALZ & DIETMAR WELLISCH

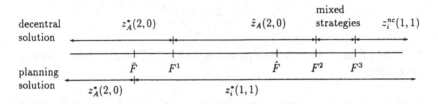

Figure 1. An overview of the results.

the restricted planning (or central government) solution. The figure is drawn for the case of small congestion costs ($\phi < \phi^*$).

5. CONCLUDING REMARKS

This paper has attempted to bring together two important elements of well-established but rather unconnected branches of literature. The first element is the relevance of imperfect competition in output markets, as emphasized in the new trade theory (see e.g. Helpman and Krugman 1989). In the new trade theory, however, firms are immobile. The second element is the competition of regions for mobile firms by providing local public goods, as emphasized in the tax competition literature. Contrary to the new trade theory, the tax competition literature commonly assumes perfect competition among private firms (see e.g. Wildasin 1986). Because one may observe both imperfect competition in the goods market and mobility of firms across countries, we have modeled the strategic interactions between oligopolistic firms and two rent-seeking regional governments as a multistage game in the presence of firm mobility.

The main results of the paper can be summarized as follows. Contrary to a related paper by Markusen et al. (1994), an agglomeration solution can emerge in our model, and is even most likely to emerge. We compare the outcome of the decentralized game with the solution that a central government like the European Union might achieve. Although the central government can provide interregionally optimal levels of local public inputs leading to an interregionally optimal spatial allocation, the decentralized solution can replicate this optimum only with very low relocation costs for building a new plant. In all other cases, excessive agglomeration and/or an oversupply of local public inputs result. Even if firms decide *not* to change their location, a strategic trade effect (à la Brander and Spencer 1985) can be expected. In order to increase the international market share of their domestic firm, regional governments tend to provide excessively high levels of local public inputs.

APPENDIX

APPENDIX 1: PROOF OF COROLLARY 1

(i) With $F > \bar{F}$, the central government provides $z_A^*(1,1) = z_B^*(1,1)$ leading to a $(1,1)$ solution. With $F > \bar{F}$, $2G_i^j(1,1,z_A^*(1,1),z_B^*(1,1)) > 2G_i^j(2,0,z_i^*(2,0)) - F$. Because, by definition, $G_i^j(2,0,z_i^*(2,0)) > G_i^j(2,0,z_i^*(1,1))$ holds, it follows that $G_i^j(1,1,z_A^*(1,1),z_B^*(1,1)) > G_i^j(2,0,z_i^*(1,1)) - F$. A $(1,1)$ solution emerges.

(ii) With $F \le \bar{F}$, the central government induces firm B to relocate by setting $z_A^*(2,0)$ and $z_B = 0$. With $z_A^*(2,0)$ and $z_B = 0$, by using (2) and (8)-(10) we obtain $\text{sign}[G_A^A(2,0,z_A^*(2,0)) - \bar{F} - G_B^B(1,1,z_B = 0,z_A^*(2,0))] = \text{sign}[162b^2 2^\phi(1+2^\phi) - 72b - 90b2^\phi + 16] > 0$. $\square$

APPENDIX 2: PROOF OF PROPOSITION 3

We proceed in four steps. First, we derive an F^3 ensuring that, with z_B^{nc} for the $(1,1)$ case, firm B will never change its location for any z_A. Hence, the best response of region A's government to z_B^{nc} is to provide z_A^{nc}; that is, the two regional governments' reaction curves intersect at this point. Second, we show that, for $F > F^3$, *no* Nash equilibrium in pure strategies exists that leads to a $(2,0)$ solution. Third, we argue that $\{z_A^{nc}, z_B^{nc}\}$ together with $z_B = 0$ form the unique Nash equilibrium in pure strategies leading to a $(1,1)$ solution. Fourth, we prove that, with $F \le F^3$, $\{z_A^{nc}, z_B^{nc}\}$ cannot be part of the Nash equilibrium of the first stage of the game.

(1) With (12) we obtain

$$\bar{\Pi}_B(z_A, z_B^{nc}) = G_B^B(1,1,z_A,z_B^{nc}) - G_A^A(2,0,z_A)$$

$$= \frac{4(a-c)^2}{(9b-2)^2} - \frac{4z_A(a-c)}{9b-2} + \frac{2^\phi}{2}z_A^2 + F. \qquad (A.1)$$

A $\bar{z}_A$ with $\bar{\Pi}_B(\bar{z}_A, z_B^{nc}) \le 0$ does not exist if the discriminant of the solution to this quadratic equation is negative. We find the critical F^3 is equal to $4(a-c)^2(2-2^\phi)/2^\phi(9b-2)^2$.

(2) In Appendix 3 we derive a critical F^2 where $\bar{z}_A$ satisfying $\Pi_B(\bar{z}_A) = 0$ exists only if $F \le F^2$. Comparing F^2 to F^3 yields $\text{sign}(F^2 - F^3) = \text{sign}(2^\phi - 2) < 0$. Thus, for $F > F^3$, a $\bar{z}_A$ does not exist and it is therefore impossible for region A to attract firm B.

(3) The unique Nash equilibrium in pure strategies leading to a $(1,1)$ solution contains $\{z_A^{nc}, z_B^{nc}\}$. The reaction functions (14) intersect only once. Hence, for any other $\{z_A, z_B\}$ combination leading to a $(1,1)$ situation, at least one government has an incentive to deviate. Blocking a $(1,1)$ solution by choosing a z_A^b slightly below $\bar{z}_A$ is not optimal. Deviating for z_A^b less (resp. greater) than z^{nc} to a $(2,0)$ (resp. $(1,1)$) solution increases A's welfare.

(4) With $F \le F^3$, $\{z_A^{nc}, z_B^{nc}\}$ cannot be part of a Nash equilibrium because region A's government has an incentive to deviate. To show this, note that $\bar{\Pi}_B(z_A, z_B^{nc})$ is minimal for z_A^r ($\partial\bar{\Pi}_B(z_A^r)/\partial z_A = 0$). If even for this z_A^r it is possible and more profitable for region A's government to opt for z_A^r for a $(2,0)$ solution rather than

134   UWE WALZ & DIETMAR WELLISCH

for z_A^{nc}, then $\{z_A^{nc}, z_B^{nc}\}$ cannot be part of a Nash equilibrium. From (A.1) we have $z_A^r = 4(a-c)/2^\phi(9b-2)$. Note that, by definition, $\bar{\Pi}_B(z_A^r, z_B^{nc}) \leq 0$ for $F \leq F^3$. Using z_A^r and (15) gives

$$G_A^A(2, 0, z_A^r) - G_A^A(1, 1, z_A^{nc}, z_B^{nc}) = \frac{(a-c)^2}{(9b-2)^2 9b 2^{2\phi}}(4(2-2^\phi)^2) > 0. \qquad (A.2)$$

Hence region A's government always deviates from $\{z_A^{nc}, z_B^{nc}\}$ for $F \leq F^3$. $\qquad \square$

APPENDIX 3: PROOF OF LEMMA 1

Inserting the reaction function $z_B(z_A)$ from (14), together with the cost functions for public inputs as well as (4) and (5), into Π_B yields (after some calculations)

$$\Pi_B = \frac{4(a-c)^2}{9b(9b-4)} + F - \frac{4z_A(a-c)(9b-2)}{9b(9b-4)} + (z_A)^2 \left(\frac{4}{9b(9b-4)} + \frac{2^\phi}{2} \right). \qquad (A.3)$$

Differentiating (A.3) with respect to z_A and solving $\partial \Pi_B(\dot{z}_A)/\partial z_A = 0$ yields $\dot{z}_A$. Suppose that $\Pi_B(\dot{z}_A) < 0$. Since $\partial^2 \Pi_B/\partial z_A^2 > 0$, it follows that $\bar{z}_A < \dot{z}_A$.

Let us now define F^2 such that no $\bar{z}_A$ exists for $F > F^2$; that is, there is no $\bar{z}_A \in \mathbb{R}$ for which (A.3) equals zero. This is the case if the discriminant of the solution to the quadratic equation being derived from $\Pi_B = 0$ is negative. Hence, the critical $F^2 = 4(a-c)^2(2-2^\phi)/(8+2^\phi(9b-4)9b)$. For $F \leq F^2$, a positive $\bar{z}_A$ exists. Since $F^2 > F^1$ and $\partial \Pi_B/\partial z_A < 0$ for $z_A < \bar{z}_A$, it follows that $\bar{z}_A > z_A^*(2, 0)$ for $F^1 < F \leq F^2$. $\qquad \square$

APPENDIX 4: PROOF OF PROPOSITION 4

We first show that, for $\bar{z}_A \leq z_A^{nc}$, it is optimal for region A's government to choose $\bar{z}_A$ in response to $z_B(\bar{z}_A)$ and thereby induce an agglomeration solution. Note that, with negatively sloped reaction curves in the case with geographically separated firms, $\bar{z}_A \leq z_A^{nc}$ implies $z_B(\bar{z}_A) \geq z_B^{nc}$ and hence $z_A(z_B(\bar{z}_A)) \leq z_A^{nc}$. Consequently, we have $G_B^B(1, 1, z_B(\bar{z}_A), \bar{z}_A) \geq G_A^A(1, 1, z_A(z_B(\bar{z}_A)), z_B(\bar{z}_A))$. Moreover, $\Pi_B(\bar{z}_A) = 0$ implies $G_A^A(2, 0, \bar{z}_A) > G_B^B(1, 1, z_B(\bar{z}_A), \bar{z}_A)$. Hence, region A will never choose $z_A(z_B)$ but rather $\bar{z}_A$. Second, $\bar{z}_A \leq z_A^{nc}$ if $\Pi_B(z_A^{nc}, z_B^{nc}) \leq 0$. Inserting z_i^{nc} into Π_B shows that this is true for $F \leq \hat{F}$ with $\hat{F} = 2(2-2^\phi)(a-c)^2/(9b-2)^2$, where

$$\text{sign}(\hat{F}-\bar{F}) = \text{sign}[81b^2(2^\phi-1)+9b(2-2^\phi)-2] > 0. \qquad (A.4)$$

The sign in (A.4) follows from the fact that the RHS increases with ϕ. Using $\phi = 0$ in the RHS give us $(9b-2) > 0$, implying that the RHS is positive for all $\phi \geq 0$. It can easily be demonstrated that $\text{sign}(F^2-\hat{F}) = \text{sign}(2-2^\phi) > 0$ for $\phi < 1$. Together with Lemma 1, this gives us the results stated in Proposition 4. $\qquad \square$

APPENDIX 5: THE MIXED STRATEGY CASE

In the absence of a pure strategy equilibrium, the reaction curves of the regions are as drawn in Figure 2. Region A's reaction curve jumps to the right at z_B^0. For

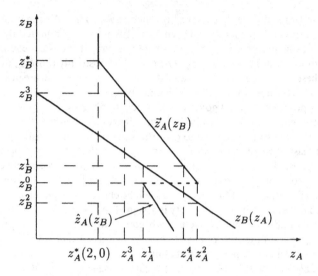

Figure 2. The mixed strategy case.

z_B greater than or equal to (resp. less than) z_B^0, it is optimal for region A to respond with its local input level for the $(2,0)$ (resp. $(1,1)$) case. The $\vec{z}_A(z_B)$ line is derived as the smaller root of the implicit solution to $\tilde{\Pi}_B \equiv G_B^B(1, 1, \vec{z}_A, z_B) - G_B^A(2, 0, \vec{z}_A) = 0$, whereas $\hat{z}_A(z_B)$ is derived from (14). To understand why A's reaction curve jumps to the right, note that, for very large z_B ($z_B > z_B^*$), region A can attract both firms with $z_A^*(2,0)$. Hence, $\vec{z}_A$ has a vertical part for $z_B > z_B^*$. If A's reaction curve jumped to the left then the regional reaction function would intersect ($\vec{z}_A$ is continuous), implying a pure strategy equilibrium and so contradicting our initial finding of the non-existence of such an equilibrium. For all z_A on $\vec{z}_A$, $\partial \tilde{\Pi}/\partial z_A < 0$. Because $\vec{z}_A$ lies to the right of $z_B(z_A)$, $\partial \tilde{\Pi}/\partial z_B < 0$, implying a negative slope for $\vec{z}_A(z_B)$. Since all conditions of the existence theorem of Dasgupta and Maskin (1986) are met, an equilibrium in mixed strategies exists.

To prove that both a $(2,0)$ and a $(1,1)$ solution can emerge with positive probability, we note that a Nash equilibrium never contains dominated strategies (cf. Fudenberg and Tirole 1992, p. 13f). We assume that region B prefers strategies that maximize its $(1,1)$ welfare. Using iterative elimination of dominated strategies, it is straightforward that B's regional government will never choose a $z_B > z_B^1$ or a $z_B < z_B^2$, whereas region A will choose z_A only in the range $[z_A^1; z_A^2]$ (see Figure 2). For instance, all $z_B > z_B^3$ are dominated by z_B^3. Consequently, $z_A > z_A^3$ is dominated by z_A^3, and so on.

Furthermore, we show that choosing (1a) only $z_B > z_B^0$ and (1b) exclusively $z_B < z_B^0$ will never constitute a Nash equilibrium. Then, we define $\check{z}_A(z_B)$ as the smallest z_A that attracts both firms to region A. We argue that (2a) $\{z_A < \check{z}_A(z_B), z_B\}$ as well as (2b) $\{z_A \geq \check{z}_A(z_B), z_B\}$ combinations will be chosen with a positive probability in the Nash equilibrium.

To prove (1a), suppose that $z_B > z_B^0$ for all $z_B \in \mathbb{R}_+$. Then A's regional government will choose z_A on $\vec{z}_A(z_B)$. But then $z_B > z_B^0$ would be dominated by $z_B \leq z_B^0$. Hence, choosing exclusively $z_B > z_B^0$ can never be part of the Nash equilibrium.

(1b) Suppose that always $z_B < z_B^0$. Then A will choose only those z_A on $\hat{z}_A(z_B)$. None of these strategies survives iterated deletion of dominated strategies, so using only $z_B < z_B^0$ does not constitute a Nash equilibrium.

(2a) Suppose A's regional government chooses only $z_A < \check{z}_A(z_B)$ (i.e., a z_A on $\hat{z}_A$). Iterative elimination of dominated strategies reveals that B will then respond with $z_B > z_B^0$ only. But, according to (1a), this does not form a Nash equilibrium. Hence, at least some of the z_A with $z_A \geq \check{z}_A(z_B)$ are selected in equilibrium.

(2b) Suppose that only $z_A \geq \check{z}_A(z_B)$ (i.e., on $\vec{z}_A$) is used. Successively eliminating dominated strategies reveals that in this case $z_B \geq z_B^0$ would be dominated by some $z_B < z_B^0$. Yet, in equilibrium, $z_B \geq z_B^0$ will be chosen with positive probability (see (1b)). Hence, a positive probability is assigned to at least one z_A with $z_A < \check{z}_A$. The Nash equilibrium thus contains both combinations: $\{z_A \geq \check{z}_A(z_B), z_B\}$ and $\{z_A < \check{z}_A(z_B), z_B\}$. We therefore have a $(1,1)$ as well as a $(2,0)$ solution occurring in the overall game with positive probability.

Because $z_A^1 > z_A^{nc} > z_A^*(2,0) > z_A^*(2,0) > z_A^*(1,1)$ (see Figure 2), at least region A provides too much in the way of public inputs.

NOTES

1. Papers such as Wildasin (1988) and Janeba (1995) eliminate one level of perfect competition by studying strategic interactions by large regions when competing for mobile capital. However, both of these contributions assume perfect competition among firms.
2. Disregarding local consumption and joint ownership of firms enables us to highlight our basic point of interest: regional competition for an oligopolistic firm. In addition, it seems plausible to neglect the small share of local consumption in a regional context. With local consumption, the problem of the inefficiency of oligopolistic output markets per se comes to the fore. By assuming away local consumption, we neglect inefficiencies in the output market and the effects of policies on this inefficiency. Assuming exclusive regional ownership of firms is less restrictive if one takes into account that local workers benefit from higher oligopolistic profits via higher wages. With an increasing degree of joint ownership, regions take increasingly greater account of the interest of the other firm. The objective functions then become more similar to that of the central government.
3. Allowing for other regional tax instruments would leave our analysis unchanged as long as the user charges for local public inputs are paid entirely by firms and shared equally by firms located in the same jurisdiction. Furthermore, firms' output decisions must be unaffected by the financing measure. An example of such a policy would be a property tax that leaves the marginal costs of firms unaltered.
4. An example of a local tax where moving costs are *not* deductible is the *Gewerbesteuer* – the basic tax source for local governments in Germany – which

mainly taxes firms' profits made within a jurisdiction. Costs for establishing firms in a locale and for relocating plants are not tax-deductible, and the proceeds of the *Gewerbesteuer* are used to finance local public infrastructure.

5. Motta and Thisse (1994) employ a similar assumption in a related paper analyzing location choices of firms and regional environmental policy. They do not model a game between regional governments, however. The major problem with mobility of both firms is the multiplicity of equilibria in the *second* (location) stage of the game; see e.g. Horstmann and Markusen (1992). With only one mobile firm, this problem does not arise. The assumption of a single mobile firm allows us to discuss some of the major economic forces at work; at the same time, we recognize the limitations of this assumption.

6. For specificity we assume that with equal welfare and equal profits the regional planner and firms prefer the agglomeration solution.

7. Note that, owing to symmetry, taxable profits are equal for the two firms, who consequently each bear half of the tax burden in the agglomeration case.

8. For this purpose we derive, using (10) and (16),

$$\text{sign}(\bar{F}-F^1) = \text{sign}[162b^2 2^\phi(2^\phi-1)+b(-126(2^\phi)+36(2^\phi)^2+72)+8(2-2^\phi)].$$

We find that

$$\text{sign}(\partial\text{RHS}/\partial\phi) = \text{sign}[(162b^2+18b)(2^\phi-1)+162b^2 2^\phi-108b+54b2^\phi-8)]$$
$$> 0,$$

since $b > 2/3$ and $\phi \geq 0$. For $\phi = 0$ (resp. $\phi = 1$), $\bar{F}-F^1$ is less than (resp. exceeds) zero. Hence, a ϕ^* exists at which $\bar{F} = F^1$. For example, if $b = 1$ then $\phi^* = 0.1188$.

REFERENCES

Aschauer, D. (1989), "Is Public Expenditure Productive?" *Journal of Monetary Economics* 24: 177-200.

Brander, J., and B. Spencer (1985), "Export Subsidies and International Market Share Rivalry," *Journal of International Economics* 18: 83-100.

Dasgupta, P., and E. Maskin (1986), "The Existence of Equilibrium in Discontinuous Games, I: Theory," *Review of Economic Studies* 53: 1-26.

Dixit, A. (1986), "Comparative Statics for Oligopoly," *International Economic Review* 27: 107-22.

Eaton, J., and G. M. Grossman (1986), "Optimal Trade and Industrial Policy under Oligopoly," *Quarterly Journal of Economics* 102: 383-406.

Fudenberg, D., and J. Tirole (1992), *Game Theory*. Cambridge, MA: MIT Press.

Helpman, E., and P. R. Krugman (1989), *Trade Policy and Market Structure*. Cambridge, MA: MIT Press.

Horstmann, I. J., and J. R. Markusen (1992), "Endogenous Market Structure in International Trade," *Journal of International Economics* 32: 109-29.

Janeba, E. (1995), "Corporate Income Tax Competition, Double Taxation Treaties, and Foreign Investment," *Journal of Public Economics* 56: 311-25.

Markusen, J. R., E. R. Morey, and N. D. Olewiler (1993), "Environmental Policy When Market Structure and Plant Locations are Endogenous," *Journal of Environmental Economics and Management* 24: 69-86.

Markusen, J. R., E. R. Morey, and N. D. Olewiler (1994), "Noncooperative Equilibria in Regional Environmental Policies When Plant Locations are Endogenous," *Journal of Public Economics* 56: 55–77.

Motta, M., and J.-F. Thisse (1994), "Does Environmental Dumping Lead to Delocation?" *European Economic Review* 38: 563–76.

Oates, W. E., and R. M. Schwab (1991), "The Allocative and Distributive Implications of Local Fiscal Competition," in D. A. Kenyon and J. Kincaid (eds.), *Competition among States and Local Governments*. Washington, DC: Urban Institute Press, pp. 127–45.

Richter, W. F., and D. Wellisch (1996), "The Provision of Local Public Goods and Factors in the Presence of Firm and Household Mobility," *Journal of Public Economics* 60: 70–93.

Wildasin, D. E. (1986), *Urban Public Finance*. New York: Harwood.

Wildasin, D. E. (1988), "Nash Equilibrium in Models of Fiscal Competition," *Journal of Public Economics* 35: 229–40.

PART III

Policy and Practice

CHAPTER 8

The Structure of Urban Governance
in South African Cities

Junaid K. Ahmad

1. INTRODUCTION

South Africa's "long walk to freedom"[1] was finally completed on November 1, 1995, with the successful holding of elections at the local government level. These elections have given the leaders of South African cities the political mandate to fundamentally reorganize the structure of urban governance. At the core of this process is the issue of how metropolitan cities in South Africa should organize themselves to finance and deliver services within their jurisdictions.

The stakes of restructuring urban governance in South Africa are high. The urban sector accounts for approximately 65% of the population and over 80% of the nation's gross domestic product. Nowhere is this concentration of people and economic activities more visible than in the major metropolitan areas, which represent over 45% of the country's population and an even higher proportion of its GDP. In addition, the urban sector represents the political fulcrum on which rests the success of South Africa's democratic experiment. How metropolitan areas will address the financing and delivery of services will, therefore, influence the economic and political condition of the country.

In Musgrave's (1959) view, the purposes of government budgets are to stabilize growth, redistribute income, and allocate resources. This view

This paper benefited from the work on intergovernmental finance in South Africa by several people, including Richard Bird, Robert Inman, Chalres McLure, Kevin Villani, and David Wildasin. In particular, the paper draws on the analysis of local government finance by Charles McLure, Kevin Villani, and David Wildasin, all of whom I would like to thank also for helping to clarify the linkages between urban governance and fiscal stability. This paper benefited from extensive comments from Richard Bird and Marianne Fay. Students in the Public Finance course at Wharton Business School helped sharpen the focus of the paper through their questions and comments.

The findings, interpretations, and conclusions expressed in this paper are entirely those of the author and should not be attributed to the World Bank, to its affiliated organizations, or to the members of its Board of Executive Directors or the countries they represent.

has influenced policy debate on the vertical dimension of fiscal decentralization – the division of fiscal responsibilities between central and local governments. According to Musgrave, the mobility of capital and labor constrains the role of local governments to the arena of allocation of resources. The objectives of pursuing economic stabilization and influencing distribution are thus the responsibility of the central government. The logic of Musgrave's principles suggests that urban governance should be guided mainly by the allocation objective of governments.

However, the economic size of South African cities suggests that how the large metropolitan cities organize themselves to finance and deliver services will inevitably have implications for macroeconomic policy and income distribution. In addition, political considerations alone mandate that cities in South Africa will inevitably play an important role in reversing the income inequalities of the apartheid era. In organizing the financing and delivery of services at the metropolitan level, therefore, policy makers will need explicitly to adapt the structure of urban governance to meet not only allocative but also stability and distributional roles of government.

This paper analyzes how the stability, distributional, and allocative objectives of government are shaping the structure of urban governance in South Africa's metropolitan areas. Section 2 describes the structure of urban governance in South Africa under apartheid. Section 3 briefly reviews the restructuring options being considered; Section 4 details the criteria used to evaluate the various options. Section 5 describes the "hybrid" structure of urban governance that is evolving in South Africa. The final section offers a summary of the conclusions.

2. INITIAL CONDITIONS: THE APARTHEID CITY

Racial segregation has been the dominant factor in shaping the structure of cities in South Africa.[2] By the early 1980s, cities were physically divided along racial lines into separate White and Black Local Authorities (WLAs and BLAs).[3] All formal economic activities were zoned in the WLAs, while residences of the black community were restricted to dormitory towns located at the urban fringe, often one to two hours away from the centers of employment.[4] In addition, the right to own property was denied to the black community.

As a result of these policies, the fiscal position of BLAs and WLAs differed significantly. WLAs had access to property taxes and various types of business taxes, including an implicit surcharge on the cost of retailing water and electricity.[5] BLAs, on the other hand, could rely only on rents from publicly owned property and some user charges. The ability to tax economic activities allowed the WLAs not only to have a larger revenue base but also to cross-subsidize their residential customers from commercial and industrial property taxes and service surcharges.[6] Depending on the extent to which the surcharges were passed on as higher commodity prices, there may also have been some level of exporting of tax burdens from WLAs to BLAs (see World Bank 1994b).

Ultimately, the difference in fiscal capacity had several important implications. First, it resulted in a significant difference in the level of services in BLAs and WLAs. In the Central Wits area in 1991, for example, the annual expenditure per capita on residential infrastructure in WLAs was about $550 (U.S.) – much higher than the level of expenditures for cities in industrialized countries – while the national average for the black community was about $60 per person (see May 1994). Second, only WLAs were able to access capital markets on the basis of their fiscal strength; on the rare occasions that BLAs raised debt, a full central government guarantee was required or the borrowing was done directly from public financial entities. Third, whereas WLAs had fiscal autonomy – fiscal transfers accounted for less than 10% of the total revenue of the WLAs – fully 80% of BLA revenues were from central transfers. The reliance of BLAs on central transfers increased over time as boycott of service payments became a fundamental instrument of protest against the apartheid regime.

In the mid-1980s, central government created Regional Service Councils (RSCs) with jurisdictions over several BLAs and WLAs. The RSCs were primarily charged with financing capital investments in the BLAs with revenues from turnover and payroll taxes collected mainly from firms in WLAs.[7] In establishing the RSCs, central government created a channel to tap into the tax base of the WLAs to finance BLAs and also to reduce the reliance on fiscal transfers from central tax bases.

Finally, an important distinction between BLAs and WLAs emerged in terms of accountability of local officials. In the WLAs, accountability was ensured through both the electoral and the local tax systems. Residents of WLAs had full political representation, and the cost of delivering services was partially passed on to the beneficiaries through increases in user charges and property taxes. Seen as an instrument of the apartheid regime, the political legitimacy of BLAs was never established. BLA officials did not represent the black community, and hence were never politically accountable. The availability of large fiscal transfers that sustained BLA administrations contributed further to the lack of accountability.

Based on one of the most inefficient and inequitable set of spatial policies in the world, apartheid created a dual system of local government. WLAs had fiscal autonomy and were politically accountable to the white residents. BLAs, crippled by lack of political legitimacy and fiscally weak, depended on central transfers for their survival. This system defined the starting point of local government reform in South African cities.

3. THE STRUCTURE OF URBAN GOVERNANCE: OPTIONS

In deciding the organization of metropolitan systems, urban political leadership faced several options. One was to maintain the status quo, albeit without the racial nomenclature, of *jurisdictional fragmentation,* or a structure of urban governance under which the responsibility for the same local functions lies with many local governments operating in the area.[8] In the case of South Africa, the proposal was to merge adjacent BLAs and WLAs into new municipalities – a twinning of sorts – and allow several of these "twins" to operate as independent municipalities. A second option was to create a *centralized metropolitan government,* with the BLAs and WLAs in each urban area being merged into a single local government having responsibility for all local functions. A third option (one that was not actively debated) was the model of *functional fragmentation,* under which the provision of services is areawide and is shared between general-purpose local government and autonomous agencies. Applied to South Africa, this model would imply that service utilities could serve several municipalities (the "twins") or a metropolitan government.

In reviewing the structure of governments in major cities of various developing countries, Bahl and Linn (1992) concluded that the choice of one form of urban governance over another will eventually be determined by the weights that policy makers accord to efficiency and equity benefits. In practice, their review suggested that – although the centralized metropolitan model seemed to dominate – the structure of urban governance is in most areas a hybrid. In South Africa's case, the emergence of a hybrid is also most probable. To understand why and what form of hybrid would be the optimal structure of urban governance requires first an analysis of the criteria most likely to influence that choice within South Africa.

4. THE STRUCTURE OF URBAN GOVERNANCE: CRITERIA

The organizational structure of metropolitan areas in South Africa will be largely influenced by political considerations, different dimensions of efficiency in the delivery and financing of services, distributional objectives, and the aim of central government that financing of local services not undermine the macroeconomic stability of the economy. These goals correspond broadly to the allocative, distributional, and stabilization functions of government used by Musgrave (1983) to discuss the optimal design of government structures in a federal system.[9]

4.1. Political Considerations

Abolishing the racial basis of the local government system is a fundamental consideration in the reform of urban governance in South Africa. A merger of BLAs and WLAs into either a metropolitan structure or as "twins" in a model of jurisdictional fragmentation will, therefore, be inevitable.

A second consideration is the creation of a system of local government through which local council members can be held accountable and responsible for their decisions. If establishing accountability is perceived as only a political goal, then the primary instrument to achieve this objective is through the *electoral system.* Ensuring that council members are directly elected rather than appointed by another tier of government provides an important basis for establishing their accountability. Not surprisingly, the direct election of local officials has been, over the last decade, an important aspect of fiscal decentralization worldwide (see Dillinger 1994).

The electoral system, however, is only one mechanism for promoting the accountability of local officials. *Efficient markets,* especially land and capital, can complement the influence of the electoral process in holding the behavior of local officials in check. Functioning urban land markets facilitate people's ability to "vote with their feet" – an important assumption embedded in Tiebout's (1956) model of local government. Similarly, the manner in which capital markets price, and thereby ration, access to capital for different local governments offers important signals to consumers about the behavior of their local officials. In South African cities, apartheid policies of zoning and discrimination in property ownership severely undermined the functioning of urban land markets. Given the constraints on property ownership and development of economic nodes in the townships, BLAs did not have access to capital markets. These measures not only resulted in welfare costs for the economy but also undermined potential instruments of accountability.

Accountability will be further influenced by the intergovernmental fiscal system that is eventually adopted and, in particular, by the extent to which the fiscal autonomy of local governments is promoted, by the design of the intergovernmental grant system, and by the type of budgeting and monitoring system adopted. Accountability is certainly enhanced through access to direct *fiscal instruments* by local authorities. Local officials can be held responsible for their actions if, at the margin, decisions to alter the level of services are reflected in increases or decreases in tax rates directly under the control of city officials. Ensuring accountability through the tax system thus favors a devolution of tax instruments to local governments, rather than a reliance on intergovernmental transfers as has been the case with the BLAs.

The *design of the intergovernmental grant system* may also increase accountability if access to fiscal transfers from other tiers of government is conditional on achieving a certain level of fiscal effort, or is driven by a formula that ensures transparency and predictability in the allocation process. Nevertheless, most systems of intergovernmental fiscal transfers suffer from the problem of incentive incompatibility because, for various reasons, tax and expenditure responsibilities are assigned to different tiers of government and transfers are needed as the residual to balance the budgets. This problem blurs accountability and places the burden of checks and balances on the effectiveness with which public officials implement various *budgeting and monitoring systems,* rather than on self-regulating processes such as markets or on the direct availability of tax instruments that avoid the incentive incompatibility problem. Although imperfect as a tool, an effective budgeting and monitoring system can add to the information base of constituencies and other tiers of government and so assist in holding local authorities accountable for their behavior.

Thus, in considering the political dimensions of structuring urban governance, policy makers have the difficult task of choosing an organization for financing and delivering services that is best able to strengthen the political institutions of democracy while enabling markets and fiscal instruments to hold local officials accountable. How this interplay between political institutions, markets, and fiscal instruments will evolve will influence the choice between jurisdictional or functional fragmentation and a centralized metropolitan form of government for the cities of South Africa.

Considerations of political accountability suggest a highly decentralized model of urban governance with elected local officials, full fiscal autonomy, limited reliance on intergovernmental transfers, and with full access to land and capital markets. Perhaps a model of jurisdictional fragmentation, as conceptualized in the Tiebout model, may best approximate this form of urban governance.

4.2. Efficiency

Efficiency can be defined over several dimensions. Economic efficiency includes how consumer preferences are reflected in the budget allocation process, how the locational decisions of households and businesses are affected, and how externalities are addressed. Finally, urban governance will also affect the technical efficiency with which services are delivered.

Consumer Preferences. Simply put, an important dimension of economic efficiency is the extent to which preferences of the constituencies can be reflected in the local budget. In reviewing the experience of urban governments in developing countries, Bahl and Linn (1992) concluded that gains in economic efficiency are the product of a system in which governments are small enough to give local residents a choice, the political process allows local voters to reveal their preferences, and the local government has the fiscal autonomy and technical capability to reflect voter preferences in its budget and service delivery. Measures to enhance the accountability of local politicians and officials (discussed in Section 4.1) thus weigh heavily in enhancing the economic efficiency of local governments.

South African cities meet the Bahl and Linn preconditions for achieving the goals of economic efficiency. The political fight against apartheid was conducted through civic and community organizations leaving behind an unusually strong tradition of grass-roots participation in political affairs.[10] In addition, there is significant technical and managerial capacity available in the WLAs that can be utilized across a metropolitan boundary. Finally, given the level of economic activities in the metropolitan areas, sufficient flexibility exists to create fiscal instruments at the local level to achieve the necessary level of fiscal autonomy. The challenge will be to choose a structure of urban governance that builds on these existing strengths.

Locational Decisions. With the pressures of urbanization and the repeal of the Group Areas Act, the allocation of population and business activities in urban areas has been in a state of flux. In the long run, if operations of land markets become more efficient then a dramatic spatial reorganization of South Africa's cities can be expected (see Bruckner 1994). In several of the major metropolitan areas there has already been a decentralization of employment from the core cities into the surrounding white municipalities. Moreover, in some cities there has been an outflow of white residents from the city center and an inflow of black residents from adjacent townships and regions.[11]

In this context, where the allocation of population and business activity over the urban areas is in a state of flux, it will be critical that any strategy chosen for financing urban services *not* distort the locational choices facing individuals and firms. A policy of amalgamating cities and adjacent townships over a narrow boundary for the purposes of financing the backlog in services may result in such inefficiencies. There is a high risk that the fiscal burden on any one individual jurisdiction will create incentives for tax-paying households and firms to escape from the taxing jurisdictions. Moreover, low-income households may be attracted to areas offering the highest level of transfer payments or public services for the poor. Because these incentives do not correspond to true economic benefits and costs, they cause misallocation of resources and hence economic inefficiency.[12]

To illustrate the problem of narrow boundaries, an exercise was undertaken to assess the potential fiscal burden of a town-twinning program in the Central Wits area. For the purposes of illustration, various BLAs were merged with their adjacent white municipalities. In this exercise, the inherited deficits of the BLAs were to be financed by property tax increases in WLAs. Owing to the large variation in these deficits, the mergers would result in an increase in property tax rates of about 9.3% in Randburg and Sandton, which is assumed to be merged with Alexandra, and of about 40% in Johannesburg, which is assumed to be linked to Soweto. On the other hand, in a combined metropolitan area the property tax increase would be approximately 30% (World Bank 1994b).

The discussion thus suggests that, in the case of the metropolitan areas, drawing of narrow municipal boundaries may result in unequal fiscal burdens in the financing of urban services. The potential for distorting locational decisions of households and firms would therefore be high. Two options are available to compensate for these effects. Central or regional fiscal transfers could be used to assist municipalities in financing the cost of the backlog and to compensate for fiscal disparities. Alternatively, the municipal boundaries could be drawn over a metropolitan area in order to equalize the tax burden across various jurisdictions. Although sufficiently high levels of taxation could well induce relocation across metropolitan (and, eventually, national) boundaries, equalizing tax burdens across adjacent jurisdictions would certainly reduce the impact of fiscal measures on locational decisions of households and firms. The tradeoffs involved in using central transfers versus relying on local finance across a metropolitan boundary have already been alluded to in the context of the discussion on accountability, and will be addressed further in the next section. However, at this stage it should be noted that, without recourse to central or regional transfers, the financing of urban services in twinned municipalities – WLAs and BLAs – may be inefficient and inequitable.

Externalities. An important aspect of achieving economic efficiency is to ensure that the system of delivery adopted is able to internalize the externalities that may characterize delivery of urban services. Otherwise, a small local community would have the incentive to under- or overproduce local goods, creating a loss in aggregate welfare. Jurisdictional fragmentation would therefore not be efficient if significant divergence exists between the social costs and benefits of services and those realized by local authorities.

Technical Efficiency. The extent to which local service delivery exhibits economies of scale is at the core of how much the structure of urban governance should be influenced by technical efficiency considerations. There is an assumption that only "hardware" services such as public utilities and transportation show economies of scale, but technological advances in recent years have certainly changed this for many services. Nevertheless, technical considerations might bias the choice toward more metropolitan-wide delivery of services.

This discussion suggests that the different models of urban governance involve tradeoffs over the various dimensions of efficiency. Consumer preferences are best reflected in homogenous and small local government structures, but could lead to overall losses in consumer welfare if fragmented local authorities attempt to deliver and finance services whose benefits and costs are areawide. On the other hand, locational distortions are minimized and technical efficiency is captured under a metropolitan structure.

4.3. Distributional Concerns

Economic analysis has long suggested that the fundamental obstacle to effective redistribution at the local level is the mobility of households and capital. As suggested in the discussion on locational efficiency, redistributive policies implemented at the local level may cause economic resources to be allocated to different jurisdictions on the basis of fiscal considerations rather than true economic costs and benefits. In addition, Wildasin (1993a) notes two other problems. First, there is an issue of fiscal sustainability. Local redistributive policies that might appear feasible initially, given some mix of rich and poor within a jurisdiction, may turn out to be unfeasible once economic resources begin to relocate in response to the redistributive policies. Second, as the poor move in and the rich move out as a result of redistributive policies, the incomes of both income groups may not change substantially, and any effects may accrue outside the jurisdiction as well as within. As a result, local redistributive policies might have little impact on local income distribution yet have widespread effects overall.

Cognizant of these important constraints in implementing redistributive policies at the local level, South Africa has begun to manage the issue of income redistribution through the intergovernmental system by coordinating redistributive policies among different levels of government. The central government has taken on the responsibility of financing a minimum standard of basic services across all jurisdictions. This includes fiscal transfers to individuals (through programs such as the housing subsidy) and also to subnational governments for financing access to basic services and infrastructure. The management of these centrally financed programs is expected to be undertaken by lower tiers of government. In addition, the center will provide "equalization" grants for the poorer jurisdictions. Finally, to avoid any adverse impact on the growth potential of the economy, a political decision seems to have been made to implement income redistribution incrementally over time.

In adopting these policies, the government is being quite pragmatic. It is depending largely on central resources to finance income redistribution, and is mixing the use of fiscal transfers to achieve both interpersonal and interjurisdictional equity. In addition, by relying on subnational governments to administer the programs, the center utilizes the generally better local-level information base on households. In fact, the informational advantage of local governments may be an important reason why they may be better equipped to meet equity goals.[13] Finally, by involving subnational governments in meeting equity objectives, the center is also diffusing the political charge that income redistribution is being used as an excuse to centralize the intergovernmental system.

Financing of income redistribution objectives is also being addressed through the structure of urban governance. In particular, to avoid the locational distortions associated with redistributive measures, a more consolidated urban governmental structure (e.g., a metropolitan system) is being advocated. A metrowide structure would minimize locational impacts, and could also achieve efficiency objectives by accommodating wide variations in levels of urban service demand without imposing a uniform level of service provision. In other words, instead of completely passing the responsibility of redistribution on to the central government, *centralization at the local level* through some form of metropolitan governance structure provides local authorities with the flexibility to implement redistributive measures without significantly reducing efficiency.

4.4. Fiscal Stability and Access to Financial Markets

Access to significant long-term finance will be required for rapid improvements in the standard of municipal services for the black community.[14] Which tier of government should have the fiscal responsibility for undertaking this borrowing? Fiscal stability concerns, as well as the objective of reducing the cost of borrowing by local governments, have often led governments in developing countries to centralize the borrowing powers of the public sector. The implications of such a policy measure are explored in this section. It is argued that centralizing the borrowing powers of government may be both inefficient and inequitable. Instead, certain structures of urban governance – while facilitating the access to capital markets by local governments – also provide a strong check on possible inefficient and fiscally destabilizing local government borrowing.

Benefits of Local Government Borrowing. Borrowing from capital markets to finance investments in urban infrastructure is justified on both efficiency and equity considerations. First, apart from the political unfeasibility of taxation, there would be significant efficiency losses if increases in local taxes were used to fund the capital investments for the black community over the next few years.[15] The tax burden would be excessive and would fall primarily on whites. Second, given that the benefits of capital investments will accrue to future generations, it is both equitable and efficient for future taxpayers to contribute to the payment stream. Capital markets, of course, provide this intertemporal link. Third, as the legacies of apartheid are removed from the economy, a larger proportion of the black community is expected to form part of the tax base and would, therefore, be in a better fiscal position in the future to pay for infrastructure investments made today.[16] Finally, as discussed previously, interaction with capital markets has the potential of creating competitive and disciplining pressures on local governments.

Fiscal Systems and Access to Capital Markets. Access to capital markets by local governments in South Africa will be difficult as long as the rules of fiscal decentralization remain in a state of flux. Capital markets need clear signals on various aspects of the fiscal system. This includes information on which tax bases are available to pay for capital investments; the legal basis on which the stream of revenue from such tax bases can be pledged as collateral; the extent to which intergovernmental grants will be available to fund local government expenditures, their predictability, and the ability of local governments to use these also as collateral or pay capital charges; the availability of transparent and externally audited financial accounts; and clear-cut definitions on the boundaries of new metropolitan governments.

The structure of urban governance is also an important determinant of local government access to capital markets. The choice of fragmented jurisdictions versus a metropolitan structure, for example, may lead to different tax capacities in different jurisdictions and hence differential access to capital markets. At one level, small fragmented local governments – Alexandra, a BLA in the current structure, for example – will not have the fiscal capacity to access capital or financial markets at all. Others would be restricted to borrowing short-term money from commercial banks. Meanwhile, some of the existing WLAs, if left intact or even if merged with some BLAs in a twin structure, would have no trouble issuing bonds or borrowing from commercial banks. On the other hand, metropolitan governments, by virtue of their economic size and diversity, may have access to more fiscal instruments and a more diversified income base.[17] Metropolitan boundaries would also allow for a better pooling of risks.[18] Finally, urban governments that adopt a model of functional fragmentation and create enterprises to finance and deliver specific services may find that access to capital markets is easier, as revenue bonds – linked to a specific payment stream and easier to evaluate as a project – are preferred over general obligation bonds of municipalities.[19]

Urban Structure and Moral Hazard. Borrowing by metropolitan governments, or indeed by any large city, raises the potential problem of moral hazard. The sheer economic size of the metropolitan areas of South Africa suggests that central government would face considerable political and financial constraints in allowing such cities to default and face bankruptcy in case of financial duress. Metropolitan governments may be "too big to be allowed to fail." In this context, capital markets would perceive the debt of urban governments in South Africa to be an implicit obligation of central government; consequently, instead of acting as a disciplining device, such markets may in fact be too generous in financing metropolitan governments. A metropolitan structure of urban governance would therefore interfere with the central government's objectives of fiscal stability.

The potential of inheriting the debt of large urban governments suggests that jurisdictional fragmentation may be a preferred option of urban governance, at least from the fiscal perspective of central government. The bankruptcy of smaller local authorities may not have significant macro implications, and central government may be in a political position to allow such local authorities to fail as a signal to both borrowers and lenders that central government is not the banker of last resort. In the case of South Africa, however, smaller local governments would result in a significant proportion of the urban jurisdictions not having the fiscal or administrative capacity to access capital markets.

Ironically, a common response by the central governments of developing countries to the problems of limited access and potential excessive debt has been to regulate heavily the borrowing of local authorities. In many countries, national government has centralized the borrowing power of all public entities by having central government borrow directly on their behalf or by creating a public financial entity that borrows from the market and then lends to subnational governments (World Bank 1990). In other countries, the borrowing is done directly from the market but only after central government approval. In some developed countries, the option has been to impose constitutional limits (von Hagen 1991). South Africa is considering variants of these controls.

For several reasons, however, centralization of borrowing powers may fail to provide the government with macro economic control over the fiscal affairs of government as a whole. First, international experience from several countries – and, indeed, the past history of South Africa – suggests that the allocation of credit through public institutions inevitably becomes embroiled in a political process (see World Bank 1994a). Capital does not necessarily flow to the most productive; often, it flows to those who are politically the most astute. In such cases, government borrowing may be inefficient and the subsequent investments generally unproductive.[20] This has the potential of contributing to a slow loss of fiscal control, as more and more borrowing is required to deliver a minimum level of public services. Second, the institutional incentives of public financial intermediaries (PFIs) are such that they may not be immune from the moral hazard syndrome. In fact, even more than in the case of subnational governments – which generally have access to tax bases and whose politicians must face an electoral process and could therefore face the consequences of their myopic decisions – PFI employees are seen as responsible to central authorities and their debt perceived as an off-budget obligation of central government. Third, the presence of PFIs may create a political channel for providing financial assistance to subnational governments or public enterprises in financial distress.[21] This process hides the problem of insolvency and eventually passes the financial burden on to the central fiscus. Finally, as discussed in what follows, by removing the direct relationship between capital markets and subnational governments, PFIs undermine a potential instrument for ensuring efficiency and accountability of local governments. Therefore, the impact of PFIs on urban governance is not neutral.

Separating Fiscal from Finance: Some General Considerations. The role of governments in the financial sector has important implications for the design of an intergovernmental fiscal system. To begin with, the fiscal base of subnational governments, which is defined by both the vertical and the horizontal dimension of fiscal decentralization, in effect establishes the "collateral" that will determine their access to financial markets. As suggested, uncertainty on the fiscal side – such as the allocation of tax bases or the predictability of intergovernmental transfers – will influence the extent to which different tiers of government can take advantage of financial markets. It may even be that the uncertainty will be read by capital markets as the national government's way of centralizing fiscal powers. Subnational debt may then be interpreted as being a direct obligation of central government. Defining the fiscal rules is therefore a necessary step in enabling access to capital markets and resolving the moral hazard problem.

More importantly, the government's involvement in the financial sector dampens the economic role of capital markets in allocating credit and

154 JUNAID K. AHMAD

signaling creditworthiness. The financial sector's ability to promote economic efficiency and the accountability of local officials, important elements of a decentralized model of government, is adversely affected. In fact, promoting fiscal decentralization only by devolving tax and expenditure responsibilities will not allow local governments to take advantage of the efficiency gains that can be achieved through the interplay of political jurisdictions and capital markets in the financing and delivery of services at the local level. To draw an analogy: would a model of decentralized local governments be effective if labor mobility between local jurisdictions were controlled? [22]

In addition, if the centralization of borrowing powers facilitates access to finance by local authorities who are not creditworthy, or makes capital more "affordable," then central government will in effect have provided an implicit subsidy through the financial sector. If the objective is to provide such subsidies, a preferable alternative would be for central government to convert the implicit *financial* subsidy into an explicit *fiscal* grant and allow local authorities to pledge such transfer as collateral when they access capital markets. Such lump-sum transfers would not distort the price of capital and would enable local authorities to establish a direct relationship with capital markets. Fiscal subsidies have the added advantage of being transparent and hence more easily monitored, and stand a greater chance of being held in check via the political process.

Centralization of borrowing powers may distort the economic incentives faced by local authorities in other ways. As von Hagen (1991) and Wildasin (1995) suggest, fiscal restraints on capital market activities are often circumvented, and the resulting behavior – for example, dipping into pension funds or engaging in off-budget activities – may affect the allocation of resources. Wildasin (1995) suggests that restricting access to capital markets may also lead local authorities to reduce their investments in local goods. In the case of South Africa, the political pressure for rapid delivery of local services is sufficiently high that central government may be forced to compensate local governments for the restriction on borrowing by ultimately funding local services through intergovernmental transfers. In effect, this would mean that central tax bases would be funding local goods – returning centralization by the back door.

In sum, the discussion suggests that keeping the fiscal and financial roles of government separate and decentralizing borrowing powers may both be fundamental in ensuring an efficient system of intergovernmental fiscal relations. In particular, such measures would provide the incentive for local governments to be more efficient in their delivery and financing of services. Equally important, the separation may be necessary to ensure that government intervention does not impede the functioning of capital markets – a distinct possibility in the context of low-income countries where financial markets are thin and government is the predominant borrower in the economy (World Bank 1990).

Resolving the Moral Hazard Dilemma. However, effectively separating the fiscal and financial roles of government and decentralizing its borrowing powers would require resolving the potential problem of moral hazard. In other words, how can the delivery and financing of services in metropolitan areas in South Africa be structured so that the costs of bankruptcy are borne by the contracting parties and not by the central government?

A possible solution would be to privatize public services or, as Baumol and Lee (1991) have suggested, to create "contestable markets" for the participation of the private sector in the financing and delivery of public goods. Simply put, changes in technology now permit the privatization of the delivery and financing of what are still considered public goods in many countries, including South Africa. These include, for example, distribution of water and electricity at the retail level, transportation services, and garbage disposal. By placing these in the private domain, governments can avoid the problem of moral hazard: [23] bankruptcy of these entities will enable other private-sector parties to bid for their assets. [24] A lack of competitive pressure and threat of takeover in the public delivery of municipal services would leave open the issue of implicit financial obligation of central government – the assumption that one tier of government under financial duress will be supported by another tier.

The privatization route has the additional advantage of enabling service deliverers both to access financial equity and to borrow in the capital markets. Because equity holders stand to lose in the case of bankruptcy, the participation of financial equity provides an incentive internal to the structure of the service provider to monitor debt, creating another layer of protection against moral hazard that is not present in a public system of delivery. In addition to reducing the current cost of services over a fully debt-financed system, equity participation improves access to and reduces the price of capital.

Shifting responsibilities onto the private sector reduces the extent to which local governments need to borrow for capital investments. But to what extent does the portfolio of public goods remaining within the responsibility of local governments (e.g., street lighting and parks) still create the problem of moral hazard? The answer is certainly significantly *less,* since these goods do not require extensive capital investments and – provided that local governments have access to adequate tax bases – can be financed on the strength of such tax bases. However, the availability of private-sector bond insurance provides an added mechanism for ensuring that central governments do not take on the role of "banker of last resort." In the event of an issuer default, the bond insurers guarantee the timely payment of interest and principal in accordance with the issuer's original payment schedule. The insurer will often work with the issuer to address financial problems and thereby minimize its own losses. The guarantee is generally irrevocable, and the instruments are guaranteed for the life of the bond, regardless of what may happen to the issuer.[25]

Overall, three important implications emerge. First, the global phenomena of technological change and availability of capital markets strongly favor the functional jurisdiction model of urban governance, but with one important caveat. Generally, areawide agencies delivering municipal services have been public corporations. The potential problem of moral hazard suggests replacing these public entities with private ownership.

Second, as implied in the foregoing discussion, the solution to the moral hazard problem requires intervention not in the financial sector but rather in the ownership structure of the service deliverer. For the public sector to benefit from the efficiency gains of fiscal decentralization, government will need to look not only at the division of fiscal and expenditure responsibilities between different tiers of governments, but also at the division of responsibilities between the public and private sectors. As Wildasin (1995) has pointed out, given that private entities are the most decentralized units of the economy, the moral hazard problem is a result not of decentralization but of insufficient decentralization. This view suggests that, in restructuring intergovernmental fiscal relations, policy makers should look at the potential of privatizing public responsibilities as an important component of the process of fiscal decentralization.

Finally, the model of private-sector delivery and the availability of bond insurance agencies suggest that decentralizing the fiscal and financial responsibilities of governments is an important component of ensuring macroeconomic stability. The structure of urban governance is thus an important tool in achieving the stability objective of central government.

4.5. Fiscal Transfers: A Final Consideration

The allocation of expenditure responsibilities and tax assignments between different tiers of government will inevitably result in a fiscal imbalance: own-revenue sources will rarely meet the funding requirements of subnational governments. Nor does the theory of fiscal decentralization suggest that each tier of government should be self-reliant. It is more efficient if certain responsibilities, such as expenditures that exhibit spillovers, are addressed through transfers.

In practice, however, the experience of central and subnational governments with fiscal transfers has been mixed. In many countries such transfers have often been determined on an ad hoc basis; even where countries have moved toward a formula system, transfers to subnational governments are often adjusted to compensate for potentially adverse fiscal shocks to the national budgets. The ensuing uncertainty and lack of predictability in the allocation of fiscal transfers limits the ability of subnational governments to plan local expenditures. From the national government's perspective, fiscal transfers have not proven to be an effective fiscal tool for ensuring efficient fiscal management by subnational governments. In fact, reliance on upper-tier financing has the potential of undermining the accountability of local politicians and officials. Finally, the problem of moral hazard, discussed in the context of financial markets, applies equally to the case of intergovernmental transfers (Wildasin 1995). It may not be credible for central government to announce a fixed level of financial support for the delivery of such basic services as health and education, for example, and then to refrain from providing additional funds under the political pressure of local politicians.[26]

Several approaches can be adopted to address these problems. At one level, legislation could be used to make the allocation process binding and transparent. Indeed, the possibility of protecting "the fiscal rules of the game" in South Africa's constitution is currently being explored. Another option is to devolve tax instruments to subnational governments, or to enable the (administratively less costly) policy of allowing subnational surcharges on national tax instruments.[27] Finally, and directly relevant to the issue at hand, is the option of shaping the organization of metropolitan governments toward reducing their dependency on fiscal transfers. The history of fiscal transfers in South Africa, embedded as it is in the politics of apartheid and the subsequent loss of accountability of subnational governments, suggests that the model of urban governance finally adopted will be designed to tackle policy issues, such as distributional concerns and spillovers, that could be effectively addressed through fiscal transfers.

5. Optional Structure of Urban Governance: A Hybrid

The optimal structure of urban governance in South Africa will eventually depend on how the political process in South Africa ranks the objectives of fiscal stability, income distribution, and efficiency in terms of their importance to public policy. In practice, the political process has given equal weight to each of these factors, and the emerging structure of urban governance in the metropolitan areas reflects this tension. Not surprisingly, a hybrid governance structure is evolving.

5.1. A Metropolitan Structure

A metropolitan government has been created in Johannesburg and is expected in Durban and Cape Town. Political considerations to ensure a nonracial structure and the recognition that urban governments will have responsibility for implementing some measure of income redistribution were two important justifications for the creation of a metropolitan government. The merger of adjacent BLAs and WLAs – the twinning option – would only partially fulfill the political objectives of creating a nonracial local government structure. In all of the major urban centers, some fiscally strong WLAs are not geographically close enough to any BLAs to justify a merger. In addition, in many cases there would be significant fiscal disparities between the newly merged BLAs and WLAs. A larger metropolitan boundary was necessary to avoid the potential locational distortions that could arise from local financing of services within narrow administrative boundaries.

Fiscal autonomy and accountability were also important in the move toward a metropolitan structure. Intergovernmental fiscal transfers could, of course, be used to compensate for the fiscal disparities between the different twinned structures and to support a more fragmented local government structure – the jurisdictional fragmentation model of urban governance. There was sufficient evidence from the past, however, to suggest that reliance on intergovernmental transfers may reduce the fiscal autonomy and accountability of local governments, two important elements in ensuring the benefits of fiscal decentralization. In addition, there was significant concern about the predictability of such transfers and the uncertainty it would create in local government planning. Finally, political leadership at the central government level was convinced that the fiscal base of the urban sector would be sufficient to support the expansion of municipal services into the black community while freeing central government fiscal resources to fund national public goods.

5.2. Two-Tier Metropolitan Structure

A metropolitan tier was perceived as necessary to achieve fiscal autonomy and accountability of local government vis-à-vis the central government, but it was nevertheless viewed as too far removed from the communities. To further enhance accountability of officials, bring government closer to the constituencies, and hence improve economic efficiency, Johannesburg has adopted a two-tier metropolitan structure: a metropolitan tier overseeing a group of twinned municipalities as the second tier. A second tier provides an additional political check on attempts by the metropolitan tier to engage in extensive redistribution. It therefore offers a level of protection for the former WLAs and may have been a necessary concession to the white community in order to form a metropolitan tier in the first place. Cape Town and Durban are expected to adopt a two-tier metropolitan system.

5.3. Assignment of Fiscal Responsibilities

Although the two-tier model has been politically accepted and is in the process of being implemented, the issue of allocation of fiscal responsibilities – expenditure and tax assignments – between the two tiers will be resolved only over time. The next section offers some options based on the earlier discussion of alternative models of urban governance. If implemented, privatization of municipal services would significantly influence the assignment of expenditure between the metropolitan and the municipal tiers, as well as the subsequent assignment of taxes.

Expenditure Responsibilities. It was suggested that concerns about fiscal stability and operational efficiency favor the privatization of municipal services. The extent of the economies of scale in the delivery process will be an important determinant of whether the municipal service should be privatized at the metropolitan or the municipal level, and whether there will be one or multiple providers within an urban jurisdiction. Where economies of scale do not exist – for example, in garbage removal – several private providers could operate in one metropolitan area, each serving a different municipality. In any case, private providers facing competitive pressures would have the incentive to respond to the willingness of customers to pay and so tailor the standard of delivery to demand. For local public goods, on the other hand, economic efficiency suggests that the division of labor between the metropolitan tier and the municipalities would depend on the jurisdictional incidence of who benefits from municipal expenditures. Street lighting, for example, could well be a municipal responsibility. On the other hand, roads – with metropolitanwide spillovers in cost and benefits – would be better financed by the metro tier.

If privatization of municipal services is accepted as part of the reform process, then a critical element of urban governance will be the regulatory function of government. In particular, this function is needed to ensure that a private monopoly does not emerge in delivery of services, especially where direct competition in the market is not possible. The general issue of whether regulatory functions should be central or local, or whether they are a concurrent responsibility of different tiers of government, is beyond the scope of this paper. However, given that most of the municipal services should be privatized at a metropolitan level, it is logical that the metro tier have regulatory responsibility for overseeing performance of the privatized entities and for managing the privatization process.

In addition to the role of regulator, a fundamental function of the metro tier would be in the area of income redistribution. Given the fiscal disparities between different municipalities, the metro tier could have the responsibility of equalizing their fiscal capacities.[28] However, if the model of functional fragmentation is accepted and municipal services are delivered through the private sector, then an additional component of the metro's distributional responsibility could be to target fiscal transfers directly to low-income households (e.g., through vouchers) to ensure access to a basic minimum level of services.[29] Because this type of fiscal assistance would be to individual households, access to a minimum level of service within a metropolitan area would not be location-specific. Locational decisions of households would therefore be undertaken on the basis of economic costs and benefits rather than fiscal considerations. In addition, by allocating the responsibility for distributional objectives directly to the public sector, the service deliverer would have the flexibility of focusing on operational efficiency and of pricing services according to economic criteria. This separation of distributional and efficiency objectives in the pricing and delivery of municipal services would also promote locational efficiency.

Tax Assignments. The discussion on tax assignment takes as its starting point the expenditure assignments discussed before, noting that the tax instruments originally assigned to the RSCs, WLAs, and BLAs will become available – in the short to medium run – to the new urban governments.[30]

Assigning payroll and turnover taxes: In the past, zoning policies separated the residences of the blacks from their places of employment and purchase of consumption goods. Yet for administrative convenience, payroll taxes are collected at the source of employment and turnover taxes in the jurisdiction in which the taxed transaction occurs; in both cases, this is primarily in the WLAs. To the extent that each metropolitan jurisdiction will include both BLAs and WLAs and hence the residences and places of employment and consumption of the black community, it would be more efficient and equitable to assign the turnover and payroll taxes to the metro tier.[31]

Although the incidence of such taxes is on residents of the former WLAs and BLAs both, most of the derived revenues will be used to fund expenditures for low-income black households. Given its potential redistributive function, the assignment of payroll and turnover taxes to the metro tier is appropriate. At the same time, given that low-income communities are part of these tax bases, there would be an incentive for metropolitan authorities *not* to be too excessive in pursuing their redistributive objectives.

Central fiscal transfers: Central transfers have traditionally been used for redistributional purposes. It is expected that in the new fiscal system the transfers will continue to be directed to achieve distributional objectives. The metro tier would therefore be the appropriate tier at the local level to manage these transfers.

Property taxes: Property taxes are a mainstay of finance in urban areas and an efficient tax instrument for financing local public goods. In addition, the autonomy to set property rates can help establish the accountability of local officials. Residential property taxes should therefore remain at the level of the municipalities to ensure that local officials can respond to the preferences of their constituencies.

However, there is an important redistributive issue regarding the use of commercial property taxes. As in the case of payroll and turnover taxes, the issue arises from the location of residences and businesses. As discussed earlier, apartheid policies zoned economic activities in WLAs and provided these jurisdictions with exclusive access to commercial property taxes. Given that economic activities will remain "locked in" in the former WLAs for some time to come, a case can be made on redistributive grounds for the sharing of revenues from commercial property between the municipalities and the metro tier.

Surcharges on municipal services: If current municipal services are privatized, local authorities could preserve their access to revenues from water and electricity by converting the implicit surcharges into explicit excise taxes on utility services. In order to minimize locational effects and tax avoidance, and given that the services will be delivered at the metropolitan level, such taxes should be assessed and collected on a uniform basis at the metropolitan rather than the municipal level. If fiscal transfers to low-income households are financed by explicit taxes on these services, it may be administratively easier to have the service providers act as administrators of the taxes and subsidies. Alternatively, the service provider could provide cross-subsidies between households with differing incomes through the pricing of the services – a less preferable option given the potential of distorting prices and, once introduced, the tendency of the public sector to "tax" private entities through greater cross-subsidies (RDP 1995).

In sum, with a two-tier metropolitan system it may be efficient and equitable to assign central fiscal transfers, payroll and turnover taxes, and excise taxes to the metropolitan tier. Residential property taxes would remain at the municipal level while taxes on commercial property could be shared between the two tiers. This tax assignment is based on the allocation of expenditure suggested earlier, which included giving the metro tier the primary role in income redistribution while privatizing the basic municipal services. The assignment is also based on minimizing potential locational inefficiencies and providing a check on the extent to which metropolitan governments can undertake redistribution of income.

6. CONCLUSION

The structure of urban governance in the major metropolitan areas of South Africa is undergoing a dramatic transformation. The model of separate municipalities has given rise to a hybrid metropolitan system in Johannesburg, and the same is expected in the other major cities. Abolishing the racial basis of the cities, distributional concerns, and the legacy of apartheid's spatial policies were major determinants of the choice of a metropolitan system. Establishing greater fiscal autonomy – for local authorities from central government and for municipalities from the metropolitan tier – was an important consideration favoring a two-tier structure. Within this structure, capital market and fiscal stability concerns suggest that the financing and delivery of municipal services should be privatized where possible. In turn, the division of labor between the public and private sector offers the metropolitan tier an exclusive redistributive function – equalizing fiscal capacity and allocating fiscal transfers to households. Clearly, no one structure of urban governance will be optimal; as the economy of South Africa changes and the legacy of apartheid disappears, urban governance will also need to change. How to induce this flexibility in the structure of South Africa's metropolises is yet one more challenge facing urban leadership.

NOTES

1. With apologies to President Mandela (1994).
2. For a detailed analysis of the history and nature of urban planning under apartheid, see Turok (1994) and Swilling, Humphries, and Subhane (1991).
3. These were often separated by tracts of empty land designed to act as buffer zones. Local jurisdictions were also created for "colored" and Indian populations. Along with the BLAs and WLAs, these will be amalgamated into the metropolitan structures described here.
4. In addition to the opportunity cost of time and the direct cost of commuting imposed on black households, the spatial policies had an economywide impact by impeding the functioning of land, labor, and housing markets (World Bank 1991).
5. To ensure access to these surcharges, WLAs were given monopoly rights to deliver municipal services in their areas.

6. See also Swilling et al. (1991) for an analysis of why the zoning of economic activities in the WLAs enabled white residents to benefit from lower per-unit charges on the price of electricity compared to black households.

7. The RSCs had additional responsibilities, which differed by province. In the former Cape Province, for example, RSCs also financed rural services. In the Natal Province, RSCs were called Joint Service Boards and differed in terms of the voting power in the Board. Across all RSCs, however, the voting power of officials representing their local authorities was based on the consumption of electricity in their jurisdictions. This obviously gave representatives of WLAs a voting majority.

8. The taxonomy adopted here to describe the various structures of urban governance is borrowed from Bahl and Linn (1992).

9. In this paper, Musgrave's original definition of the stability function of government has been extended to include macroeconomic instability as described in Section 4.4. I would like to thank David Wildasin for emphasizing this point.

10. Community leaders now face the challenge of harnessing this tradition and converting it into active political participation, rather than maintaining rent and payments boycotts that were characteristic of the fight against apartheid.

11. Although residential relocation will dominate as a means for the black community to access better employment and service opportunities, job relocation toward the township is also beginning to emerge. Data on this issue is rather sparse, but recent surveys from Soweto, for example, suggest that land prices over the last two years have increased significantly at the center of the township, with some land values similar in magnitude to the land prices in Johannesburg and its rich northern suburbs. It is hypothesized that most of this appreciation is a result of increased commercial activities (Eckert 1994). Nevertheless, it is quite likely that formal manufacturing and service industries will move into the black communities at a slow pace. The substantial infrastructure advantage, preexisting economies of agglomeration, and perceived racial and security issues will continue to "lock in" industries and business in the former white areas.

12. They may also impact adversely on equity. There is no obvious reason why taxpayers with similar preferences and in the same income bracket should have to bear higher fiscal burdens depending on the place of residence; conversely, there is no reason why the benefits provided to the poor in some localities should be more generous than the benefits provided to the poor in other areas.

13. Particularly relevant in the case of South Africa is the local government's ability to respond rapidly to emerging squatter camps and other emergency population movements, which will likely require redistributive measures (Wildasin 1993b).

14. Preliminary estimates suggest that for Johannesburg, Cape Town, Durban, and Port Elizabeth, investments in the order of 4–8% of annual GDP will be required to improve the level of basic residential services being received by the black community (World Bank 1994b). South Africa is unique in Africa, and also relative to its stage of economic development, in having a relatively

well-developed private financial system capable of mobilizing such funds. In addition to a well-developed commercial and merchant banking structure, South Africa has particularly strong contractual savings institutions – private insurance companies and pension funds. In fact, assets of insurance companies and pension funds correspond to 80% of GNP – higher than in the United States and Canada – and South Africa has the highest level of insurance premium relative to GNP in the world (Vittas 1994). Local capital markets therefore have long-term money that can be invested in municipalities and cities.

15. See Wildasin (1995) for a general discussion of possible savings and consumption response to public-sector borrowing by households in the case of South Africa.

16. The importance of urban investments is underscored by the fact that such capital investments are a prerequisite for fostering improvements in the economic status of the black community (RDP 1995).

17. See Bahl and Linn (1992) and McLure (1994) for a discussion of different tax instruments available for urban governments.

18. In an interesting study of cities in the United States, Rusk (1993) shows that cities with both vacant land to develop and the political and legal tools to annex adjacent areas had higher bond ratings. In other words, flexible boundaries and existing wider boundaries were perceived by capital markets to have *reduced the risk* of a loss of fiscal capacity as a result of locational decisions by businesses and firms. This will be an important consideration for institutional investors in the case of South Africa.

19. See Villani (1994) on the benefits of project finance and revenue bonds over general obligation borrowing by local governments.

20. In a global review of the experience of government intervention in credit allocation, a World Bank (1990) report concludes as follows: "It is clear that they [directed credit programs] have damaged financial systems. . . . The distorted allocation of resources and the erosion of financial discipline have left intermediaries unprofitable and, in many cases, insolvent. . . . The adverse impact is clearest in the case of development finance institutions."

21. The development finance institutions in South Africa that were designed to prop up the apartheid structure are examples from the country's recent past.

22. Such control of the functioning of labor markets was, of course, precisely the objective of the spatial polices of apartheid.

23. Furthermore, competitive pressure improves the operational efficiency of the delivery system, another important factor favoring privatization of public functions.

24. Klein and Roger (1994) provide an excellent discussion of how the public sector can stimulate competition in sectors that exhibit lumpiness in investment. They call this competition *for* the market as opposed to competition *in* the market. A critical prerequisite includes multiple service providers in the same sector or a system to regulate "natural monopolies" (see the discussion in Section 5.3).

25. See FGIC (1992, 1993) for a detailed analysis of the mechanism behind bond insurance. As summarized in FGIC (1992), bond insurance is a form of credit

enhancement. An insured bond receives a higher rating than it would on its own merits, and consequently has a lower total interest cost and greater marketability. Rating agencies judge the quality of insured bonds not on the strength of the issuer but rather on the claims-paying capacity of the insurer. In effect, bond insurers let issuers "borrow" their credit ratings and collect insurance premiums in return (FGIC 1993). In the United States, bond insurance has become a common feature in the bond market. In 1992, approximately 40% of the new bond issues were insured; in 1982, the figure was only 8.7%.

26. Overall, problems of incentive incompatibility and asymmetric information between different tiers of government are important determinants of the problems associated with fiscal transfers.

27. A surcharge on the national tax base may be the best option for accessing "own revenues" for the newly formed provinces in South Africa (McLure 1994). Otherwise, there will be a significant difference in fiscal autonomy between the provinces and their metropolitan areas. Indeed, the fiscal relationship between the metropolitan areas and the provinces may be a source of political tension in the future. The root of the problem is the political decision to create regional state governments in a predominantly urbanized society (McLure 1994).

28. The experience of Minneapolis–St. Paul in metropolitan tax-base sharing provides an interesting case study of how fiscal disparities were reduced across 188 municipalities (Rusk 1993).

29. It may be more appropriate for the national government to *finance* a voucher program; its *implementation* could be a metropolitan responsibility.

30. See Wildasin (1993b), McLure (1994), and Ahmad (1995) for an analysis of (i) the efficiency of existing local taxes; (ii) alternate fiscal instruments for local governments; and (iii) the efficiency and equity implications of relying on central tax bases for financing local infrastructure investments.

31. The incidence of payroll and turnover taxes will, in fact, be spread more widely than within the metro area, as in the case of Johannesburg. Hence there may be a case for sharing these revenues nationally and not just on a metropolitan basis. However, this might reduce the fiscal autonomy of the metropolitan tier, as the metros would then rely more on transfers from other tiers. This tradeoff between the efficiency of tax instruments and the autonomy of metropolitan governments is better addressed by replacing payroll and turnover taxes with alternative fiscal instruments. For a discussion of this point see Wildasin (1993b) and McLure (1994).

REFERENCES*

Ahmad, Junaid (1995), "Funding the Metropolitan Areas of South Africa," *Finance and Development* 32: 50-3.

Bahl, Roy, and Johannes Linn (1992), *Urban Public Finance in Developing Countries*. Oxford University Press.

Baumol, William, and Kyu Sik Lee (1991), "Contestable Markets, Trade and Development," *World Bank Economic Observer* 6: 110-23.

Bruckner, Jan K. (1994), "Welfare Gains from Removing Land-Use Distortions," AF1EI Working Paper, World Bank, Washington, DC.
Dillinger, W. (1994), "Decentralization and Its Implication for Service Delivery," Working Paper, World Bank, Washington, DC.
Eckert, J. (1994), "Land Prices in Greater Johannesburg," AF1EI Policy Note, World Bank, Washington, DC.
Financial Guarantee Insurance Company [FGIC] (1992), "An Introduction to Financial Guarantee Insurance Company," FGIC Report, GE Capital, New York.
Financial Guarantee Insurance Company [FGIC] (1993), "Municipal Bonds: Investing in America's Future," FGIC Report, GE Capital, New York.
Klein, Michael, and Neil D. Roger (1994), "Back to the Future: The Potential in Infrastructure Privatization," *Finance and International Economy* 8: 1-28.
Mandela, Nelson (1994), *A Long Walk to Freedom*. Boston: Little, Brown.
Mayo, S. (1994), "Housing Policy Reform in South Africa," in *AF1EI Housing Aide Memoire - South Africa*. Washington, DC: World Bank.
McLure, Charles (1994), "Intergovernmental Fiscal Relations in South Africa," AF1EI Working Paper, World Bank, Washington, DC.
Musgrave, Richard A. (1959), *The Theory of Public Finance*. New York: McGraw-Hill.
Musgrave, Richard A. (1983), "Who, What, Where?" in C. McLure (ed.), *Tax Assignment in Federal States*. Canberra: Australian National University.
Reconstruction and Development Program [RDP] (1995), "Urban Infrastructure Program," Draft Report, State President's Office, Pretoria, South Africa.
Rusk, David (1993), *Cities Without Suburbs*. Princeton, NJ: Woodrow Wilson Center Press.
Swilling, Mark, Richard Humphries, and Khehla Subhane (1991), *Apartheid City in Transition*. Cape Town: Oxford University Press.
Tiebout, Charles (1956), "A Pure Theory of Local Expenditures," *Journal of Political Economy* 64: 416-24.
Turok, Ivan (1994), "Urban Planning in the Transition from Apartheid," *Town & Planning Review* 65: 355-65.
Villani, Kevin (1994), "Financing Infrastructure," AF1EI Working Paper, World Bank, Washington, DC.
Vittas, Dimitri (1994), "Policy Issues in Contractual Savings in South Africa," Informal Paper, World Bank, Washington, DC.
von Hagen, Jurgen (1991), "A Note on the Empirical Effectiveness of Formal Fiscal Restraints," *Journal of Public Economics* 44: 199-210.
Wildasin, David E. (1993a), "Local Finance of Urban Infrastructure in South Africa," AF1EI Working Paper, World Bank, Washington, DC.
Wildasin, David E. (1993b), "The Economics of Urban Governance in South Africa," AF1EI Working Paper, World Bank, Washington, DC.
Wildasin, David E. (1995), "Financing Local Government Capital Outlays in South Africa," AF1EI Working Paper, World Bank, Washington, DC.
World Bank (1990), "Financial Systems and Development," Policy and Research Series no. 15, World Bank, Washington, DC.
World Bank (1991), *AF1EI Urban Sector Aide Memoire - South Africa*. Washington, DC: World Bank.

World Bank (1994a), *AFIEI Housing Aide Memoire – South Africa.* Washington, DC: World Bank.

World Bank (1994b), "Financing Metropolitan Areas," South Africa Informal Discussion Paper no. 8, World Bank, Washington, DC.

* AFIEI aide memoires and working papers may be obtained from the Southern Africa Department of the World Bank. Other World Bank papers may be obtained directly from their respective authors.

CHAPTER 9

Computable General Equilibrium in Local Public Finance and Fiscal Federalism:
Applications to Local Taxation, Intergovernmental Aid, and Education Vouchers

Thomas Nechyba

1. INTRODUCTION

Beginning with Harberger's (1962) two-sector investigation of the incidence of the corporate income tax, and culminating in the more recent and more involved applied general equilibrium models reviewed in Shoven and Whalley (1984), computable general equilibrium (CGE) models have a long and rich history in public finance. With the increasing power of computers, these models are now capable of incorporating a level of detail and complexity that is unreachable in simple analytic frameworks. They further reduce the need for economists to restrict themselves to one-dimensional simplifications of multidimensional problems and allow for the analysis of difficult general equilibrium questions and large policy proposals beyond the restrictive context of looking exclusively at "marginal changes."

The intricate and elaborate relationships between national, state, and local governments make research in the areas of fiscal federalism and local public finance a natural candidate for application of this new CGE technology. For example, local governments must balance political interests and the strategic decisions of competing jurisdictions, on the one hand, with the impulse of agents to migrate to other communities – and the effect this has on endogenously determined property values – on the other.[1] In dealing with local communities, state and national governments are forced to take as given these complex determinants of local government behavior and all the implicit constraints they impose on local pol-

The author thanks Marcus Berliant, Jan Brueckner, David Wildasin, Robert Inman, Hideo Konishi, participants of the 1994 ISPE Conference on "Fiscal Aspects of Evolving Federations," and two anonymous referees for helpful comments and discussions, as well as Nathan Hatch for assistance with SAS. The author is particularly indebted to Robert P. Strauss for the generous use of his VAX. All remaining errors are the author's.

168

iticians. Therefore, any serious long-term inquiry into the *hierarchical* government interactions known as fiscal federalism must be based on an informative model of the *horizontal* interactions between local governments known as local public finance. Although it makes analytic treatment of the topic difficult, the complexity of such an approach paves the way for a flexible CGE framework. Such a model may hold the key to answering many open conceptual questions in fiscal federalism and local public finance; moreover, its capacity for evaluating large policy changes is of increasing practical importance as states and nations consider radical ways of changing the nature and mix of state and local roles in providing public goods and services. In addition, a properly parameterized CGE model not only allows us to make qualitative predictions, but also opens the gate for a quantitative evaluation of the microeconomic effects and welfare changes of regional policy proposals in specific state or metropolitan areas.

This paper intends to make a case for CGE models in the area of fiscal federalism and local public finance by first presenting a fairly general model that captures many important features, then summarizing results obtained elsewhere (Nechyba 1997a, 1996a,b) with this framework, and finally pointing to a large number of other potential applications of the model. In the process we hope to show not only that CGE approaches to fiscal federalism are feasible, but also that they offer excellent prospects for gaining greater insights into open questions and quantifying the effects of particular, region-specific policy proposals.

Section 2 begins by formally defining a theoretical model of fiscal federalism as well as a CGE derivative. At the base of the model's fiscal federalism pyramid is an interconnected web of local governments. This local public sector contains all three main features pointed to by Rose-Ackerman (1979) as essential for any satisfactory positive model of local government behavior: mobile residents choosing between multiple communities, a political model of local government decision making, and a land market that can capitalize local policy choices through a competitive price system. To this base of local communities is added a state (or national) government encompassing all local jurisdictions.[2] The model is currently parameterized to micro tax data from several school districts in Camden County, New Jersey, but in principle it can be fitted to a variety of different metropolitan, regional, or state settings. In the public finance literature, this is the first such CGE model based entirely on individual behavior.[3] Section 3 discusses the computation of equilibria for this model, and Section 4 summarizes applications to a variety of research questions as well as potential future directions. In the process, a few illustrative examples are given, but the bulk of the results are reported elsewhere

Table 1. *Summary of computable general equilibrium model including parameter values*

	General model	CGE version and parameters
Community structure	$C = \{C_{mh} \subset N \mid (m,h) \in M \times H\}$	$N = [0,1]$; $M = \{1,2,3\}$; $H = \{1,2,3\}$; $\mu(C_{mh}) = 1/9 \ \forall(m,h)$
Endowment types	$E = \{E_{mhi} \mid (m,h,i) \in M \times H \times I\}$	$I = \{1,2,3,4,5\}$; $\mu(E_{mhi}) = 1/45 \ \forall(m,h,i)$; $(z(e_{mh1}),\ldots,z(e_{mh5})) = (2,3.5,5,6.5,8) \ \forall(m,h)$
Preferences	$U = \{u^2 : M \times H \times \mathbb{R}_+^{\bar{m}+2} \to \mathbb{R}_+ \mid n \in N\}$	$u^n(m,h,x,z) = k_{mh} x_0^\alpha x_m^\beta z^\gamma, \ \forall n \in N$, where $(\alpha,\beta,\gamma) = (0.13, 0.06, 0.64)$ and $(k_{11},\ldots,k_{13},k_{21},\ldots,k_{33})$ $= (0.82, 0.89, 0.96, 0.85, 0.95, 1.05, 0.93, 1.03, 1.13)$
Production of LPGs	$F = \{f_m : \mathbb{R}_+ \to \mathbb{R}_+ \mid m \in M\}$	$f_m(Z_m) = \dfrac{Z_m}{\mu(C_m)} \Rightarrow x_m(t_m) = \dfrac{t_m\, p(C_m)}{\mu(C_m)}$
Production of SPG	$f_0 : \mathbb{R}_+ \to \mathbb{R}_+$	$f_0(Z_0) = \dfrac{Z_0}{\mu(N)} \Rightarrow x_0(t_0) = \dfrac{t_0\, z(N)}{\mu(N)}$

due to space constraints here. Results thus far seem to indicate that this CGE approach offers great prospects for gaining better insight into both theoretical and applied policy questions. Section 5 concludes with some closing remarks.

2. THE MODEL

The computable general equilibrium model developed here is calibrated to New Jersey data and is based on the theoretical model in Nechyba (1994, 1997b), where the existence of an equilibrium is proved.[4] The model takes as given a set of community boundaries that divides a large set of different houses into local political entities, which produce public goods funded through a property tax. An additional political unit called the state (or nation) encompasses all communities and provides a state public good funded through income taxation. There are no a priori restrictions on the mix of house types across communities; that is, some communities may have a fairly homogeneous housing stock while others have both "good" and "bad" houses. Similarly, some communities may be inherently more preferred because of particular community qualities.[5] Hence, the model makes no attempt to explain either the evolution of the housing stock or the formation of communities. Rather, it takes these as having evolved exogenously and resulting from some given history. The model's potentially heterogeneous intracommunity housing structure allows for the possibility of the coexistence of rich and poor sectors within a particular community, a feature not possible in models that view housing as a perfectly divisible, homogeneous good (Epple, Filimon, and Romer 1993; Rose-Ackerman 1979). Consumers own houses and a certain level of private good, both of which are tradeable at market prices, and choose their optimal place of residence given their preferences and budgets. The existence of a land market – rather than housing exogenously supplied by absentee landlords, as is common in the literature (see e.g. Epple et al. 1993) – enables the model to seriously investigate capitalization and its impact on communities. Finally, each agent also votes on the level of local property and state income taxation.

The main elements of the general model and its CGE derivative are summarized formally in Table 1. The set N represents both the set of agents and the set of houses in the model, where $n \in N$ is defined as that agent who is initially endowed with house n.[6] A fixed community structure C is imposed on this set of houses, partitioning it into a set of house types $H = \{1, ..., h, ..., \bar{h}\}$ spread over a set of communities $M = \{1, ..., m, ..., \bar{m}\}$. Thus C_{mh} denotes the set of houses of type h in community m as well as the set of agents initially endowed with such houses. The CGE version presented here defines $N = [0, 1]$, $H = \{1, 2, 3\}$, and $M = \{1, 2, 3\}$, which implies the existence of nine different house endowment types (three house types in each of three communities). Each of these is, for illustration, assumed to be represented in the economy in equal numbers; that is,

$$\mu(C_{mh}) = 1/9. \tag{1}$$

In addition to a house endowment, each agent n is also endowed with a strictly positive amount of private good $z(n)$, called *income*. The set of income levels is assumed to be finite, which gives rise to a set of income classes $I = \{1, ..., i, ..., \bar{\imath}\}$. This implies that the house and income endowments jointly define a set of endowment types

$$E = \{E_{mhi} \,|\, (m, h, i) \in M \times H \times I\}, \tag{2}$$

where $e_{mhi} \in E_{mhi}$ is an agent who falls into income class i and is endowed with a house of type h in community m. Our CGE model contains five of these income classes (with incomes of 2, 3.5, 5, 6.5, and 8 roughly corresponding to household income levels scaled by \$10,000), which – when combined with the three house types in each of three communities – generates 45 endowment types, each of which is (again, for purposes of this illustration) represented equally in the economy:

$$\mu(E_{mhi}) = 1/45 \quad \forall (m, h, i) \in M \times H \times I. \tag{3}$$

Agents are endowed with a utility function $u^n \colon M \times H \times \mathbb{R}_+^{\bar{m}+2} \to \mathbb{R}_+$, which takes as its arguments the community and house type the agent lives in, private good consumption $z \in \mathbb{R}_+$, and a vector of public goods $(x_0, x_1, ..., x_{\bar{m}}) \in \mathbb{R}_+^{\bar{m}+1}$, where x_0 is the state public good (SPG) and x_m (for $m \in M$) is the local public good (LPG) produced in community m. In the CGE version, all agents have the same utility function, which is defined so as to exclude the possibility of spillovers between jurisdictions:[7]

$$u^n(m, h, x, z) = k_{mh} x_0^\alpha x_m^\beta z^\gamma \quad \forall n \in N.[8] \tag{4}$$

State and local public goods are, for now, produced according to production technologies defined by a set of production functions

$$F = \{f_i \colon \mathbb{R}_+ \to \mathbb{R}_+ \,|\, i \in 0 \cup M\}$$

that convert private goods directly into public goods. Suppose that total spending on the national public good level is Z_0 and that total spending on the public good in community m is Z_m. In the CGE model, we define public good levels as per-capita spending on the good:[9]

$$f_0(Z_0) = \frac{Z_0}{\mu(N)}, \qquad f_m(Z_m) = \frac{Z_m}{\mu(C_m)} \quad \text{for } m \in M,[10] \tag{5}$$

where $\mu(N)$ is the size (measure) of the total population and $\mu(C_m)$ is the size (measure) of the local population. (For local public goods, for example, $f_m(Z_m)$ can be interpreted as per-pupil spending on education.) The SPG is financed through a proportional income tax t_0; LPGs are funded through proportional property taxes. All tax rates are set through absolute majority-rule voting by members of the relevant constituencies, who are assumed to be myopic in the sense that they take community composition and property values as given when they go to the polls. (This is, however, restrictive only out of equilibrium.[11]) Because local budgets must balance, the relationship between t_m and x_m is one-to-one and is defined by

$$x_m(t_m) = \frac{t_m \, p(C_m)}{\mu(C_m)} \quad \forall m \in M. \tag{6}$$

Here $p(C_m) = \Sigma_{h \in H}(\mu(C_{mh})\bar{p}(C_{mh}))$ is the local property tax base. This tax base varies with the endogenously determined house price function $\bar{p}: M \times H \to \mathbb{R}_+$ and so gives rise to a house price vector $\mathbf{p} \in \mathbb{R}_+^{\bar{m}h}$; that is, the function $\bar{p}$ assigns a unique price to each house type in each jurisdiction. This, combined with myopic voting and standard assumptions on preferences and technologies, is shown in Nechyba (1994, 1997b) to yield single-peaked preferences over LPG levels (or, equivalently, over local property tax rates), which in turn implies the existence of local voting equilibria.[12]

Agents are also assumed to be myopic in their location decisions: they take prices, other public good levels, and other agents' locations as given. An equilibrium is simply defined as follows.

Definition. An *equilibrium* (J, p, t, x) is a list of population assignments to communities J, prices p, tax rates t, and public good levels x such that:[13]

(i) prices clear the market (i.e., there is no excess demand or supply for any house);
(ii) all government budgets balance;
(iii) consumers cannot gain utility by moving; and
(iv) local property and state income tax rates are determined through majority-rule voting.

Calibration of the Model

The utility function is parameterized to be consistent with data from several school districts in Camden County, New Jersey. Other parameters, such as endowments and community sizes, were arbitrarily fixed. The calibration described here is therefore "partial" in the sense that, whereas

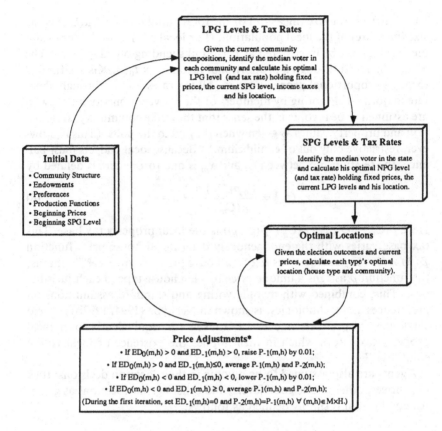

Figure 1. CGE program to calculate an equilibrium. *Note:* $ED_0(m, h)$ and $ED_{-1}(m, h)$ stand for excess demand for (m, h) during the current and previous iterations, respectively. $P_{-1}(m, h)$ and $P_{-2}(m, h)$ stand for the prices of (m, h) one and two iterations prior to the current iteration.

parameter values are picked to be consistent with data, the benchmark equilibrium (reported in Table 2A) is *computed* and then observed to be consistent with the data. Owing to space considerations, the specifics of this parameterization are not reported here; they can be found in Nechyba (1994, 1997a).

3. COMPUTATION OF EQUILIBRIA

The CGE program (illustrated in Figure 1) begins with the information contained in Table 1 as well as a vector of initial house prices and an initial level of the SPG. It iterates to an equilibrium by first finding local and

Table 2

	Income	Wealth	Property	Con-sumption	Property tax	LPG
A. Benchmark equilibrium with local property taxes						
Community 1	3.3000	4.3900	0.6550	2.9462	0.4247	0.2782
Community 2	5.2000	6.3027	1.0250	4.0753	0.3880	0.3977
Community 3	6.5000	7.5573	1.5700	4.5568	0.2706	0.4248
B. GE effect of community 2's unilateral introduction of a 3% income tax						
Community 1	3.8000	4.6447	0.6538	3.1093	0.4433	0.2989
Community 2	4.2000	5.5670	1.0153	3.5667	0.2019	0.3310
Community 3	7.0000	8.0309	1.5737	4.8659	0.3185	0.5012
C. GE effect of simultaneous introduction of a 3% income tax						
Community 1	3.2840	4.2865	0.6234	2.8839	0.2618	0.2617
Community 2	5.5123	6.4362	1.0323	4.1052	0.2565	0.4301
Community 3	6.2038	7.5188	1.5858	4.5337	0.1485	0.4217

Note: For a more complete set of results, see Nechyba (1997a).

state election outcomes, then determining equilibrium prices given those outcomes, then using those prices (and the new community compositions) to update election results, and so forth. During each major iteration, the program iterates to find prices for given election outcomes.[14] Throughout, the value of each agent's *initial* house is used to determine that agent's budget. Values typically converge within ten major iterations and – owing to the uniqueness of equilibrium assignments of agents into house types and communities – are only slightly sensitive to initial prices.[15]

Average community values for several variables are reported in Table 2A.[16] Local and state public good levels can be interpreted as per-capita spending by local and state governments. The LPG figures fall within the actual range of per-pupil spending on education (roughly between $2,500 and $5,000 in 1987) for Camden County, and the SPG level (of 0.7737, not reported in the table) is close to the combined per-capita state and national spending. Agents in the model separate into low-, middle-, and high-income communities, with higher-income communities tending to have higher LPG levels and lower property tax rates, and with property values (the value of yearly housing services) tending to increase in community wealth. Although there is significant stratification along income and wealth levels, the overlapping values of the k_{mh} (see Table 1) prevent this stratification from being complete. The resulting intracommunity mixing of income types makes many policy questions significantly more interesting, as we can now investigate to what extent government action can facilitate or discourage such mixing. It may, for example, be desirable to encourage wealthy agents to migrate to poor communities since this would tend to equalize fiscal disparities. On the other hand, some policies may unintentionally encourage migration in the opposite direction and thus cause unforeseen inequities. A model whose equilibria were completely stratified along income lines could not address such issues.[17]

4. Applications of a CGE Model of Fiscal Federalism and Local Public Finance

The CGE model outlined here can be used to investigate a variety of conceptual and policy-related questions. Carefully defined simulations begin at the benchmark equilibrium and proceed by introducing a discrete policy change at the local and/or state level. A new equilibrium is then calculated in the same manner as in Figure 1, except that the "Initial Data" is now the benchmark equilibrium.

Thus far, three sets of issues have been addressed in Nechyba (1997a, 1996a,b) using this CGE simulation approach – one conceptual, the others policy-oriented. The first begins with the following old (but still open) question in public finance: Why, despite evidence indicating strong voter dissatisfaction with it, do local governments in the United States use property taxes to the virtual exclusion of all other forms of taxes? Furthermore, when public sentiment against the property tax gain sufficient momentum, why is it that state rather than local governments give in to voter demands to change the local tax systems?[18] The second set of questions deals with the relative effectiveness – in a general equilibrium world – of such state or national programs as redistributive revenue sharing, district power equalization, deductibility of local taxes, and the creation of enterprise zones. Particular attention is paid to questions concerning the extent to which various formulations of these programs achieve the dual policy goals of increasing the overall level of local public goods while decreasing their interjurisdictional variance. Finally, the third set of questions surrounds the effects of private school vouchers on a local public finance economy. In particular, when the model is expanded to allow for both the entrance of private (cream-skimming) schools and the presence of peer externalities in the production of schooling (the LPG), what will be the effect of private school vouchers on both public school quality and community compositions? We will begin with an overview of past results (Sections 4.1–4.3) and proceed by speculating on future applications (Section 4.4). We are constrained by space limitations to only summarizing results here, but complement that summary with occasional numerical examples. For the full simulation results and procedures see Nechyba (1997a, 1996a,b).

4.1. Local Income and Property Taxation

The use of property taxes to finance local public goods in general and education in particular is so predominant in the United States that it can hardly be dismissed as a mere historical accident. In 1988–89, for example, over 97% of local tax revenues raised by politically independent U.S. school districts were raised through property taxes (Strauss 1993). At the same time, however, public disdain for this method of taxation and its alleged inequities is widespread and growing. Although voters seem to be demanding a change (rather than a reduction) in the funding of public goods (Courant, Gramlich, and Rubinfeld 1980), local politicians are leaving it to higher levels of government to respond to these demands (through tax limitations and grants-in-aid). The result of such tax limitation measures in the United States has been a shift from financing LPGs solely through property taxation to using state income taxes as well (De Tray and Fernandez 1986).[19] We therefore must explain not only (i) why the property tax (rather than something like an income tax) has become the primary local tax strategy,[20] but also (ii) why, when confronted with political pressures against the property tax, local governments leave the response to states and stubbornly refuse to change their local tax apparatus.

A slight modification to the theoretical model of the local public sector outlined in Section 2 provides a partial explanation to this puzzle. In particular, suppose that we endogenize the choice over local tax systems by placing a nonmyopic community planner in charge of setting a local income tax rate and then allowing the local electorate to set the property tax.[21] Under certain restrictive conditions,[22] it can be shown that a unilateral increase in the local income tax by a single community planner would cause a pattern of migration in which every agent who leaves the community as a result of the tax policy change is replaced by an agent with less income (Nechyba 1994, 1997a). Note that this does not imply that high-income agents leave to be replaced by low-income agents, but rather that a low-income agent who leaves will be replaced by someone with still less income. The intuition for this is straightforward: a revenue-neutral tax policy shift away from the property tax and toward the income tax will benefit those residents (and potential residents) whose income/property ratio is low at the expense of agents whose income/property ratio is high. Thus we can look at each house in the community that is imposing a higher income tax and, if prices are sticky in the short run, determine that a current resident who leaves must be replaced by someone with less income. (If this were not true then the latter agent would have preferred this house to his or her original house even without the tax change, which would imply that we were originally not at an equilibrium.) A unilateral shift from the local property tax to a local income tax is therefore equivalent to a shift toward a tax base that is shrinking. On the other hand, a unilateral move away from the income tax and toward the property tax causes precisely the opposite: every agent that leaves the community as a result of the policy change is replaced by someone with more income.

As we have indicated, this analytic explanation is derived under rather restrictive conditions. In particular, these restrictions preclude general equilibrium adjustments in property values and local public good levels, both of which may be of interest to a farsighted community planner and would be part of a long-run general equilibrium explanation. However, the complexity of the factors involved in choosing local tax systems precludes us from fully treating the problem analytically and also from quantifying the predictions that we can make. Furthermore, in the presence of opposing forces within the model, theoretical treatments can give neither quantitative nor qualitative answers. For example, a move away from the property tax may raise property values, but the loss in community income (and thus the loss of part of the community tax base) due to migration may cause a drop in the level of local services and an increase in local taxes, both of which would cause property values to fall.

The CGE model from Section 2, however, can shed further light on these issues. In particular, simulations (in Nechyba 1994, 1997a) of different actions by the local community planner demonstrate that a unilateral move toward a local income tax lowers not only community income but also property values and average community wealth, as well as utility, consumption, and local public good levels. The general equilibrium migration effects that decrease community income and wealth thus actually cause a *reduction* in property values when local income taxes are introduced (despite the fact that property is now taxed at a lower rate) as well as a reduction in the size of local government. Most agents from the community (including the median voter) end up paying more local taxes in the long run even if their income/property ratio causes their tax burden initially (before migrations) to fall. In addition, they are receiving lower levels of public services. On the other hand, a unilateral move away from income taxation and toward property taxes has precisely the opposite effect: community income rises together with all other variables, including property values (despite the fact that property is now taxed at a higher rate) and local public good levels. Sample values for a unilateral income tax of 3% (in "community 2") are provided in Table 2B.[23]

The combination of the analytic approach – which provides hints at a possible answer to our puzzle – and the CGE simulations therefore provides a powerful argument against local communities making unilateral use of the income tax, even if a myopic local electorate is dissatisfied with the property tax. Because the results are driven by general equilibrium migration effects, the only effective way for a community to introduce a local income tax is to prevent its residents from migrating. Aside from undemocratic restrictions on the freedom to move, this can most easily be accomplished by colluding with other communities to raise local income taxes jointly (so that agents cannot avoid the local income tax by moving). However, such a collusive agreement is not enforceable because, as demonstrated by the CGE simulations, it would always be in each community's best interest to violate this agreement. Thus, the uniform introduction of local income taxes can most effectively be achieved by a state or national government that imposes an income tax and then distributes revenues back to local communities. Such a scheme can be shown in this CGE model to eliminate adverse general equilibrium migration and price effects, and represents precisely what has happened to school districts in states like Michigan and California. (Table 2C reports the general equilibrium effects of a statewide income tax of 3% where all revenues are returned to local jurisdictions.) The model therefore offers one explanation for both the limited local use of income taxes and the widespread efforts by states to undermine local property tax systems. Yet the explanation can arise only in a general equilibrium model rich enough to include: many communities among which agents can choose, the possibility of both income and property tax systems, and an initial equilibrium in which communities are not completely homogeneous. The CGE model thus makes possible an interaction between theory and simulation results, which can yield new insights that would be difficult to obtain with a purely analytic approach.

4.2. Redistributive Grants, District Power Equalization, and Local Deductibility

The stated intention behind most intergovernmental programs is twofold: (i) to correct for the underprovision of LPGs by raising their production in all communities,[24] and (ii) to adjust perceived inequities in the provision of LPGs.[25] The following three categories of intergovernmental grants have been evaluated in the context of the model outlined in Section 2 in terms of their effectiveness in achieving these goals (Nechyba 1994, 1996a): redistributive state grants, district power equalization, and the deductibility of local taxes. Again, a combination of theory and simulation results are used to illustrate the differences in these programs with respect to their structure and effects. That different levels of government use different tax bases, a fact usually ignored in the analysis of governmental interaction, plays a crucial role in both interjurisdictional and interpersonal redistribution. Furthermore, when these programs are defined broadly, it is demonstrated analytically that for every matching grant system there exists both an equivalent district power equalization program and an equivalent deductibility scheme, and vice versa.

In the simulations, previous partial equilibrium results are shown to be robust under general equilibrium simulations that allow for property value adjustments and migration. Programs that focus on lowering tax prices, for example, are shown to be significantly more effective at raising LPG levels than equally funded programs that merely transfer revenues among jurisdictions. Thus, because of their price effects, matching grants are substantially more effective than block grants in persuading voters to lower their private consumption in favor of LPGs; however, unlike block grants, they may cause voters to significantly reduce the SPG. Furthermore, since grants must be funded endogenously in the general equilibrium model, block grants can never raise LPG levels in all communities and produce only slight increases in some communities. In contrast, matching grants can – owing to their strong price effects – achieve dramatic universal increases in LPGs. In addition, by causing relatively larger price effects in poor communities, they are also more effective than block grants at reducing interjurisdictional variance in public spending. Neither grant type shows much consistent superiority in reducing disparities in fiscal capacities, but both (and especially matching grants) benefit residents of poor districts at the expense of residents elsewhere by raising their property values relative to those in other communities. Tables 3A and 3B report equilibria for one example of equally funded block and matching grants. More detailed results are reported elsewhere (Nechyba 1994, 1996a).[26]

Because the results thus far indicate superior performance by matching grants in the dual policy goal of increasing overall LPG spending and decreasing interjurisdictional variance, a focus on specific types of matching grant programs is warranted. One program often proposed is district power equalization (DPE), under which the state sets a guaranteed tax base for communities by transferring tax bases from rich to poor districts. This program can focus solely on interjurisdictional redistribution when it relies on transferring local tax bases between communities *without* using the state income tax system, or it can lift tax bases in low-income communities without lowering bases in wealthy districts by subsidizing the system through the state income tax. It is essentially a matching grant program with possibly negative matching rates for wealthy communities, so both the former (revenue-neutral) and latter types of DPE are shown to be quite effective in reducing the variance of LPG levels across jurisdictions – both in the short run and, contrary to past findings (Inman and Rubinfeld 1979), in the long run.[27] In fact, when bases are equalized completely, LPG levels actually vary *inversely* with community income and wealth, a result consistent with Feldstein's (1975) estimates. (Table 3C presents such an equilibrium with full revenue-neutral DPE.) When DPE is modified to ensure positive matching rates everywhere (and is thus funded through the state income tax), variance in local fiscal variables across juris-

Table 3

	Income	Wealth	Property	Con-sumption	Property tax	LPG
A. GE effect of a redistributive block grant funded by a 3% state income tax						
Community 1	3.2000	4.2962	0.6745	2.9074	0.1711	0.2654
Community 2	5.3000	6.3926	1.0226	4.1007	0.2714	0.4275
Community 3	6.5000	7.5624	1.5542	4.5207	0.1744	0.4211
B. GE effect of a redistributive matching grant funded by a 3% state income tax						
Community 1	3.6000	4.4412	0.6866	2.8336	0.3880	0.3736
Community 2	5.3000	6.3145	1.0198	3.9495	0.3753	0.4977
Community 3	6.1000	7.4919	1.5420	4.4312	0.2656	0.5263
C. GE effect of full revenue-neutral DPE						
Community 1	3.8000	4.7165	0.7462	3.0848	0.3916	0.4073
Community 2	4.9000	6.1059	1.0322	3.9225	0.3741	0.3891
Community 3	6.3000	7.3916	1.4356	4.5439	0.2985	0.3104
D. GE effect of 100% deductibility of local taxes when bottom ⅓ do not itemize						
Community 1	3.1500	4.2142	0.6598	2.7965	0.4292	0.2832
Community 2	5.0500	6.2721	1.0250	4.0495	0.4109	0.4212
Community 3	6.8000	7.7685	1.5700	4.6538	0.3196	0.5018

Note: For a more complete set of results, see Nechyba (1996a).

dictions does not fall by as much but LPG levels rise higher in wealthier communities. At the same time, however, the SPG level may suffer. Thus, by varying matching rates – even allowing them to become negative – the gains in equity and general LPG levels can be traded off easily, and the cost to the state government in terms of its reduction in size can be adjusted to desired levels. This CGE treatment therefore represents a first step in setting up a framework to analyze these tradeoffs in a general equilibrium environment, and so provides a tool for policy makers to analyze competing proposals.

Finally, making local tax payments deductible on state income tax forms constitutes yet another popular form of matching grants (where grants here are given to voters directly rather than to the local government). Uniform deductibility causes no migration and no changes in property values when all agents itemize, and, through uniform matching rates, produces relatively equal increases in LPGs and decreases in private good consumption in all communities. However, in the presence of poor residents who do not itemize deductions on their income tax returns, uniform deductibility causes increases in interjurisdictional inequities: fewer residents in poor communities benefit from the program (which causes LPG levels to rise substantially faster in wealthier communities), and income and wealth migrate from poor communities to wealthy ones as the latter become relatively more desirable (owing to relatively higher LPG levels). (Table 3D reports the equilibrium when local taxes are fully deductible and the bottom third of the income distribution does not itemize.) On the other hand, targeting deductibility to needy "enterprise zones" can have substantial positive equity implications.

4.3. Education, Peer Effects, and Private School Vouchers

Thus far, we have reported results that inform on theoretical questions (Section 4.1) as well as traditional applied questions in the study of fiscal federalism (Section 4.2). We proceed by discussing a final set of results that deals with a more recent policy issue in local public finance: the impact of private school vouchers on public school quality. Since there exists virtually no empirical evidence on this issue, we consider it an ideal candidate for applied research using our methodology. In this section, we will sketch a few results from ongoing CGE research applied to this model (Nechyba 1996b).

In the previous literature (see e.g. Manski 1992), two effects of a voucher policy have been hypothesized: (i) increased competition from private schools could cause higher productivity of public schools as they put forth greater effort (and seek fewer rents) in order to retain students; and (ii) private schools might "cream-skim" the best students from the public schools. The first of these effects implies that public school quality would improve as a result of private school vouchers, whereas the latter – assuming peer quality is an important input to the quality of school output – implies that private school vouchers may worsen public schools. Disagreement as to which of these effects dominates is central to the policy debate surrounding vouchers.

In Nechyba (1996b) we use a modification of the CGE framework to demonstrate that additional effects are present when we explicitly model not only the public–private choice currently modeled in the literature but also the public–public choice inherent in a Tiebout economy with free mobility. In other words, we extend previous work of Epple and Romano (1994) and Manski (1992) by incorporating the choice parents face between public and private schools into our Tiebout economy, in which parents can choose to relocate. Furthermore, we add school peer effects to the Tiebout model by assuming that both per-pupil spending and peer quality (represented by average family income of those attending the school) enter into school production functions.[28]

The presence of these school peer effects causes substantial increases in interjurisdictional stratification and inequities in the provision of public

Table 4

	Income	Wealth	Property	Property tax	School quality[a]	LPSpend[b]	% private
A. Benchmark equilibrium without peer effects							
Community 1	3.3000	4.3900	0.6550	0.4247	0.2782	0.2782	0.0000
Community 2	5.2000	6.3027	1.0250	0.3880	0.3977	0.3977	0.0000
Community 3	6.5000	7.5573	1.5700	0.2706	0.4248	0.4248	0.0000
B. Equilibrium with peer effects but without private schools							
Community 1	3.0000	3.8773	0.4983	0.5671	0.2377	0.2826	0.0000
Community 2	5.0000	6.1405	1.0325	0.4017	0.3718	0.4147	0.0000
Community 3	7.0000	8.2925	1.7800	0.2863	0.4877	0.5097	0.0000
C. Equilibrium with peer effects and private schools							
Community 1	3.4000	4.3009	0.5325	0.5325	0.2523	0.3109	0.0667
Community 2	4.6000	5.7523	1.0075	0.3976	0.3505	0.4006	0.0000
Community 3	7.0000	8.2684	1.7683	0.2861	0.4859	0.5060	0.0000
D. Equilibrium with peer effects, private schools, and vouchers = $1,000							
Community 1	4.0000	4.7591	0.5783	0.5207	0.2798	0.4517	0.3333
Community 2	4.8000	5.8057	1.0325	0.3449	0.3431	0.4856	0.2667
Community 3	6.2000	7.7313	1.6833	0.2730	0.4359	0.4596	0.0000

Note: For a more complete set of results, see Nechyba (1996b).
[a] Public school quality.
[b] Per-pupil spending in the local public school.

schools. (See e.g. the results reported in Tables 4A and 4B.) Even under zero peer effects (Table 4A), we expect disparities to arise owing to different demands for public spending by different income groups in different communities; the presence of peer effects that are correlated with socioeconomic status provides additional incentives for high-income types to separate into their own communities.[29] Thus, all else being equal, peer effects cause increases in income stratification.

As peer effects become more important, however, all else does not remain equal. In particular, high–peer-quality effects give an added incentive to high-income individuals to opt out of the public system and create private schools that cater to their peer quality (Table 4C). The first to opt out of the public system are high-income parents who live in high-income communities. Once they choose not to take advantage of the relatively good public schools in their community, these high-income residents choose to outbid current residents of good houses in the lower-income communities because it no longer makes sense to pay higher (capitalized) house prices and higher tax payments in the high-income community to support a public school system they no longer take advantage of. So long as there exists some relatively desirable housing in lower-income communities, those (high-income) agents who choose private schools therefore settle in poorer communities. They typically replace relatively higher-peer-quality agents from those communities (who formerly lived there in the more desirable houses). Private schools therefore appear first in poor communities, but they cater not to those originally residing in those communities but rather to high-income immigrants.

General equilibrium simulations show similar patterns of private school development as private school vouchers are introduced into a locally financed public education system (see e.g. Table 4D). As the face value of a voucher (which can be used toward tuition in a private school) rises, private schools arise in the poorer communities as high-income residents migrate to those communities in order to take advantage of lower house prices. These immigrants tend to replace the relatively high-income residents of that community, residents who formerly sent their children to the local public schools. Thus, *while residential stratification decreases, school stratification increases.*[30] It is only when all the "desirable" houses in the poor and middle income communities are occupied by parents of private school attendees that private schools begin to appear in the richest community.

Because private schools appear in low-income communities first, the public school population in those communities shrinks. Furthermore, since those attending private schools are immigrants who replaced former residents of the most desirable houses in the community, average peer quality in the public schools declines. At the same time, however, the tax base increases (property values and community income are higher) while the number of students to be served by the public schools in the poor community declines. Therefore, our simulations demonstrate that, so long as a sufficiently large political constituency for public schools exists, per-pupil spending on public education in the poor community will rise. Even in the absence of any positive competitive effects, public schools in poor communities may therefore improve in quality as the effect of increases in per-pupil spending outweigh those resulting from the loss of high-quality peers. At the same time, both the spending effect and the peer effect imply that public schools in high-income districts will become unambiguously worse with the introduction of vouchers. The peer quality in those districts falls because some high-income agents migrate to the low-income communities to send their children to private schools, while per-pupil spending falls as this same political constituency favoring high public school spending is leaving the community. This model therefore gives a somewhat counterintuitive result: *public schools in poor communities may benefit from the introduction of private school vouchers, whereas public schools in rich communities are made unambiguously worse.*

Computable general equilibrium simulations further demonstrate that the extent to which this loss in public school peer quality in low-income communities affects public school output quality depends on the institutional setting used to finance public education in the state. (These simulations are unreported here.) Whether schools are funded by state or local sources, per-pupil spending rises in the poor community and more than offsets the loss in peer quality (this can be seen in Table 4D). However, under foundation grants and DPE, local public schools worsen in the poor community because per-pupil spending either remains constant or does not rise sufficiently to offset the losses in peer quality.

4.4. Potential Applications of the Computable General Equilibrium Model

We have summarized three very different applications of a CGE model to issues in fiscal federalism and local public finance. One approached a precise analytic question and utilized both theory and simulation evidence to arrive at a plausible explanation for an unexplained institutional phenomenon. The second asked a set of more applied questions concerning the precise general equilibrium effects of various state or national government programs that we observe in the real world. Finally, the third application demonstrated how the CGE framework can be modified to address very specific policy questions (the effect of private school vouchers) related to very precise types of local public goods (schools with peer effects). All three of these types of applications could be used to address a variety of other issues.

Current research is directed mainly at expanding the CGE framework in several new directions. Incorporating interjurisdictional spillovers, for example, can shed light on the extent to which higher governments can use programs to achieve more efficient outcomes. Although the use of matching grants has long been advocated, it is not clear to what extent these grants will be effective in long-run equilibria in which agents vote with both their ballots and their feet. A national grant program may, for example, raise public good levels in one community whose spillovers may cause another community to lower its public good levels. A thorough general equilibrium analysis of an entire set of national grants can lead to a better understanding of both the nature and limitations of optimal grant systems.

Although intercommunity spillovers may be important, intracommunity externalities such as those discussed in Huizinga (1994) may play an even larger role. To some extent, this work has begun with the incorporation of peer effects in the production process of local public schooling, which was addressed in the previous section. In addition, however, neighborhood effects can be important (Durlauf 1992) and can play a significant role in community development. The composition of the community – or, more precisely, the level of community income (which is correlated with adult education levels) – may therefore play an important role not only in the production functions for local public goods but also in the desirability of the community in and of itself. The effects of such population externalities and of various government policies on the nature of the general equilibrium are still relatively unknown.

An interesting conceptual question concerns the extent to which various often-used assumptions about the objective function of local governments matter. In our model we have assumed simple majority voting as the social choice rule. Others (see e.g. Wildasin 1986) have argued that maximization of property value may also be a reasonable objective function to apply. A modification of the CGE model could allow for an explicit comparison between these and other approaches to modeling local government behavior. This could generate insights into the extent, if any, to which researchers need to be concerned with the precise community objective functions when modeling local behavior.

On a more empirical level, the CGE model could be modified to predict long-run effects of a variety of real-world policies. Many states, most recently Michigan, have enacted sweeping finance reforms that have fundamentally changed the roles played by states and local communities. Although the simple CGE model presented here lacks certain potentially important empirical features, it should be noted that there is much room for added institutional detail and complexity, for increasing the number of communities and house types, for adding agents with multiple preferences, and for incorporating a commercial sector that is equally mobile.[31] These features can be calibrated to the particular state or region in question, and long-run policy effects can be simulated in the manner demonstrated here. Since the model is entirely micro-based, these simulations will be capable of predicting not only aggregate community trends but also individual migration behavior and welfare effects.

Furthermore, this applied analysis need not be limited to local issues in the United States. For example, Ahmad and McLure (1994) have detailed policy debates, within the emerging federation of South Africa, in which decentralization and fiscal federalism are proposed as tools for achieving interjurisdictional and interpersonal redistribution. By redrawing local political boundaries to merge parts of wealthy suburbs with poor townships, tax bases can be shared and used to fund desperately needed social services in fiscally distressed areas. A CGE approach could be applied to simulate the long-run general equilibrium effects of such boundary changes, of the migration decisions by members of the respective communities, and of the evolution of property values. Similar issues (albeit of lesser magnitude) arise in many U.S. states that are considering the consolidation of local school districts.

5. CONCLUSION

This paper presents a new theoretical and a related CGE model of fiscal federalism that includes a rigorous specification of local public finance. The model still has room to grow, yet it already incorporates a variety of important institutional features: (i) multiple agents who vote with both ballots and feet, (ii) local governments that respond to majority-rule voting, (iii) property taxes at the local level, (iv) income taxes at the state or national level, and (v) a heterogeneous land market. It is argued throughout that the complexity of the fiscal interaction between local, state, and national governments often makes purely analytic approaches difficult and thus leaves room for fruitful research that combines theoretical analysis with computational general equilibrium simulations. The CGE model presented here has been applied elsewhere to the study of several theoretical and applied issues and thus has been proven to be suitable for such research. Results from these studies have been summarized and new directions for future research discussed. Some of these directions are currently being explored, whereas others await further attention. By no means, however, is the list of potential applications offered here exclusive. As federations develop and evolve, complicated new questions are likely to arise and so provide fruitful avenues for further research. In addition, the CGE model offered here focuses on only some aspects of fiscal federalism and local public finance. Other features that are now central to debates over free trade and the European Union, such as labor and firm mobility, may be similarly well-suited for CGE analysis.

NOTES

1. Because of this propensity of residents to "vote with their feet" (Nechyba and Strauss 1994; Tiebout 1956), local policy decisions are reflected in equilibrium property values as these adjust to changes in demand (Oates 1969; Rosen and Fullerton 1977).
2. More precisely, the model includes (i) multiple communities producing local public goods funded through a property tax, (ii) a state (or national) government producing a national public good through income taxation, (iii) different types of mobile voters who cast ballots in local and state (or national) elections, and (iv) a discrete land market with heterogeneous houses that are traded at market prices.
3. Inman (1977) and Inman and Wolf (1976) have previously used a computable model with behavioral equations. Our approach differs in that it starts with economic primitives and traces individual rather than aggregate behavior. Richter

(1978) suggests a computational approach based on Scarf's algorithm for an economy in which one central authority sets tax rates for all communities. This model is not applicable here because of our focus on autonomous local governments.

4. The sufficient conditions for the existence of an equilibrium in this model are fairly weak compared with others in the literature. In particular, they include standard assumptions on preferences and technologies without the usual single crossing conditions (Epple et al. 1993; Westhoff 1977) and without Dunz's (1985) independence assumption.

5. Although not discussed in this section, the general model also allows for population externalities.

6. More precisely, the set of houses and consumers is defined as part of a measure space $(N, \mathfrak{N}, \mu)$, where μ is taken to be the Lebesgue measure. All subsets referred to are henceforth assumed to be measurable.

7. As demonstrated in Nechyba (1994, 1997b), there is no technical problem in including spillovers or population externalities in the model. These have been omitted for our current illustration.

8. This utility function satisfies all conditions necessary for the existence of an equilibrium (see Nechyba 1994, 1997b). The parameters are set to be consistent with New Jersey micro tax data as described in Section 3. Preferences are assumed to be identical in this way not only for computational convenience but also because stratification results in Nechyba (1994, 1997b) imply that, under these conditions, the equilibrium assignment of agents into house types is unique.

9. Again, including externalities in production (it may be easier to produce education when the majority of parents in the community are educated) poses no major technical problems; see e.g. Nechyba (1996b). This is discussed further in Section 4.3.

10. Note that this formulation of public production implicitly ignores the important issue – highlighted in Ladd and Yinger (1989, 1994) – of cost differences between jurisdictions as well as the role of peer effects (see Nechyba 1996b).

11. This is because all expectations implicitly held by myopic voters are fulfilled in equilibrium when voters vote while holding levels of public goods, community compositions, and property values fixed at the *actual equilibrium values*. Thus, in equilibrium, voters correctly take current levels of these variables into account. Myopic voting of this kind is common in the literature (see e.g. Dunz 1985; Epple et al. 1993; Westhoff 1977).

12. Voters are assumed to vote separately on local and national issues. This produces a *structurally induced equilibrium* (Shepsle 1979) in which voters hold fixed local public goods when voting in national elections and vice versa. The same conditions that guarantee a local voting equilibrium then also guarantee a national voting equilibrium.

13. Note that $J = \{J_{mh} \subset N \mid \mu(J_{mh}) = \mu(C_{mh}) \; \forall (m, h) \in M \times H\}$ and C are both partitions of N. The difference, however, is that C assigns houses (and the *initial* distribution of agents) to house types and communities, whereas J gives the *equilibrium* assignment of agents to houses and communities.

14. The program is written in GAMS. Solvers in GAMS are used to partition agents into communities and house types but not (for technical reasons that

involve a high degree of nonlinearity in the problem) to determine equilibrium prices. An alternative approach to calculating equilibrium prices is outlined in Figure 1. Although this approach is fairly simple and does not in itself guarantee convergence, it has worked extremely well in all simulations. For other approaches, some of which are now being considered for this model, see Kimbell and Harrison (1986).

15. In particular, as mentioned before, stratification results in Nechyba (1994, 1997b) imply that, when preferences are identical and there are no spillovers (both of which are true in the CGE model), agents will separate into house types and communities in a way that makes this separation unique. Therefore, although the set of equilibria is not necessarily a singleton, it is unique in certain important dimensions (e.g., in the assignment of agents into communities). The limited number of house types means that prices still can vary within intervals, which implies that majority-rule tax rates and public good levels can vary within intervals. As the number of types increases, these intervals become smaller. Experiments within the context of the 45–agent type model of this paper indicate that equilibrium house price intervals are generally smaller than 0.01. The program simply picks the first set of prices, public good levels, and tax rates that satisfy the equilibrium conditions, but the assignment of agents is the same for any potential equilibrium in these price intervals. Policy simulations are conducted for various different levels of policy parameters, and each of these simulations starts at the same equilibrium.

16. Property tax figures in the table are taxes levied on yearly housing services, not on the total value of the house.

17. In fact, Epple and Platt (1992) go to considerable lengths to achieve such mixed equilibria by allowing agents' tastes to vary along one dimension. Although introducing heterogeneous preferences will certainly reduce stratification along income lines, the model here achieves such stratification simply by allowing a heterogeneous housing stock.

18. In California, for example, a state initiative in the 1970s capped local property tax rates and increased the role of state income taxation (passed back to jurisdictions in the form of grants) in local fiscal matters. A similar revolt against property taxation has occurred in many other states, most recently in Michigan, where the state legislature abolished the local property tax to finance public education (leaving a revenue shortfall in excess of $6 billion) without even having an alternative proposal to raise the required funds.

19. In addition, the presence of the "flypaper" effect (see Gramlich 1977) provides some evidence that this change in tax policy is consistent with local voting. The flypaper effect states that state governments can raise income taxes in a community, hand the revenues to the local government, and thereby effect higher local spending. In Nechyba (1994) we demonstrate that, in the context of our model, often a majority of residents is better off under such a scheme.

20. A primary argument in favor of the local property tax has been the relative ease with which buildings can be observed by local authorities. With a well-established system of state and national income taxes, however, incomes are now perhaps even more easily observed by local authorities than are property values. It therefore seems eminently feasible for local communities to simply

"piggyback" on the state or national income tax, a process that could be relatively costless and politically acceptable in light of the high costs of administering local property tax systems with perpetual reassessments that incur an endless flow of allegations of unfairness.

21. The addition of a nonmyopic planner to a model of myopic voters is intended to approximate the way in which tax bases are often determined in the United States. In particular, voters are often asked to vote directly on property tax rates in special local school referenda, whereas local income tax rates are usually set either by the state government or by local planners. Alternatively, one can view the introduction of a nonmyopic planner as a theoretical tool for approximating what tax bases would evolve in the long run. If communities that deviate toward property taxes and away from income taxes consistently "do better" than communities that deviate toward income taxes and away from property taxes, then one would expect property taxes to evolve as the universal local tax instrument. The results of such evolution are, in that sense, comparable to decisions made by nonmyopic local planners.

22. The crucial assumptions we have made are that (i) housing is a normal good in fixed supply and available in discrete units, (ii) agents have reasonably attractive opportunities outside their community, (iii) reform proposals are revenue-neutral, and (iv) prices are sticky. For specifics, see Nechyba (1994, 1997b).

23. Further simulation results with different income tax values, as well as simulations treating the unilateral introduction of property taxes in the presence of local income taxes, can be found in Nechyba (1994, 1997a).

24. Underprovision of LPGs may occur for several reasons. For example, in Zodrow and Mieszkowski (1986) it is due to fiscal competition. It can, of course, also result from spillovers.

25. A series of state court decisions beginning with *Serrano v. Priest* in California have held that large interjurisdictional variance in primary and secondary educational quality (often interpreted as per-pupil spending) violates the equal protection clauses of state constitutions.

26. Block grants are here defined to be lump-sum grants given to local governments independent of local government spending, whereas matching grants are grants that match local spending according to some ratio. Both grants reported in Table 3 distribute an equal amount of total tax revenues from a 3% state income tax to each jurisdiction. This is redistributive because high-income districts pay more for the grant programs than they receive.

27. Mieszkowski's (1994) survey of school aid programs in the United States confirms the relative effectiveness of DPE in equalizing school spending.

28. Although empirical evidence on peer effects is difficult to come by, such effects are generally thought to be of great importance in the educational process. In order to incorporate them into the current framework, the production function for the LPG in Table 1 may be modified as follows:

$$f(\text{per-pupil spending, peer quality})$$
$$= (\text{per-pupil spending})^{(1-\rho)}(\text{peer quality})^{\rho},$$

where peer quality is measured by average parental income and ρ determines the strength of the peer effect. The production function for private schools is identical. Note that we therefore assume away any competitive effects and thus bias the results against vouchers. For a more detailed explanation of private school behavior and voting decisions in the presence of private schools, see Nechyba (1996b).

29. As perceived peer effects become unrealistically high, individuals abandon the public schools to attend private schools that are more tailor-made.

30. To the extent that peer quality matters not only in schools but also in communities in general (as suggested by Durlauf 1992 and others), this is a positive effect of vouchers.

31. Most simulations take only a few minutes on a SUN Sparc-20® workstation. Adding these additional elements therefore seems computationally feasible.

REFERENCES

Ahmad, J., and C. McLure (1994), "Fiscal Federalism in South Africa: Challenges for Analysts," Paper presented at the ISPE Conference on "Fiscal Aspects of Evolving Federations" (26–28 August, Nashville, TN).

Courant, P., E. Gramlich, and D. Rubinfeld (1980), "Why Voters Support Tax Limitation Amendments: The Michigan Case," *National Tax Journal* 33: 1–20.

De Tray, D., and J. Fernandez (1986), "Distributional Impacts of the Property Tax Revolt," *National Tax Journal* 39: 435–50.

Dunz, K. (1985), "Existence of Equilibrium with Local Public Goods and Houses," Discussion Paper no. 201, Department of Economics, SUNY – Albany.

Durlauf, S. (1992), "A Theory of Persistent Income Inequality," Working Paper no. 4056, National Bureau of Economic Research, Cambridge, MA.

Epple, D., R. Filimon, and T. Romer (1993), "Existence of Voting and Housing Equilibrium in a System of Communities with Property Taxes," *Regional Science and Urban Economics* 23: 585–610.

Epple, D., and G. Platt (1992), "Equilibrium Among Jurisdictions when Households Differ in Preferences and Income," Working Paper, Carnegie-Mellon University, Pittsburgh, PA.

Epple, D., and R. Romano (1994), "Competition between Private and Public Schools, Vouchers and Peer Effects," Mimeo, Carnegie-Mellon University, Pittsburgh, PA.

Feldstein, M. (1975), "Wealth Neutrality and Local Choice in Public Education," *American Economic Review* 65: 75–89.

Gramlich, E. (1977), "Intergovernmental Grants: A Review of the Empirical Literature," in W. Oates (ed.), *The Political Economy of Fiscal Federalism.* Lexington, MA: Lexington, pp. 219–39.

Harberger, A. (1962), "The Incidence of the Corporation Income Tax," *Journal of Political Economy* 70: 215–40.

Huizinga, H. (1994), "Migration and Income Transfers in the Presence of Labor Quality Externalities." [Chapter 6 in this volume]

Inman, R. (1977), "Micro-Fiscal Planning in the Regional Economy," *Journal of Public Economics* 7: 237–60.

Inman, R., and D. Rubinfeld (1979), "The Judicial Pursuit of Local Fiscal Equity," *Harvard Law Review* 92: 1662–1750.

Inman, R., and D. Wolf (1976), "SOFA: A Simulation Program for Predicting and Evaluating the Policy Effects of Grants-in-Aid," *Socio-Economic Planning Science* 10: 77–88.

Kimbell, L., and G. Harrison (1986), "On the Equilibrium Solution of General Equilibrium Models," *Economic Modelling* 3: 197–212.

Ladd, H. F., and J. Yinger (1989), *America's Ailing Cities: Fiscal Health and the Design of Urban Policy.* Baltimore: Johns Hopkins University Press.

Ladd, H. F., and J. Yinger (1994), "The Case for Equalizing Aid," *National Tax Journal* 47: 211–24.

Manski, C. (1992), "Educational Choice (Vouchers) and Social Mobility," *Economics of Education Review* 11: 351–69.

Mieszkowski, P. (1994), "Tiebout Stratification, Fiscal Federalism, and School Finance," Paper presented at the ISPE Conference on "Fiscal Aspects of Evolving Federations" (26–28 August, Nashville, TN).

Nechyba, T. (1994), "Fiscal Federalism and Local Public Finance: A General Equilibrium Approach with Voting," Ph.D. dissertation, University of Rochester, New York.

Nechyba, T. (1996a), "A Computable General Equilibrium Model of Intergovernmental Aid," *Journal of Public Economics* 62: 363–97.

Nechyba, T. (1996b), "Public School Finance in a General Equilibrium World: Equalization, Peer Effects and Private School Competition," Working Paper no. 5642, National Bureau of Economic Research, Cambridge, MA.

Nechyba, T. (1997a), "Local Property and State Income Taxes: The Role of Interjurisdictional Competition and Collusion," *Journal of Political Economy* 105: 351–84.

Nechyba, T. (1997b), "Existence of Equilibrium and Stratification in Local and Hierarchical Tiebout Economies with Property Taxes and Voting," Technical Working Paper no. 190, National Bureau of Economic Research, Cambridge, MA; forthcoming in *Economic Theory.*

Nechyba, T., and R. Strauss (1997), "Community Choice and Local Public Services: A Discrete Choice Approach," Working Paper no. 94-45, School of Public Policy and Management, Carnegie-Mellon University, Pittsburg, PA; forthcoming in *Regional Science and Urban Economics.*

Oates, W. (1969), "The Effect of Property Taxes and Local Public Spending on Property Values: An Empirical Study of Tax Capitalization and the Tiebout Hypothesis," *Journal of Political Economy* 77: 957–71.

Richter, D. (1978), "Existence and Computation of a Tiebout General Equilibrium," *Econometrica* 46: 779–805.

Rose-Ackerman, S. (1979), "Market Models of Local Government: Exit, Voting, and the Land Market," *Journal of Urban Economics* 6: 319–37.

Rosen, H., and D. Fullerton (1977), "A Note on Local Tax Rates, Public Benefits, and Property Values," *Journal of Political Economy* 85: 433–40.

Shepsle, K. (1979), "Institutional Arrangements and Equilibrium in Multidimensional Voting Models," *American Journal of Political Science* 23: 27–59.

Shoven, J., and J. Whalley (1984), "Applied General-Equilibrium Models of Taxation and International Trade: An Introduction and Survey," *Journal of Economics Literature* 22: 1007–51.

Strauss, R. (1993), "Reforming School Finance in Illinois: Some Observations on Principles, Practicalities, and Politics," *State Tax Notes* 5: 351–60.

Tiebout, C. (1956), "A Pure Theory of Local Expenditures," *Journal of Political Economy* 64: 416–24.

Westhoff, F. (1977), "Existence of Equilibria in Economies with a Local Public Good," *Journal of Economic Theory* 14: 84–112.

Wildasin, D. (1986), *Urban Public Finance.* London: Harwood.
Zodrow, G., and P. Mieszkowski (1986), "Pigou, Tiebout, Property Taxation, and the Underprovision of Local Public Goods," *Journal of Urban Economics* 19: 350–70.

CHAPTER 10

"One People, One Destiny":
Centralization and Conflicts of Interest
in Australian Federalism

Jeffrey D. Petchey & Perry Shapiro

1. INTRODUCTION

As part of the Australian federation celebrations almost 94 years ago, the Sydney Town Hall was lit with electric lights proclaiming the message, "One People, One Destiny." Presumably, this was intended to convey the new mood of the new Australia: the coming together of disparate peoples and states and the dawning of nationhood (Coper 1987, p. 82). Tired of parochial thinking and colonial selfishness, leaders of the time called on the new Australia to enter a wider national life and achieve honor and dignity among the world's nations.

Since that time, Australia has become increasingly centralized. State powers have been greatly diminished, and the economic and political power of the central government – the "Commonwealth" – have been substantially increased. Although this has been a trend in most federal countries, many argue that centralization has gone much further in Australia. In many respects, Australia resembles a unitary state more than a federation (see Walsh 1990 for discussion). Indeed, in the current debate over whether Australia should become a republic, serious consideration is being given to whether the states should be abolished. In Australia, nationhood – and the accompanying erosion of state determination – have been pursued with a tenacity seemingly unequaled elsewhere.

The reasons behind this shift of power are complex. However, it is commonly recognized that the financial dominance of the Commonwealth, much of which was granted at federation, has been paramount in the centralization process. In this regard, the states have been excluded from two crucial tax bases. One, the sales tax base, has been denied by the High Court's interpretation of Section 90 of the Constitution.[1] This is unlike most other federations, where states can impose sales taxes. Second, the income tax base was taken by the Commonwealth during World War II

194

and has never been returned, despite numerous proposals for income tax sharing and High Court challenges launched by the states.

Thus, the states are financially weak, and this has been the main reason for their loss of self-determination since federation. Alfred Deakin, one of the key architects of Australian union, foresaw the consequences of financial dependence as early as 1902. In an article in the *London Morning Post* he stated:

As the power of the purse in Great Britain established by degrees the authority of the Commons, it will ultimately establish in Australia the authority of the Commonwealth. The rights of self-government of the states have been fondly supposed to be safeguarded by the Constitution. It left them legally free, but financially bound to the chariot wheels of the central government. Their need will be its opportunity. The less populous will first succumb; those smitten by drought or similar misfortunes will follow; and, finally, even the greatest and most prosperous will, however reluctantly, be brought to heel. Our Constitution may remain unaltered, but a vital change will have taken place in the relations between the states and the Commonwealth. The Commonwealth will have acquired a general control over the states, while every extension of political power will be made by its means and go to increase its relative superiority.[2]

Many arguments have been put forward to support the centralization of powers in federations. One is that central control is needed in order to take into account the national implications of public policy decisions. It is argued that states care only about their own citizens and hence pursue local or state interests. This means that they ignore important national implications flowing from their policy decisions (i.e., cross-jurisdictional effects or externalities). On the other hand, since they care about all citizens in the federation, central governments take account of the national ramifications of public policy decisions and can achieve Pareto-superior outcomes.

The fiscal federalism literature is replete with models that characterize the superiority of central control in such a world (see e.g. Oates and Schwab 1988). It is usually assumed that states have homogenous populations and that the welfare or interests maximized by the state are characterized by the preference function of a representative individual citizen. Thus, state interests can be thought of as the interests of a representative individual resident. Similarly, the welfare or interests of the nation are characterized as a combination of the preferences of representative individuals from each state (the Samuelson condition). If there are externalities flowing between states, then state provision of public goods will be suboptimal from a national perspective. Because it adopts the Samuelson condition, the center takes account of these externalities, leading to an unambiguous Pareto improvement. Centralization leads to an allocation on the contract curve where the Samuelson condition holds.

Here we develop a model where state residents have different preferences and where public choices are made by majority rule. This means that only the wishes of the majority preference group are implemented at the local level. State interests are the preferences of the local majority (rather than the preferences of one representative citizen within a homogenous state), and the national interest is characterized by the preferences of the national majority. In this world, the various policy regimes – from decentralized state provision to central provision – yield welfare outcomes that differ from those found in models with beneficent governments and homogenous state populations. In particular, the clear preference for centralization when there are interstate externalities disappears because, in our analysis, centralism has a cost attached to it: a tension between state and national interests. The interests of local majorities can be overridden in the centralization process, making at least one state worse off under central control. We show that interstate treaties emerge as a way of securing the gains from coordination without this conflict of interests. The analysis is linked with a debate in U.S. Constitutional history over state interests, and the implications for Australian federalism are examined. We also draw some more general conclusions for emerging federations such as the European Union.

The discussion is organized as follows. In Section 2, we develop a model that shows the potential costs of centralization by examining three policy regimes for the provision of a public good: decentralized provision, treaties, and centralized supply. We use the model to demonstrate how conflicts of interest occur under each regime in the presence of diversity and majoritarian considerations. In Section 3 we show how centralization has taken place in Australia as an illustrative example, and link the Australian experience with the theoretical analysis. Section 4 discusses the implications for emerging federations; conclusions are presented in Section 5.

2. THE MODEL

Consider a federation of two states, $i = 1, 2$. Each state is assumed to have a government that makes a voluntary contribution to a public good, denoted as q_i. There is a perfect externality associated with provision by state i. This means that the provision by state 1 benefits not only citizens of state 1 but also citizens of state 2, and vice versa. Therefore, the total consumption of the public good in state 1 is $Q_1 = q_1 + q_2$; in state 2, $Q_2 = q_2 + q_1$. There are two types $t = h, l$ of citizens in state 1: high demanders ($t = h$) who want high public spending and low demanders ($t = l$) who prefer a low level of public spending. The number of high demanders,

$n_{1,h} = 20$, exceeds the number of low demanders, $n_{1,l} = 5$. In other words, because the states care only about their own citizens (or state interests), they ignore the external effects of local decisions.

We suppose that the states implement a majority-rule (direct democracy) public choice mechanism.[3] This means that the government of state 1 implements the preferences of the majority in state 1, the high demanders in this case, and hence adopts a high spending posture. In state 2 there is a group of high demanders, who are identical to the high demanders in state 1 in terms of preferences and incomes, as well as a group of low demanders, whose preferences and incomes are identical to the low demanders in state 1. In state 2, however, the low demanders outnumber the high demanders: $n_{2,l} = 15 > n_{2,h} = 5$. With majority rule in state 2, the preferences of the low demanders are implemented and state 2 adopts a low public spending stance. The total population of state 1 is $n_1 = n_{1,h} + n_{1,l} = 25$ and in state 2 it is $n_2 = n_{1,l} + n_{2,h} = 20$; the fixed population of the federation is $N = n_1 + n_2$. There is no migration between states. Citizens also have preferences over a private good. Each citizen in both states has an income of unity.

Assuming Cobb–Douglas preferences (this facilitates numerical solution), the per-capita utility of type-t citizens in state i is

$$u_{i,t} = \left(1 - \frac{q_i}{n_i}\right)^{(1-\lambda_t)} Q^{\lambda_t}, \quad \text{where } x_i = 1 - \frac{q_i}{n_i} \tag{1}$$

and λ_t is the preference parameter of a type-t individual. Notice that, because there are perfect externalities, total consumption of the public good is identical across states even though individual contributions may differ.

Competitive Federalism

We now characterize the competitive provision of q by the two states. This can be thought of as the provision of the public good under a regime of "competitive federalism." Since states are majoritarian, the public spending of each is made to enhance the welfare of the dominant preference group. In state 1 this is the group of high demanders; in state 2, the low demanders. Therefore, under competitive state provision of q_i, state 1 maximizes (1) where $t = h$ (i.e., the utility function of a representative high demander). That is, it chooses q_1 according to

$$\text{MRS}_{Q,x}^{1,h} = \frac{1}{n_1}, \tag{2}$$

where $\text{MRS}_{Q,x}^{i,t}$ is the marginal rate of substitution between the public and private good for a type-t citizen in state i and where the right-hand side is the tax share per capita in state i. Similarly, state 2 chooses q_2 according to

$$\text{MRS}_{Q,x}^{2,l} = \frac{1}{n_2}. \qquad (3)$$

Using (1) to solve for $\text{MRS}_{Q,x}^{1,h}$ and $\text{MRS}_{Q,x}^{2,l}$, and then substituting into (2) and (3), we can solve for two reaction functions describing each state's optimal choice of public good provision:

$$q_1 = n_1\lambda_h - q_2(1-\lambda_h), \qquad (4)$$

$$q_2 = n_2\lambda_l - q_1(1-\lambda_l). \qquad (5)$$

Equation (4) expresses state 1's optimum choice of q_1 as a function of q_2. Similarly, equation (5) expresses state 2's optimum choice of q_2 as a function of q_1. Hence, there is interdependence between the voluntary contributions of each state owing to the presence of a positive public good externality. This introduces the potential for strategic behavior. Adopting the Nash behavioral assumption (zero conjectures), solving (4) and (5) simultaneously yields the Nash equilibrium contributions to Q as follows:

$$q_1^* = \frac{n_1\lambda_h - (1-\lambda_h)n_2\lambda_l}{1 - (1-\lambda_h)(1-\lambda_l)}, \qquad (6)$$

$$q_2^* = \frac{n_2\lambda_l - (1-\lambda_l)n_1\lambda_h}{1 - (1-\lambda_h)(1-\lambda_l)}. \qquad (7)$$

Here q_1^* and q_2^* are the levels of provision by states 1 and 2 acting competitively; q_1^* is the level of provision preferred by the high demanders in state 1. The low demanders in state 1 must contribute their per-capita share to q_1^*, and consume $Q^* = q_1^* + q_2^*$. In state 2, q_2^* is the equilibrium voluntary contribution based on the preferences of the low demanders in that state. The high demanders in state 2 must contribute their per-capita share to q_2^*, and consume Q^*. Per-capita utilities with competitive behavior are given by equation (1).

Cooperative Federalism

The states may take externalities into account by cooperating through a treaty or compact, that is, adopting a "cooperative federalism" policy regime. Any treaty would be between the two state majorities, as they control the respective local polities. There is, of course, the issue of whether states can negotiate, maintain, and enforce such agreements. Indeed, it may be that in some circumstances such agreements cannot be maintained. In the discussion here we do not examine these issues. Rather, we ask: If interstate agreements *can* be negotiated and maintained, then what characteristics might they have?

First, the treaty should be *welfare-improving* from the point of view of the two state majorities, relative to the noncooperative outcome; that is, it should make at least one group better off without making the other worse off. Second, the treaty should be *efficient*. Because the treaty would be between the majority of state 1 (high demanders) and the majority of state 2 (low demanders), the condition for efficiency is

$$n_1(\text{MRS}^{1,h}_{Q,x}) + n_2(\text{MRS}^{2,l}_{Q,x}) = 1. \tag{8}$$

Equation (8) defines a "utility possibilities frontier" between the two state majorities. Allocations on the curve will be Pareto-optimal, relative to noncooperation, but only from the point of view of the state majorities. We can characterize at least two allocations on the frontier. The first assumes that the high demanders in state 1 are held to their competitive utilities and characterizes the level of utility achievable by the low demanders of state 2 – that is, the low demanders of state 2 take all the cooperative surplus. The second allocation assumes that the low demanders of state 2 remain at their competitive utilities and characterizes the utility achievable by the high demanders of state 1 – that is, the high demanders in state 1 take all the cooperative surplus.

There may be a range of outcomes between these two points. However, we do not have information on the bargaining strength of the two states and so have no particular reason to choose any point on the curve. For this reason, we examine these "endpoint" allocations only.

The first allocation, in which the low demanders of state 2 take all the surplus from cooperative federalism, is obtained by solving

$$n_1\left(\frac{\lambda_h x^T_{1,h}}{Q(1-\lambda_h)}\right) + n_2\left(\frac{\lambda_l x^T_{2,l}}{Q(1-\lambda_l)}\right) - 1 = 0, \tag{9}$$

$$u^T_{1,h} - u^*_{1,h} = 0; \tag{10}$$

the superscript T denotes allocations in the treaty. Equation (9) is the MRS condition in a treaty between the two state majorities (obtained by using (1) to derive the MRS conditions and substituting them into (8)). Equation (10) requires that the utility of a representative high demander in state 1 remain, in the treaty, at the level achieved in the noncooperative outcome. Equations (9) and (10) can be solved simultaneously (numerically) for private and public good provision and per-capita utilities in such a treaty. We can also use (9) and (10) to solve for the second allocation, where the low demanders in state 2 remain at their competitive utilities and the high demanders of state 1 take all the cooperative surplus.

Centralization

Confronted with inefficient local policies under competitive federalism – due here to a majoritarian collective choice process and externalities – it may also be argued that central intervention is welfare-improving if the center is beneficent, cares about the welfare of *all* citizens, and seeks to find efficient and equitable outcomes. Thus, centralizing provision of the public good is an alternative way of taking account of interstate externalities.

In this case, the center would choose the national level of the public good using the Samuelson condition, which sums the marginal rates of substitution between the public good and the private good for both the high and low demanders in each state and then equates this sum to marginal cost. It is likely that the outcome would Pareto dominate the competitive and cooperative outcomes. Indeed, this is the basis of the standard result in the federalism literature – that centralization in the face of inefficient state behavior is preferable to either competitive or cooperative federalism.

If the center knows the number of citizens of each preference type then it can implement efficient policies. With such information it could, for example, implement an efficient Lindahl equilibrium, with each preference type facing individual tax shares equal to their marginal rates of substitution for the public good. Under this system, all individuals would consume the same socially optimal supply of the public good but face different tax shares depending on the diversity of preferences. But, as noted earlier in discussing the states' collective choice problem, this is a demanding informational requirement.

In the absence of such information, the center must rely on citizens to reveal their preferences truthfully if it is to implement efficient policies. However, it is well known that there is an incentive for individuals to act strategically by misrepresenting their true preferences. By misrepresenting their marginal rates of substitution, individuals are able to reduce their tax share and "free ride" on the contribution of others. Thus, with an informational constraint, the center would *not* be able to implement an efficient Lindahl equilibrium, and instead would have to rely on mechanisms for encouraging people to reveal their true preferences. Many such mechanisms have been proposed, and all have the feature of breaking the link between the tax share faced by individuals and their marginal rate of substitution (see e.g. Groves and Ledyard 1977 or Groves and Loeb 1975). Acting strategically with regard to preferences would then have no effect on the tax share.

Another rule that encourages truthful revelation of preferences would have the center announcing that it will provide public goods according to the Samuelson condition, with equal cost sharing across both preference types and states; that is, $q_1/n_1 = q_2/n_2$. From the budget constraint this implies that consumption of the private good is also equal for both preference groups. If the center adopts this tax rule then truthful revelation of preferences will be incentive-compatible (although this may not be the only rule available).[4]

Thus, even if the center is beneficent, choosing to adopt such a preference revelation rule may constrain the center to equal per-capita cost shares unless it has full information on preferences. Of course, the center may also implement equal cost sharing as a result of such institutional constraints as political limitations on its ability to differentiate between types and of constitutional constraints barring it from discrimination between states. Indeed, in the Australian Constitution there is an explicit prohibition on the Commonwealth's ability to treat the states differentially in terms of taxation matters. Equal per-capita cost shares for individuals who have the same incomes but different preferences for public goods is also something we observe in practice. Thus, apart from being one rule that could result from informational constraints, equal cost sharing may also have origins in institutional arrangements and conventions.

The center may also be subject to the same majoritarian forces as the states and simply act in the interests of the national majority. Thus, there are at least two central outcomes of potential interest: a constrained efficient central solution where the center must impose equal tax shares, and a majoritarian outcome where the preferences of the national majority are implemented. These outcomes will be discussed in turn.

Constrained Efficient Provision. With equal cost sharing, the federal government would solve (simultaneously)

$$(n_{1,l} + n_{2,l})\mathrm{MRS}^l_{Q,x} + (n_{1,h} + n_{2,h})\mathrm{MRS}^h_{Q,x} - 1 = 0, \tag{11}$$

$$\frac{q_1}{n_1} - \frac{q_2}{n_2} = 0. \tag{12}$$

Choosing the provision of the public good according to (11) and (12) will result in a level of provision consistent with the Samuelson condition, which is preferable to the state majoritarian decision-making rule but at the same time imposes the constraint that each preference type must face the same tax share. This places a cost on each preference group, which – as will be shown in the numerical solutions that follow – can be sufficient to mean that central provision does not Pareto dominate competitive or cooperative provision by the states. Of course, if the center had full information on preferences then it could implement (11) without the constraint implied by (12) and instead tailor individual tax shares for each preference group, thus achieving a Pareto optimum.[5]

Majority Rule (Direct Democracy). Alternatively, the federal government may not attempt to act efficiently and instead be subject to the same majoritarian forces as the states (direct democracy). Under majority rule, high demanders are in the majority at the *national* level. If the provision of the public good is centralized then the center will sum the marginal rates of substitution of all the high demanders in the federation in determining the total marginal benefit of the public good, equate this to marginal cost, and ignore the preferences of the low demanders. Thus, the national interest is the interest of the national majority – the high demanders. The low demanders of state 2, who are in the majority in that state, will not be a part of the national majority. We shall see that this makes them worse off under majoritarian central provision than they would be under cooperative or competitive federalism. That is, for state 2 there is a clear conflict between its own interests and those of the national majority.

Under central provision with majority rule, the central government chooses q according to

$$n_1(\text{MRS}^h_{Q,x}) + n_2(\text{MRS}^h_{Q,x}) - 1 = 0$$

or

$$N(\text{MRS}^h_{Q,x}) - 1 = 0, \tag{13}$$

because it takes into account the MRS of high demanders in states 1 and 2 and *ignores* the low demanders' preferences. Equation (13) defines a utility possibilities frontier between the high-demand types in the two states (because they are the national majority). Thus, under majority rule, the center solves

$$n_1\left(\frac{\lambda_h x^c_{1,h}}{Q(1-\lambda_h)}\right) + n_2\left(\frac{\lambda_l x^c_{2,h}}{Q(1-\lambda_l)}\right) - 1 = 0, \tag{14}$$

$$\frac{q_1}{n_1} - \frac{q_2}{n_2} = 0, \tag{15}$$

where again there is a uniform cost-sharing condition. This is part of the majoritarian central solution because there is no reason to expect the national majority (the high demanders) to do anything other than charge all high-demand citizens the same tax share.

Numerical Solutions

Numerical solutions for the three policy regimes are presented in Table 1. The overall conclusion is that no policy regime Pareto dominates another. In particular, if we take competitive federalism as a benchmark, then moving to a treaty or centralized provision will not be Pareto-improving because at least one group is always made worse off.[6] This is in contrast to our usual intuition that cooperation or centralization is desirable when

Table 1. *Welfare effects of competitive, cooperative, and centralized policy regimes*

	$u_{1,h}$	$u_{1,l}$	$u_{2,h}$	$u_{2,l}$
Competitive federalism	4,454	118	8,994	238
Cooperative federalism				
Option 1	4,454	89	15,165	302
Option 2	7,080	137	253	238
Central provision				
Constrained	9,484	180	9,484	180
Majoritarian	9,000	185	9,000	185

Note: Solutions assume $\lambda_h = 0.75$ and $\lambda_l = 0.65$. Under Option 1 of the compact, the majority in state 1 (the high demanders) are held to their noncooperative utility and all the cooperative surplus goes to the majority of state 2. Under Option 2, the majority of state 2 (the low demanders) are held to their noncooperative utility and all the cooperative surplus goes to the majority of state 1 (the high demanders).

there are externalities associated with decentralized provision or with inefficient collective choice mechanisms at the local level. This is so because the potential policy options of the central government are constrained by informational limitations and hence the center is unable to implement a Pareto-optimal outcome.

For example, it is clear that centralization, either constrained efficient or majoritarian, does not Pareto dominate competitive federalism. Constrained efficient central provision makes one group, the low demanders in state 2, worse off even though all others are better off. This is because, in the noncooperative solution, the low demanders in state 2 are in the majority and reach their optimum. Under the constrained efficient central solution, the level of central provision is weighted more toward the preferences of the high demanders, and as a consequence is higher than under the noncooperative outcome (for state 2). Hence, the low demanders in state 2 are worse off because they must contribute to a higher level of public good than they would otherwise choose. In contrast, the low demanders in state 1, who are a minority in the noncooperative outcome, are better off under constrained efficient central provision. This is because, with centralization, the preferences of the low demanders in state 2 come into play in the public choice decision. The high demanders in state 1 and state 2 are better off under the constrained efficient central solution.

Similar conflicts occur when we compare the competitive and majoritarian central outcomes. Again, all groups except the low-demand majority in state 2 are made better off in any move to centralize. Now, however, the low-demand group in state 2 is worse off because, under majoritarian central provision, they are not part of the national majority. Their preferences are ignored by the central government, and there is a conflict between the interests of the majority at the state level and the national majority; that is, a conflict between state and national interests arises. The majoritarian centralization regime does not Pareto dominate the competitive equilibrium.

Thus, with any move from competitive federalism to either of the centralized outcomes, although we do take account of the externality (as argued in the federalism literature), this benefit is achieved at a cost because centralism has its own inefficiency due to informational constraints. What is particularly interesting here is that, even when competitive federalism is weighted down with two significant inefficiencies – majority rule and perfect externalities – the welfare costs of these informational constraints make centralizing unattractive if we are interested in welfare-improving policy changes.

Next, consider any move from the competitive to the treaty outcomes. Both treaty outcomes are welfare-improving from the point of view of the two state majorities but not from the point of view of all groups. In particular, any move from competition to a treaty makes one local minority worse off. Moreover, at least one local majority, the low demanders of state 2, have an incentive to prefer treaties to any form of centralization. In contrast, the other state majority, the high demanders of state 1, have an incentive to support either form of centralization in preference to a treaty.

Our results highlight a tension in federations where different preference groups have an incentive to favor alternative policy regimes. This tension, or competition over the degree of centralization and decentralization, results from diversity of preferences, inefficient collective choice processes, and informational constraints. It is likely to be present in federations where collective choices are being made by more than one level of government over the same group of citizens.

A final point to note here is the possibility that voluntary transfers undertaken by the states, or mandated by the center, could secure welfare improvements under all three policy regimes. But again this would require that the states and the center know the number of individuals in each preference group. Otherwise, governments cannot identify who should contribute to transfers and who should be the beneficiaries. Because we characterize decision making where governments face informational constraints, we do not address the issue of transfers.

Calhoun and Webster

Tensions between state and national interests are at the heart of the theory of federalism. This was, for example, central in the debate between two of the most prominent U.S. political thinkers of the nineteenth century, Daniel Webster and John C. Calhoun.[7] On the one hand, Webster argued that the federal government was created by the American people as one indivisible whole and not by state parliaments or state residents as separate sovereign groups. It was as citizens of the United States that individuals established the Constitution and the federal government and indeed the state governments. Each sphere of government was created for specific purposes and each with its own set of powers. Neither can call itself master of the other, and the people were seen as the master of both. Webster also believed that the distribution of power between the two governments, and hence the tradeoff to be made between state versus national interests, was to be decided by the federal legislature and that the will of the national majority should prevail. He asserted

that the Constitution of the United States confers on the government itself, to be exercised by its appropriate department, and under its own responsibility to the people, the power of deciding ultimately and conclusively upon the just extent of its own authority. If this had not been done, we should not have advanced a single step beyond the old Confederation. (Forsyth 1981, p. 119)

John C. Calhoun differed sharply from Webster.[8] His view was based on a very different interpretation of what constitutes a federation. In Calhoun's theory, the American Constitution was a *compact* between the sovereign states and their respective peoples, not a creation of the American people as one indivisible whole, as Webster argued. The compact entailed the states retaining sovereignty in certain areas and delegating other powers to a central government. Thus, each sovereign state (and its people) created two governments, one for itself (the state government) and the other in conjunction with other sovereign states.

To Calhoun, the issues of how to protect the reserved powers of each government from encroachment by the other, and solving the problem of conflict of interest, were crucial. If one government had the right to decide on this distribution of power (Webster proposed that this right should reside with the center) then, Calhoun argued, the balance of power between governments would be destroyed. To stop this, Calhoun proposed that each government should have the power to "nullify" the acts of the other; that is, each government should be given negative powers, one of which would be the right to secede.

In particular, Calhoun was suspicious of central power because of the threat to national minority interests (see Calhoun 1953). He believed that the interests of national minorities were safeguarded by individual states and would not be taken into account by a national government. Calhoun's solution to this problem was to maintain the power of the states. He proposed the idea of the "concurrent majority" as an explicit limit on the power of the center to override local majority interests. The notion was that, for something to become a national law, the majority in all states would need to pass it. If a particular state did not approve of the law then it would be passed nationally only if a majority of the states approved; dissenting states would have the right to secede from the union.[9]

Calhoun's concurrent majority was a mechanism designed to address the conflicts of interest analyzed here. He may also have been comfortable with our results suggesting that the states would prefer cooperative federalism over centralism, simply because cooperative federalism can be welfare-improving from the point of view of the states but avoids the problem of local majority interests being overruled by national majorities (which occurs with centralization). Cooperative federalism protects the interests of local majorities (though not, of course, those of local minorities). A strength of Calhoun's proposal is that, like the analysis here, it recognizes the diversity of interests inherent in federal systems and the constant tension that exists between such interests. This tension arises from majoritarian forces combined with diversity of preferences.

3. CENTRALIZATION IN AUSTRALIA

The discussion so far has emphasized the potential costs of centralizing the provision of public goods, that is, expenditure decisions. We now turn to a discussion of the mechanism through which centralization of expenditure decisions has occurred in Australia as an illustrative example of centralization in practice.

The Australian experience is particularly interesting for two reasons. First, centralization of expenditure powers in Australia came in through the "back door" in the sense that – by gaining exclusive control over the major tax bases (in particular, the sales and income tax bases) and through use of conditional grants and other means – the central government has gained control over many of the expenditure powers that the Constitution had actually left to the states. Thus, it is through tax powers that the center has achieved centralization of expenditure powers. Second, centralization in Australia has gone much further than elsewhere (see Walsh 1993 for international comparisons of centralization). Therefore, one would expect the potential costs of centralizing expenditure powers, highlighted in the model developed here, to be of greatest interest in a country such as Australia. Interestingly, we argue that this has not been the case.

Taxation Powers

As noted, a key factor behind the effective concentration of policy making in Australia has been the transfer of tax powers to the Commonwealth. In the last century, the states have lost two important tax powers: excise taxes (and, because of the High Court's interpretation of the meaning of "excise," sales taxes as well) and income taxes. The circumstances surrounding these events are discussed next.

Excise and Section 90. Customs and excise powers were relinquished to the Commonwealth at federation in Section 90 of the Constitution, which reads: "On the imposition of uniform duties of customs the power of the Parliament to impose duties of customs and of excise, and to grant bounties on the production or export of goods, shall become exclusive."

The motives of the Founders and the interpretation of the meaning of "excise" were not specified in the Constitution, and have been difficult to glean from Constitutional debates. This omission is possibly one of the greatest gaps in the Constitution. It has meant that the High Court has been left with the role of interpreting what is to be included under the term "excise" and hence, in effect, of determining the distribution of tax powers. This has conferred enormous influence on the Court, which has determined the relative strength of states versus the Commonwealth in a way that has diminished the states' role. Indeed, the role of the Court has been highly controversial, and the issue of excise hotly debated.

Much of the debate has been over the Founders' motives and the meaning of "excise." It turns out that the various views on the meaning of this term depend on one's view about the *motives* behind Section 90. According to Coper (1987), one of the major motives of the Founding Fathers in making the excise tax exclusive to the Commonwealth had to do with federal tariff policy. He notes:

The consensus of opinion amongst informed scholars and right-thinking judges is that, historically, the ban on State excise duties was intended, as an adjunct or corollary to the ban on State customs duties and State bounties on production or export, to protect Federal tariff policy from State interference. (p. 226)

This argument, though it does not emerge strongly from the federation debates, has merit. State power over excise duties would enable them to change the intended effect of federal tariff policy. For example, by imposing an excise duty on its producers, a state could *reduce* the effect of a federal tariff designed to lower the domestic price of the good relative to the price of imports. In other words, state excises could offset the intended effect of a federal tariff policy. A free-trading state could use power over excise to frustrate a protectionist Commonwealth.

Moreover, this added level of protection (or reduced level, if the excise tax is positive) would differ across states according to how each state set its excise tax policy. It would therefore have an impact on interstate trade and so run counter to the intent of Section 92, which guarantees free trade between states. Insofar as one of the main motivations for Australian federation was to obtain the benefits of a customs union – with a common external tariff and free interstate trade – it seems reasonable that the power to impose excises should also be made exclusive to the Commonwealth.

If this was in fact the motive behind centralizing excise, then the meaning of "excise" to be adopted (in order to satisfy the Founders' intent) would be extremely *narrow*. It would include production taxes on internationally traded goods subject to federal tariffs. Other indirect taxes might be available to the states. For example, it may be possible for states to impose production taxes on goods and services for which there are no competing imports or for which there is no Commonwealth tariff (i.e., goods that were internationally traded but imported tariff-free).[10] It is likely, however, that under this interpretation states would be free to impose taxes that affected imports (from interstate and overseas) and domestically produced goods equally. This would leave the states free to impose, for example, a *general nondiscriminatory sales tax* because such a tax would not interfere with federal tariff policy though it may affect the freedom of interstate trade.

Another view is that – in giving the Commonwealth control over both customs and excise duties, two of the most important taxes of the time – the Founders intended to grant the Commonwealth a *general* control over taxes on goods for reasons of macroeconomic policy. Supporters argue that this means we must adopt a *wide* interpretation of the meaning of "excise" to include taxes on the production, distribution, or sale of goods because taxes on the latter have the same effect as excise taxes on production – that is, they all affect the price of goods. If the Founders intended, in Section 90, to give the Commonwealth general control over taxes in order to have control over fiscal policy, then it follows that taxes on sales and distribution would have to be centralized.

Shapiro and Petchey (1994) have identified what they believe to be an important additional motive behind the centralization of excise duties: a desire to ensure both free internal trade and the unity of the federation. In their view, it is possible to discern such motives from the Constitutional debates. They note that a discriminatory excise tax has the potential to distort interstate trade patterns and that – since Australian federation was primarily motivated by a desire to promote free internal trade together with a common external tariff (i.e., to achieve the benefits of a customs union) – the Founders centralized excise to ensure that the "free internal trade" end of the federal compact was upheld.

To Shapiro and Petchey (1994), centralizing excise taxes went hand-in-hand with centralizing the customs tariff: one secured a common external tariff and the other helped secure free interstate trade. Without a centralized excise tax there was always the possibility that states could use discriminatory excise taxes to interfere with trade across state boundaries. They argue that the concern of the Founders for free interstate trade derived from their desire to preserve federal unity and the need for states to act cooperatively. Adopting this motive for Section 90, one would still be led to the narrow view of an excise tax as a discriminatory tax on production. General nondiscriminatory taxes would not distort interstate trade and would therefore be allowable.

Given the puzzle over what was to be included as an excise, it was not long after federation that the High Court was asked to adjudicate and interpret the Constitution on this matter. In the first case to be considered, *Peterswald v. Bartley* (1904), the Court adopted the narrow view of excise as a tax on the quantity or value of goods produced in a state. This left states free to impose taxes on goods that did not discriminate between states; that is, the narrow definition did not pose a threat to state tax powers. But this was gradually expanded to the broad interpretation of the meaning of "excise" in a series of cases during the 1920s and 1930s – in particular, *John Fairfax and Sons Ltd. v. New South Wales* (1927), *A.G. (NSW) v. Homebush Flour Mills Ltd.* (1937), and *Mathews v. Chicory Marketing Board* (1938). All subsequent Section 90 cases before the High Court have seen the adoption of a wide definition of an excise as *any* tax on the production, distribution, or sale of goods. This has meant the end of state taxes on goods with three notable exceptions. The states are allowed to levy franchise fees on tobacco, alcohol, and petroleum products, alhough their hold on these tax bases has been somewhat tenuous in recent years, owing (again) to various High Court decisions.

The wide view of excise has been highly contentious. A detailed discussion of the Court's reasons for taking the wide view would take us too far afield for present purposes. Excellent surveys can be found in Coper (1987) and Hanks (1986).[11] Briefly, the main reason for the reversal of the earlier interpretation of excise is that the Court changed its mind over the motives behind Section 90. In the early years, judges accepted the "tariff policy" motive. This, as discussed before, implies a narrow interpretation of the meaning of excise. Eventually, however, the "general control over taxation" motive gained prominence, and the wide interpretation of excise that this implies was adopted. It remains this way today, although only a small majority of judges voted for the broad view in the most recent

Section 90 case to be heard. This has left the states with the hope that the Court may reverse its interpretation at some stage in the future.

We already know that the Founders realized Section 90 gave the Commonwealth considerable financial power. As Deakin observed in 1902, Section 90 tied the states "to the chariot wheels of the central government." However, if the Founders intended "and of excise" to be included in Section 90 purely because of the tariff motive, or because they were concerned about interstate free trade and federal unity, then they would be shocked to see how it has contributed to the financial dependence of the states. On the other hand, if they really meant to give the Commonwealth a general power over taxation of commodities, then perhaps what we have today was intended.

There are at least two points against this latter interpretation. First, why would the Founders go to all the trouble of specifying the division of powers in the Constitution (the Constitution of Australia was settled on after 30-odd years of tough intercolonial negotiations from the 1870s onward) *and then* give the Commonwealth so much control over taxation that it is effectively able to destroy that division of power? This seems to make a mockery of the Constitution. Second, if the Founders intended to give the Commonwealth a broad power over taxation of goods, why then did they not centralize all the other powers that states use to influence the price of goods? State decisions still have plenty of scope for influencing prices without sales taxes.

Our view is that the federal tariff, interstate trade, and federal unity motives were really behind including "and of excise" in Section 90, and that excise should therefore be interpreted narrowly as a discriminatory tax on local production. This interpretation would leave the states free to impose sales taxes.

Income Tax. In 1942 the Commonwealth passed federal legislation decreeing that, for the duration of World War II and one year afterward, the Commonwealth would have the sole authority to impose income taxes. This legislation made invalid all state income taxes in effect at that time and established a uniform Commonwealth income tax regime across all states. Four states unsuccessfully challenged this in the High Court (see *State of South Australia and the Others v. Commonwealth of Australia* 1942) and in 1946 all states were informed by the Commonwealth that the uniform Commonwealth income tax system, and the prohibition on state income taxes, would continue indefinitely. The Commonwealth has retained exclusive access to the income tax base ever since.

However, there have been other state challenges to the loss of the income tax power to the Commonwealth. For example, in *Victoria v. Com-*

monwealth (1957), the state of Victoria unsuccessfully challenged certain aspects of the Commonwealth's uniform income tax legislation. Also, in 1978 the Commonwealth offered the states an income tax–sharing arrangement in which the states would actually be able to levy their own income taxes using the Commonwealth's existing legislation. But the Commonwealth did not "make room" in the income tax base for the state tax. This made it very difficult for the states to proceed with their own income taxes without bearing the political cost of increasing the overall income tax burden. In addition, there seems to have been a more general reluctance on the part of the states to take additional responsibility for raising their revenue. It appears they preferred to let the Commonwealth bear the political costs of revenue raising, at least as long as the Commonwealth remained generous in its treatment of the states with tax reimbursment grants. As a result, the 1978 proposal produced nothing and the offer was rescinded by the Commonwealth in the 1980s.

By 1990, following a long period during which the Commonwealth cut back heavily in real terms on tax reimbursment transfers to the states and a period of budgetary problems at the state level, state enthusiasm for income tax sharing resurfaced. During 1990–91, the states developed their own plan for income tax sharing with the Commonwealth. This intially met with considerable approval at the national level. There was an admission by the Commonwealth that the centralization of powers in the Australian federal system was a serious issue in state–federal relations and that attempts should be made to redistribute tax powers to the states. A change of prime ministership in 1993, and a reversal of the Commonwealth's attitude, resulted in the tax-sharing proposal being shelved (see Moy 1993 for discussion of this episode). Despite this, the states appear to have remained keen on some form of income tax sharing with the Commonwealth, or the return of sales tax powers to the states through a reversal of the High Court's interpretation of excise.

Expenditure Powers

In contrast to tax powers, most *expenditure* powers remain, in spirit at least, decentralized. Section 51 of the Australian Constitution gives about forty powers to the Commonwealth. All powers not listed in Section 51 are, by implication, left to the states as a residual (although they are not specified explicitly as in the Canadian Constitution). This effectively gives the states responsibility for such big-spending items as education, health, roads, and so on. In reality, however, the High Court's wide interpretation of excise and the loss of income tax powers have meant that the Commonwealth has also been able to centralize expenditure powers. Because of its fiscal power, the Commonwealth has extended its general influence over expenditure responsibililties supposedly left to the states by the Constitution. However, the center has also increased its influence over state expenditure decisions by using conditional grants to control state behavior and through legislative dominance – policies that will now be examined.

Specific Purpose Transfers. Taxation powers are highly centralized, so the Commonwealth collects much more revenue than it needs for its own purposes while the states rely on a relatively narrow tax base and collect much less than they need to meet their commitments. This has created a large "fiscal gap," meaning that the Commonwealth makes large tax reimbursment grants each year to meet the states' revenue shortfall. These grants compensate the states for the centralization of tax powers. If this were as far as it went, then centralization of tax powers per se would not result in centralization of expenditure powers. The Commonwealth would simply collect revenue on behalf of the states and hand it back to them as untied grants.

This, however, is not how matters developed. Because of a key High Court decision, *Commonwealth v. Victoria* (1926), the Commonwealth was given the power to attach any conditions it liked to these grants, regardless of whether the conditions had anything to do with the Commonwealth's constitutional powers. As a result, it is possible for the Commonwealth to influence state behavior directly by increasingly attaching conditions to what previously were unconditional grants necessitated by centralized tax powers.

The Commonwealth now has a strong influence over almost all areas of state responsibilities.[12] The greatest expansion of conditional or specific purpose transfers to the states, and hence of Commonwealth influence over state functions, came in the 1970s under the Whitlam Labor government. Indeed, specific purpose transfers as a proportion of total payments to the states have increased from 25% in the early 1960s to 55% in 1993–94. There are now extensive Commonwealth and state bureaucracies devoted to conditional transfers, and the breadth of their coverage is a contentious issue in state–federal relations.

Legislative Dominance. The Commonwealth's legislative dominance has also contributed to the "back door" concentration of expenditure power in Australia. In this regard, Section 109 of the Constitution provides that where a state law is inconsistent with a valid Commonwealth law, the latter prevails and the state law is invalid to the extent of the inconsistency. Thus, the Commonwealth is able to overrule the states in any area where it enacts valid legislation; that is, legislation where it has a Constitutional responsibility.

One of the areas defined as a Commonwealth responsibility in Section 51 of the Constitution is the "external affairs" power. Supported by High Court decisions, the Commonwealth has been able to use this power to ratify international treaties in areas such as human rights, labor relations, and the environment. By appealing to Section 109, the Commonwealth has used these treaties as a basis for national legislation that overrules state laws. This process has been relied on extensively to negate state policies, especially in environmental matters and industrial relations (see Coper 1987 for discussion). It is another major source of friction between the states and the Commonwealth.

State and National Interests

It can be seen from this brief overview that the concentration of taxation powers, the use of conditional transfers to exercise influence over the states, and the legislative dominance of the Commonwealth have facilitated the process of centralizing public-sector decision making in Australia. Yet our theoretical analysis highlighted that centralization may *not* be welfare-improving, because of the very concerns expressed by Calhoun. If one adopts a Calhounian view of federation as a compact between sovereign states, then the high degree of centralization in Australia is a concern because it raises the questions of (1) whether important local majority interests have been, and are still being, compromised; and (2) whether the checks on central power that exist in Australia are sufficient to protect local majority interests. Surprisingly, and to the best of our knowledge, these issues have never been addressed in Australia.

However, one commentator has raised the issue, at least indirectly. Sharman (1983) has argued that, in contrast to the United States, there is no tradition in Australia of concern over state interests and the concentration of central power. He sees this as a missing ingredient from Australian federalism, suggesting that this omission occurred because Australian federalism is a grafting of elements of the U.S. model of federalism onto a Westminster model, which is traditionally less concerned about limits to power. As long as the federal government operates with support of the national majority and within its legislative powers, no need is seen for placing further restraints on federal power. Sharman also suggested that Australia has no tradition of seeing the states as the basic units on which the federation is built – that is, no interstate compact theory of federation such as that underlying the Calhounian view.

Yet one can argue that the major episodes of discontent in Australia's short federal history have been driven by concerns of some of the smaller states that their interests were being overruled by national majority views.[13] Such concerns also seem to underpin current disillusionment with Australia's federal affairs. This has seen the open expression of discontent with centralization and the loss of state self-determination. Australia is entering a period of conflict between states and the Commonwealth. This debate is centered on questions regarding the degree of centralization, the use of central powers, and clashes between local and national interests.[14]

Our analysis suggests that dissatisfaction would be experienced in states with relatively small populations, such as Western Australia, South Australia, and Tasmania, since they are the least likely to have a voice at the national level and hence the most likely to have their interests overridden. It does seem that the least populous states are expressing the greatest dissatisfaction at present. Calhoun was likewise concerned about protecting the interests of the smaller southern states against the concentration of federal power in Washington.

If we are to be concerned about the protection of local majority interests, another question is whether Australia has sufficient *constraints* on central power. There are three at present, all of which are arguably inadequate. The first is democracy itself, which (as shown here) will not protect local majority interests against the will of the national majority. The second is the Senate (Australia's upper house). It is commonly recognized, however, that the Australian Senate has not performed this role, mainly because it is organized along political party lines. Finally, the states themselves may be protectors of local majority interests, as Calhoun argued they should be. The Australian states, however, have been greatly weakened by the concentration of power, as discussed in Section 2. Their ability to protect national minority interests in a Calhounian sense is limited. Thus, in Australia there are only very weak constraints to shield local majorities from the rule of national majorities. In any conflict of interest between local and national majorities, the latter have the upper hand.

If – rather than the contractual view of Calhoun – one adopts the view of Webster and sees the Commonwealth and the state governments as the creations of one Australian people, then we need not be so concerned about the effect of centralization on state interests since the will of the national majority would be paramount. Of course, one may still wish to be concerned about centralization for other reasons. State interests, however, would not be one of them.

One final point of interest relates to interstate compacts. Our results suggest that states which lose self-determination in the centralization process have an incentive to find other ways of securing gains from cooperative behavior. The model suggests that compacts between states may be such an alternative, as they allow the pursuit of national interest without sacrificing local majority interests. Compacts are in the Calhounian tradition, since he emphasized the desirability of cooperation through compromise rather than coercion from the center.

Interestingly, there have been tentative moves toward such forms of cooperation in Australia.[15] Indeed, Courchene (1993) alludes to this alternative. In his paper on the effects of globalization in federal systems (especially regarding the power of the center relative to the periphery), Courchene argues that Canberra's most important power is its ability to harmonize and manage policy interdependencies *between* levels of government (in order to take into account the national interest), rather than the direct provision of public goods. In Courchene's own words, "Canberra should ensure that programs are national and should not be overly preoccupied about whether these national programs are state or Commonwealth delivered" (1993, p. 101).

4. Implications for Emerging Federations

Our analysis on conflicts of interest, and the discussion of the Australian experience, have implications for emerging federations such as the Economic Union in Europe. There, an important question seems to be: If Europe becomes federal, then who would make up the national or European majority? One possibility is that the national majority would be dominated by the interests of countries with the largest populations, such as Germany. If this is so, Germany has an incentive to support the formation of a European federation, as indeed they seem to in practice, because their interests will dominate any European majority.

Countries with smaller populations, such as Britain and Italy, may have an incentive to resist centralization because they would lose local autonomy to the European majority. For these countries, the critical issue is how to find ways of obtaining the benefits of coordination throughout Europe *without* the loss of sovereignty inherent in forming a federation with a central government.

The results here suggest that interstate compacts between the nations of Europe may achieve these benefits without the loss of national sovereignty. Interestingly, some European countries, especially the United

Kingdom, seem to favor these looser confederal arrangments over federation for precisely this reason (i.e., fear of losing self-determination). This is an issue that the European nations will need to confront: what functions can be coordinated through treaties, and what they might need to centralize in a federal arrangment.

5. CONCLUSIONS

We have argued that, in federations characterized by informational constraints and inefficient collective choice mechanisms, there can be no clear preference for central control over competitive state provision or interstate treaties. This is because of a conflict of interest among different preference groups over policy regimes. Our analysis has shown how such conflicts of interest may be at work in the Australian federation, where centralization has progressed much further than elsewhere. It was suggested that the nations of Europe will need to come to terms with such issues if they are to contemplate a federal compact.

We conclude by noting that these are also important issues for countries that are presently reforming their systems of government and facing the issue of how best to allocate powers between the center and state or local governments. Australia seems to be going through this self-examination process, but so too are other countries. For example, removal of the old apartheid political boundaries in South Africa is likely to create new conflicts between regional and national interests.[16] In Canada, too, conflicts of interest driven by diversity are the key to the issue of Quebec's relationship with the rest of the country.

The Australian experience provides many lessons for countries facing these issues. In particular, Australia is a country that has not traditionally been concerned about the concentration of power, state interests, and constraints on centralism. In Australia, centralization has been a self-perpetuating force that followed federation, largely facilitated by the loss of major tax powers by the states. In the process it is likely that many state interests have been overruled. If federalism is seen as a compact between states in a Calhounian sense, then this is a matter of some concern that needs to be addressed at the Constitution drafting stage. It suggests that there is a need for clear constitutional and other mechanisms to protect the interests of national minorities (local majorities) against the ability of national majorities, through central governments, to wield power.

Our results also suggest that interstate compacts are a viable alternative to centralization because they can achieve the same benefits of centralization, taking into account the common interest, without the conflict between state and national majorities inherent to centralism.

NOTES

1. Australia's High Court has a role similar to the U.S. Supreme Court.
2. Reproduced from Prest and Mathews (1980, p. 17).
3. It is assumed here that the states do not have sufficient information on the two preference types to implement, for example, a Lindahl equilibrium (which is Pareto-optimal) and so are forced to an inefficient mechanism such as majority rule. This feature of our model is discussed more extensively when we characterize the central outcomes.
4. This idea was first proposed in Shapiro (1993) and can be illustrated by noting that the center chooses q by solving

$$(n_{1,l} + n_{2,l})\text{MRS}^l_{Q,x} + (n_{1,h} + n_{2,h})\text{MRS}^h_{Q,x} - 1 = 0,$$

which is the Samuelson condition yielding a set of efficient policies along a utility possibilities frontier defined between the low- and high-demand groups for the nation. Suppose now that the allocation on the frontier selected by the center yields equal consumption of x and hence an equal q/n for each type. Because $\text{MRS}^h_{Q,x} > \text{MRS}^l_{Q,x}$, the choice of q/n will be smaller than is optimal for the type-h individuals and larger than is optimal for the type-l citizens. If a type h claims to be a type l, then the center will change the allocation on the frontier to one where there is an even smaller q and hence lower q/n (from application of the Samuelson condition). This makes type-h individuals worse off. Similarly, if a type l pretends to be a type h then the center will change its provision to one where there is a higher q/n, making the type l worse off. It is therefore in the interests of both types to reveal their preferences accurately (under equal per-capita cost sharing) because they are made worse off by misrepresenting their preferences.
5. We could also have characterized "constrained efficient" state provision with an equal per-capita tax sharing constraint. We have not done this because we wish to show that, even when the states have the liability of two sources of inefficiency – majority rule and perfect externalities – central provision with just *one* informational constraint may still not Pareto dominate competitive or cooperative state provision.
6. Similarly, commencing with centralized provision as a benchmark, any moves to decentralize toward a treaty or competitive provision will not be Pareto-improving.
7. See Forsyth (1981) for a detailed analysis of this debate and its important contribution to our understanding of federalism.
8. Calhoun has been associated with the defense of slavery in the South, with the result that much of his work on the theory of federation has received less attention than it might otherwise have.

218   JEFFREY D. PETCHEY & PERRY SHAPIRO

9. The advisability of such easy secession, and a similar proposal by Buchanan (1990), is examined in Shapiro, Petchey, and Coram (1996).
10. The only difficulty with such taxes is that they would still interfere with inter-state trade by altering relative prices between states. Hence they could be struck down for contravening Section 92, which guarantees free interstate trade.
11. For an excellent and detailed analysis of the High Court's arguments, see Coper (1987, pp. 224–42) and Hanks (1986, pp. 365–85).
12. Thus, not only did the Court's wide interpretation of excise squeeze the states out of much of the indirect tax base, in *Commonwealth v. Victoria* (1926) a link was made between this taxation power and expenditure responsibilities. This enabled centralization of tax powers to *lead to* effective centralization of spending decisions, regardless of the division of powers implied by the Constitution.
13. See Sharman (1994) for discussion.
14. This dissatisfaction, and the view that decisions made in Canberra often over-ride state interests, are expressed in various policy documents released at the state level in recent years. For example, see Government of Western Australia (1994).
15. For a brief discussion of this process see James (1992).
16. See Ahmad and McLure (1994) for a discussion of these changes.

REFERENCES

Ahmad, J. K., and C. E. McLure (1994), "Intergovernmental Relations in South Africa: A Case Study," Paper presented at the ISPE Conference on "Fiscal Policy in Emerging Federations" (26–28 August, Nashville, TN).
Buchanan, J. M. (1990), "Europe's Constitutional Opportunity," in *Europe's Constitutional Future*. London: Institute of Economic Affairs.
Calhoun, J. C. (reprinted 1953), *A Disquisition on Government and Selections from the Discourse* (C. Gordon Post, ed.). Indianapolis, IN: Bobbs-Merrill.
Coper, M. (1987), *Encounters with the Australian Constitution*. North Ryde, NSW: CCH.
Courchene, T. J. (1993), "Globalisation, Institutional Evolution and the Australian Federation," in B. Galligan (ed.), *Federalism and the Economy*. Canberra: Australian National University Federalism Research Centre, pp. 64–123.
Forsyth, M. (1981), *Unions of States: The Theory and Practice of Confederation*. New York: Leicester University Press / Holmes and Meier.
Government of Western Australia (1994), *Rebuilding the Federation: An Audit of State Powers and Responsibilities Usurped by the Commonwealth in the Years Since Federation*. Perth, Western Australia.
Groves, T., and J. Ledyard (1977), "Optimal Allocation of Public Goods: A Solution to the 'Free Rider' Problem," *Econometrica* 45: 783–809.
Groves, T., and M. Loeb (1975), "Incentives and Public Inputs," *Journal of Public Economics* 4: 211–26.
Hanks, P. (1986), "Section 90 of the Commonwealth Constitution: Fiscal Federalism or Economic Unity," *Adelaide Law Review* 10: 365–85.

James, D. W. (1992), "Intergovernmental Financial Relations in Australia," Information Series no. 3, Australian Tax Research Foundation, Sydney, NSW.
Moy, P. (1993), "Vertical Fiscal Imbalance: The State's View," in D. J. Collins (ed.), *Vertical Fiscal Imbalance* (Conference Series no. 13). Sydney, NSW: Australian Tax Research Foundation, pp. 301-14.
Oates, W. E., and R. M. Schwab (1988), "Economic Competition Among Jurisdictions: Efficiency Enhancing or Distortion Inducing?" *Journal of Public Economics* 35: 333-54.
Prest, W., and R. L. Mathews (eds.) (1980), *The Development of Australian Fiscal Federalism.* Canberra: Australian National University Press.
Shapiro, P. (1993), "Which Level of Government Should Be Responsible for Environmental Regulation? Alexander Hamilton and John C. Calhoun in the Environmental Protection Agency," Paper Presented at the Symposium on "Environmental Policy with Economic and Political Integration: The European Community and the United States" (30 September – 2 October, Urbana-Champaign, IL).
Shapiro, P., and J. Petchey (1994), "'Shall Become Exclusive': An Analysis of Section 90," *Economic Record* 70: 171-82.
Shapiro, P., J. D. Petchey, and B. T. Coram (1996), "Federal Stability, Secession and Uniform Tax Sharing: An Application of the Theory of the Core," Federalism Research Centre, Australian National University, Canberra.
Sharman, C. (1983), "Calhoun: A New Perspective on Theories of Australian Federalism," *Strathclyde Papers on Government and Politics* 22: 2-27.
Sharman, C. (1994), "Discipline and Disharmony: Party and the Operation of the Australian Federal System," in C. Sharman (ed.), *Parties and Federalism in Australia and Canada.* Canberra: Australian National University Federalism Research Centre, pp. 23-44.
Walsh, C. (1990), "State Taxation and Vertical Fiscal Imbalance: The Radical Reform Options," in C. Walsh (ed.), *Issues in State Taxation.* Canberra: Australian National University Centre for Research on Federal Financial Relations, pp. 53-92.
Walsh, C. (1993), "Vertical Fiscal Imbalance: The Issues," in D. J. Collins (ed.), *Vertical Fiscal Imbalance* (Conference Series no. 13). Sydney, NSW: Australian Tax Research Foundation, pp. 31-53.

Index

accountability
  under apartheid system in South Africa,
    143, 145
  means to achieve political and fiscal, 41
  proposals to improve South African,
    145, 158-9
  see also fiscal responsibility
action, joint
  moral hazard dynamic game, 92-3
  moral hazard static game, 87-9
adverse selection, 96
*A.G. (NSW) v. Homebush Flour Mills
  Ltd.* (1937), 209
Agarwal, V., 21
Agarwala, R., 26
Ahmad, J., 29, 186
apartheid, South Africa, 142-3
Argentina, 23-4
Arnott, R., 105
Artis, M., 17
Aschauer, D., 122
Atkinson, A. B., 47
audit policy, optimal, 74-8
Austin, D. A., 31
Australia
  centralization in, 194-6, 206-15
  as customs union, 208-9
  tax policy, 207-11

Bahl, R., 26, 28, 144, 147
banking system
  Argentina, 23-4
  Brazil, 24-5
Baumol, W. J., 155
Berkowitz, D., 31
Besley, T., 17
Bird, R. M., 20
Black Local Authorities (BLAs), South
  Africa
  under apartheid system, 142-3

in emerging metropolitan structures,
  158, 160
lack of accountability in, 143
Borjas, G., 103
Brander, J., 120, 123, 132
Brazil, 24-5
Brown, C. C., 104, 113, 115
Bruckner, J. K., 147
Burbidge, J. B., 31
bureaucracy, U.S. state and local
  education, 19
Burgess, R., 21

Calhoun, J. C., 205-6
Canada
  fiscal equity and efficiency issues, 17-18
  fiscal policy, 29
Casella, A., 31
central bank
  Argentina, 24
  Brazil, 25
centralization
  Australia, 194-6, 206-16
  decentralization as subset of, 96
  preferences with, 195
centralization cost model
  numerical solutions to policy regimes
    in, 202-4
  policy regimes analyzed in, 196-206
Cheng, T., 26
China, 26-7
Coase theorem, 94
Commonwealth v. Victoria (1926), 212
communes, France, 83
competition
  fiscal competition for mobile capital, 9
  in France among subcentral
    jurisdictions, 84
  games of regions competing for mobile
    firms, 120-32